P9-CSE-307

Unleashing the hidden power of adversity

Coming Back

TYNDALE HOUSE PUBLISHERS, INC., CAROL STREAM, ILLINOIS

STRONGER

DREW BREES

WITH CHRIS FABRY

Visit Tyndale's exciting Web site at www.tyndale.com.

Visit Drew Brees's Web site at www.drewbrees.com.

TYNDALE and Tyndale's quill logo are registered trademarks of Tyndale House Publishers, Inc.

Coming Back Stronger: Unleashing the Hidden Power of Adversity

Copyright © 2010 by Brees Company, Inc. All rights reserved.

Front cover photo and author photo of Drew Brees by Stephen Vosloo copyright © 2010 by Tyndale House Publishers, Inc. All rights reserved.

Back cover photo copyright © 2010 AP Photo/Eric Gay. All rights reserved.

Insert photo of Drew holding a rose in his teeth copyright © 2000 AP Photo/Tom Strattman. All rights reserved.

Insert photos of Drew and Marty Schottenheimer; and of Drew, LaDainian Tomlinson, and Lorenzo Neal copyright © Mike Nowak. All rights reserved.

Insert photo of Drew being helped off the field by Dr. Chao copyright © 2005 AP Photo/Denis Poroy. All rights reserved.

Insert photo of boat rescue in St. Bernard Parish copyright © 2005 AP Photo/Eric Gay. All rights reserved.

Insert photo of National Guard truck outside the Superdome copyright © 2005 AP Photo/Eric Gay. All rights reserved.

Insert photo of aerial view of New Orleans post-Katrina copyright © 2005 AP Photo/David J. Phillip, file. All rights reserved.

Insert photos of the Saints home opener in 2006; Drew shaking hands with Sean Payton; Drew leading the pregame chant; Drew dropping back to pass against the Redskins; Drew diving in for a touchdown against Miami; the Saints fan shots; Jon Stinchcomb blocking for Drew; Drew holding the Lombardi Trophy; Drew holding Baylen; and Drew riding in the Super Bowl parade used with express permission of copyright holder New Orleans Louisiana Saints, L.L.C. and taken by Saints Director of Photography Michael C. Hebert copyright © 2006, 2009, 2010. All rights reserved.

Insert photo of Drew and Brittany kissing Baylen in front of the green wall copyright © 2009 by Marie-Dominique Verdier, www.mdvphoto.com. All rights reserved.

Insert photo of Brittany kissing Drew after Super Bowl win copyright © 2010 AP Photo/Mark Humphrey. All rights reserved.

Insert photo of Drew holding up Baylen ("We did it, little boy!") copyright © 2010 AP Photo/Paul Spinelli. All rights reserved.

All other interior photos are from the Brees family collection and are reprinted with permission.

Cover designed by Jacqueline L. Nuñez

Interior designed by Dean H. Renninger

Published in association with Encore Sports and Entertainment.

All Scripture quotations, unless otherwise indicated, are taken from the New King James Version.® Copyright © 1982 by Thomas Nelson, Inc. Used by permission. All rights reserved.

Scripture quotations marked NIV are taken from the Holy Bible, *New International Version,*® *NIV.*® Copyright © 1973, 1978, 1984 by Biblica, Inc.™ Used by permission of Zondervan. All rights reserved worldwide. www.zondervan.com.

Library of Congress Cataloging-in-Publication Data

Brees, Drew, date.
    Coming back stronger : unleashing the hidden power of adversity / Drew Brees with Chris Fabry.
        p. cm.
    ISBN 978-1-4143-3943-6 (hc)
    1. Brees, Drew, date.   2. Suffering—Religious aspects—Christianity.   I. Fabry, Chris, date.
II. Title.
BV4909.B73 2010
248.8'6—dc22   2010016560

Printed in the United States of America

16   15   14   13   12   11   10
 8   7   6   5   4   3   2

To my wife, Brittany, my little boy, Baylen, and our children yet to come. You have brought more joy into my life than I ever thought possible. You are my inspiration.

CONTENTS

FOREWORD

IN THE NFL, there are a lot of good quarterbacks. And very few that can be considered *great*. But what defines greatness in that position? Are the great quarterbacks those who have won Super Bowl championships? Is greatness reserved for the quarterbacks who have broken passing records or have been to multiple Pro Bowls? In my opinion, a truly great quarterback is one who plays at a very high level on the field—and off the field as well. A guy who plays like a champion, not only on Sundays, but also on every other day of the week.

I met Drew Brees at the beginning of the 2003 season, when he was the starting quarterback for San Diego. His Chargers were coming to play the Jacksonville Jaguars, and both teams were 0–4. I didn't know much about Drew at the time other than the successful career he'd had at Purdue. He clearly was talented, yet he and his team were struggling. Many critics wondered if Drew Brees was good enough to be successful in this league. Some thought he was too short. Some considered him a bust. Little did they know. . . .

Seven years later, it's clear: Drew has silenced his critics. He is at the top of his game and without a doubt one of the best quarterbacks in the NFL today. The guy who fought to hold on to his job in San Diego now holds the Lombardi Trophy as a champion. I was fortunate to share that experience with him, and I can honestly say that Drew Brees is a champion in every sense of the word. I have never been around anybody more focused, more competitive, and more driven to succeed than Drew.

That passion is by no means limited to the football field. His commitment to his family, his friends, and the kids and communities he supports is positively unmatched. Drew is a man on a mission. For him there are no wasted days, no wasted hours, no wasted minutes. I am continually impressed by how willing Drew is to sacrifice his time and energy to help those around him succeed—both on and off the field.

He'd cringe to hear me say this, but in many ways, Drew is a modern-day hero. It's difficult to describe what he has meant to the city of New Orleans. I guess the best way to say it is that, in many ways, he has brought hope to this city. He gave fans hope in the form of a Super Bowl championship. And with the work he and his wife, Brittany, have done through their foundation, he has given the city hope for better neighborhoods and has provided programs that give kids, families, and previously shattered communities the hope of a brighter future.

Simply put, Drew is making a difference. The Bible is clear that God has a purpose for each of our lives, and I wholeheartedly believe that God has brought Drew to New Orleans for a specific purpose—a purpose that goes far beyond winning football games. God is using Drew in a powerful way to make a difference in the lives of so many people in New

Orleans. While the city has come a long way since 2005, most would agree that there is still much more that needs to be done. While many have given up, Drew has not. He never quits on the field, and he will never quit working to help this community that has so openly embraced him.

It is a privilege to have Drew as a friend, and I consider myself extremely fortunate to have had the opportunity to play alongside him and to be a part of what he has accomplished— in his career, on this team, and for New Orleans. Drew Brees is truly a *great* quarterback.

Mark Brunell

ACKNOWLEDGMENTS

FIRST OF ALL, writing a book is an interesting process. The time and effort required to put together a memoir like this was extensive. I really had no idea what I was getting myself into when I took on this challenge, but it has been one of the most rewarding experiences of my life. I hope that those who read this book are motivated and inspired by the experiences that are shared and the lessons learned. I talk about many things I have not talked much about before, at least not in this great of detail all at once. Writing this book was an emotionally freeing experience and truly a labor of love. I hope you enjoy reading it as much as I did writing it.

I would first like to thank Chris Fabry for all his help in writing this book. We did not have a lot of time to put this collaboration together, but our ability to trust each other and communicate helped us through it all. I would also like to thank the staff at Tyndale House Publishers for all their hard work. I know it was not easy at times, but they handled everything with great respect and professionalism, and as a result we were able to put together a tremendous book.

I would also like to thank my family, friends, chaplains, teachers, mentors, teammates, and coaches for believing in me and being a part of this journey. I think about you all every day.

Then there is Chris Stuart. We have been through a lot together in a short amount of time. You are a true friend and a special person. Thanks for teaching me how to "win the day."

And last but certainly not least, I would like to thank the city of New Orleans for embracing me at a time when I needed it most. You saved me.

PROLOGUE

Eight seconds was all it took to change my life forever. Eight seconds at the end of the second quarter, in the middle of a meaningless game. Of course it wasn't meaningless to me. No game in the NFL ever is, especially when you have something to prove.

It was the final game of the season. With 4:22 left in the first half, our offense had taken over at our own eight yard line. The Broncos, our archrivals, had already sealed a playoff berth. At 9–6, we'd been eliminated from playoff contention a week earlier. Some said we should rest our starters and avoid any unnecessary injuries, but our coach, Marty Schottenheimer, disagreed. He believed that closing out a tough season with a victory on our home field was important—especially if that victory came against the Broncos. I knew he was right, and I also had my own reasons for wanting to be on the field.

A younger quarterback was waiting in the wings, and this was my chance to prove once again that I deserved to lead this team as we looked to the future.

The Broncos were up 7–0. The slight drizzle that fell over Qualcomm Stadium echoed the mood of the Chargers fans. In fact, there seemed to be as many people cheering for *Denver* as there were for San Diego. Denver certainly had a lot to cheer about that year; they had already clinched the number two seed in the AFC. Plus, their fans always travel well.

On first and ten, I handed off to LaDainian Tomlinson, who ran off left tackle for a one-yard gain. Running the ball wasn't going to be easy. The Denver defense was one of the best in the league against the run.

Second down was a pass to Keenan McCardell that fell incomplete. Champ Bailey broke up the play, as he always seemed to do. Early in the season he had picked off one of my passes in Denver and run it back for a touchdown. I wish I had that pass to do over again. But you can't live in the past in the NFL. And you can't live too far in the future. You have to live in the now.

Cam Cameron, our offensive coordinator, called in another pass play, and I surveyed the defense from the shotgun. I noticed John Lynch, All-Pro safety, creeping toward the line of scrimmage off left tackle. I knew what that meant: he was going to blitz. We had the correct protection called to block him, but there was still a sense of urgency for me to get rid of the ball. If we could get a first down, we would still have around 3:30 left on the clock to tie the score, or at the very least, attempt a field goal. Anything to take some momentum into the locker room at the half.

Nick Hardwick gave me a clean snap, and I dropped back in the pocket, going through my read. *Take care of the football. Make a good decision. Trust your progression on this play.* My feet were in our end zone as I scanned the receivers running their routes. The coverage was good, but I anticipated the opening as Keenan McCardell ran into the clear. Just as I pulled the ball back to throw, John Lynch, who was blitzing from my blind side, swiped at my arm before I was able to get the throw off. Lynch had fought through his block, and he got just enough of my arm to knock the ball loose. It wobbled out like a wounded duck and rolled to a dead stop right in front of the goal line.

The last thing a quarterback ever wants to see is a football lying loose on the ground. It should be either in your own hands, in the arms of your running back, or on the way to your receiver. But never on the ground. Ever. I knew my arm wasn't going forward when the ball was stripped—it was going back—so it was definitely a fumble, a live ball.

Lynch was behind me, and Sam Brandon and Gerard Warren of the Broncos were in front of me, moving to recover the ball. I had been coached to never jump into those loose ball situations on the ground, because bad things happen to quarterbacks who dive into a pile. Jim Harbaugh broke his arm jumping into a pile when he played quarterback at Michigan, and I had seen Kurt Warner dislocate his elbow trying to pull in a fumble. A dropped snap is one thing. You fall on it and cover up, and you're okay. But a loose ball is different. With several three-hundred-pound guys converging from different angles in a matter of seconds, there's a high risk for injury. But in that moment, instinct kicked in. It was my responsibility to get that ball back. I had lost it. And I was going to recover it.

As I dived for the ball, I saw defensive tackle Gerard Warren coming toward me—all 330 pounds of him. I jumped toward the ball, extending my right arm to scoop it up and pull it in. As I hit the ground, Warren did what every defensive player does when he has a chance to take a legal shot at the quarterback. He took it. He drove into my left side, jolting me backward. The blow spun my body around on the ground, while my right arm was stuck in an awkward position above my head.

The force of Warren's hit, and then the others who piled on, twisted my arm in a direction it is not supposed to go. The collision was ferocious, and it happened in a matter of milliseconds. And then there was silence—a stunned silence for me. The only way I can describe it is that the entire stadium became still. It wasn't just pain in my arm and shoulder—there was a signal that went to every part of my body telling me something was off. Way off.

When the whistle blew, the Broncos had the ball, and thanks to me, they were less than a yard away from another touchdown. Their defense celebrated and ran off the field. As our offense hurried off the field and our defense ran in, I rolled over, pushed myself up with my left arm, and struggled to stand. I couldn't move my right arm at all. When I looked down, it was tilted at a disturbing angle—stuck out to the side in an unnatural L. There was no movement and not much feeling.

As much as I didn't want to admit it, I knew exactly what I had done. This wasn't just a separation. I had separated my left shoulder in 2004, so I knew what that felt like. This was something with much graver implications. I was in absolute shock. I stood in the end zone looking up but not seeing anything. I glanced into the stands and tried to focus, but a million thoughts raced through my mind. I didn't need to hear it from a doctor: deep down I sensed how serious this was.

I started for the sidelines, and all of a sudden I became sick to my stomach. *This may be the last time I'll ever wear a Chargers uniform.* Fear rose up. *Maybe this is the last time I'll ever wear a football uniform. This could be the end of my career.* The feeling was real. I could taste it. And it was terrifying.

By the time I took a handful of agonizing steps, the medical staff had flown into action.

"It's my arm," I said. "I can't move it. It's stuck."

They took me behind the bench, and Dr. David Chao felt around the injury. He winced as he examined me, and then he looked straight at me. "Drew, you've dislocated your shoulder. I need to pop it back in place. You ready?"

I nodded as his prognosis confirmed my worst fear. He extended my arm and pulled until it slipped into place. I held it close to my body and sat on the bench. I've heard that one of the most painful things to experience is having a shoulder put back into the socket, but I wasn't feeling much of anything. I was focused on what had just happened and the implications of the injury—for me, for my family, and for my team.

I thought about my future and how long it might take to come back. Then I thought about Brittany, my wife. She had to be freaking out. We had plans for that night, New Year's Eve, and plans for the off-season. I had my contract to think about. And next year. There were a lot of good, positive things going on in our lives, and in an instant, with one play, it could all be gone.

"You have to call my wife and tell her I'm okay," I said to James Collins, our head trainer.

"Sure thing, Drew."

We took that long walk from the field to the locker room, and I had an X-ray. That's when the reality started to set in. And with reality came the pain . . . and the emotions. My shoulder started to throb, and with each wave I thought of Brittany. It's one thing to go through an injury when you're the one on the field, but it's excruciating for family and friends who are watching from the stands.

"I have to get a cell phone and call my wife," I said to one of the doctors. "I need her to hear my voice. To let her know I'm okay."

The cell service was bad in the locker room because it's nothing but concrete down there. I was moving around trying to get a good signal, and I had to call Brittany three times before the phone finally connected. As soon as she answered, I heard the fear in her voice.

"Babe, I'm okay," I said. I didn't want her to know how bad it was, so I tried to keep my emotions in check.

"The trainer said it was your throwing shoulder, but he wouldn't tell me any more than that."

"We don't know anything yet. I'm just getting the X-rays now. It probably looked a lot worse than it really is."

She asked me what had happened, and I tried to explain it without letting on how bad the injury was. She's been around football long enough to know it's not a good sign if you're taken to the locker room and you don't come back out. And an injury to the shoulder of the throwing arm is never good news for a quarterback.

It didn't take Brittany long to figure out things weren't okay. That's when the tears began running down my cheeks. My arm was throbbing. And the dreams we'd built seemed to come crashing down right in front of me.

I'm not one of those people who can keep the tears back once they start. When the emotion begins, it's hard for me to control. So as we talked, I was trying to tell myself, *Be strong for her. Tell her it's going to be okay. We're going to be fine. Reassure her. You're supposed to be strong here.* I tried to hold it together, but I don't think I did a very good job.

I told Brittany I loved her and said good-bye. The second I disconnected, I just lost it. All of that stuff inside— the uncertainty and fear and questions—swirled around and came out. Part of the intensity behind those emotions was the amount of work I had put into the 2004 and 2005 seasons. I had trained and practiced and done everything I could to establish myself as the quarterback and leader of the San Diego franchise. I had fought to earn respect from my team and from the Chargers faithful. But I didn't want them just to accept me as their quarterback; I wanted everybody—from the players on the field to the owner in the box upstairs to the fans in the stands—to believe *I* was the guy who could lead the Chargers to a championship. I felt like I had a lot of believers; I had convinced a lot of people. But there were still those who doubted, and unfortunately they were the ones making the decisions. I constantly felt like I had to look over my shoulder. I needed to fight and prove to them every day that I was their guy. Then, in the blink of an eye, in one play, everything seemed to have slipped through my fingers. I should have known better than to jump on the ball, but I never would have imagined something like that could possibly end my career.

Here's the thing. I truly believe that God can use anything—even an injury—for good. I believe that God has a plan for people's lives, even when that plan doesn't work out the way we think it should. I don't think God dislocated my shoulder, but in the normal processes of life, he allowed that to happen. And I have the faith to believe there was a reason for it. But in that moment in the middle of the exam room with the tears flowing, my worldview was clouded. I was struggling. I felt right on the edge. Other than maybe breaking my neck or getting paralyzed, a throwing-shoulder dislocation is pretty much the worst thing that could happen to a quarterback.

So sitting there with my shoulder in absolute agony, I remember thinking, *God, I know that if you bring me to it, you will bring me through it. I know you have a plan, but quite honestly I don't see it right now. But I know it's there. I know I have to believe.*

I know I need to have faith. I have to trust you. And I do trust you. But it's hard right now.

After the X-rays, my shoulder was absolutely throbbing. The pain was really starting to set in. I took a shower, and Brittany came and was waiting outside the locker room.

"Drew, you and your wife need to go home now," the doctor said. "Just take it easy and ice that shoulder, and we'll get you in tomorrow for an MRI."

I thought about it a minute and gritted my teeth. "You know what? I'm not leaving until I get to see my teammates again."

It was really important to me to stay until the end of the game. I wanted to be there for my teammates when they came into the locker room. I needed to show them that their leader would always be there for them. I wanted to look them in the eye and let them know that this might have knocked me down, but it didn't knock me out. I would be back, and I would still be their quarterback.

I don't remember the final score of the game—I just know we lost. It was miserable. From the weather to the final score to my injury, it was all miserable. Second-year quarterback Philip Rivers ended up filling in for me, and he played fine despite the circumstances. The second half was a blur for me, as I was getting my shoulder treated and slowly trying to gather my things. I tried to watch some of the game from the locker room, but it was difficult. I should have been out there playing, but I couldn't. Once the game ended, the guys started to flow into the locker room with that defeated, end-of-the-season look on their faces. As they filtered in, they looked surprised to see me. I didn't say anything. It was enough for me to be there when they came inside.

The guys didn't know the extent of the injury then—and neither did I. Maybe that was part of why I felt I had to be there with them. I knew this was really bad, and it might be the last time I'd get to be in that locker room as a member of the San Diego Chargers. I was trying to fight back the emotions, but it was hard. I didn't want my last memory or theirs to be of me walking off the field with my arm out of socket. If anything, I wanted that final moment to be in the locker room with all those guys who had been through so much with me. As they walked in one by one, I felt like something I'd been working toward my whole life was evaporating. This was not how it was supposed to end.

The next day I would have an MRI and then another exam that would confirm a 360-degree tear of the labrum and a torn rotator cuff. Basically, everything that held my shoulder together was shredded. I would learn later that only one out of five hundred shoulder dislocations were like mine. That translates to 0.2 percent—almost like winning the lottery. But without the cash.

There was a chance I would never play in the NFL again.

I was knocked down. My future was uncertain. Had I just played my final game as a Charger? Was my career over? This injury was the worst thing that could possibly happen to me.

Or so I thought.

MARK OF A CHAMPION

CHAPTER ONE

WHEN I HELD UP MY SON, Baylen, after the fourth quarter of Super Bowl XLIV, with confetti streaming down all around us, it was the fulfillment of a dream. But what I've discovered along the way is that the road to success is usually a pretty bumpy one. And there are no shortcuts.

They say you need three skills to be a great quarterback: toughness, intelligence, and heart. Although I didn't officially start training to become a quarterback until I was in high school, in a way, I guess God has been preparing me for that role all my life.

I had a great childhood, but it wasn't always easy. Then again, neither is life. And neither is football. As a kid, I got teased a lot because of a distinguishing birthmark on my right cheek. My mom and dad used to tell me that was where an angel had kissed me, but the kids at school didn't quite see it that way. They used to tease me and take jabs at me in the classroom and on the playground, saying things like "What happened to your face?" or "Wipe that stuff off your face." I couldn't help but get in a few scraps over it.

When I was little, the pediatrician gave my parents the option of having it removed because there was a chance it could become cancerous, but in spite of all the harassment I took at school, I decided to keep it. Instead of seeing it as a bad thing, I chose to see it as something that made me unique and special. It set me apart from everyone else. In a way, it became my trademark.

Looking back, I guess it might have been smarter to remove it, because why take a chance on it becoming cancerous? I even had it biopsied a few years ago, and I still see the dermatologist every once in a while to make sure it's okay, but now it's just a part of who I am. I wouldn't consider cutting off my arm. Neither would I cut off my birthmark. If I had ever been forced to remove it, I would have been devastated. My good friends who have known me a long time say they don't even see it anymore. If I had it removed, they would notice, but now they don't see it at all. They just see me.

In some ways, I guess you could say it was a character builder that helped me develop an inner toughness and an ability to shake off jabs and criticism. Not a bad trait to have as a quarterback in the NFL—or in any job, for that matter.

A Lineage of Competition

If you look at pictures of me as a child, you'll see the birthmark, but you'll also almost always see me holding a football or a baseball. As far back as I can remember, football has been a part of my life.

When I was growing up, my father would throw to me in the yard, but my constant playmate was my brother, Reid. He's two and a half years younger than I am, and we played all the time in our little yard in Austin, Texas. Our "field" was a patch of grass that was about as big as a good-size living room. Trees bordered the yard, and those were our sidelines. The invisible goal lines were clearly defined in our minds, so we knew when we scored.

There's a big gap when a fifth grader plays against a second grader or when a sixth grader plays against a third grader, so to make it fair, I would get down on my knees and Reid would try to run around me. And it wasn't touch football—we were really tackling each other, and I would try anything I could to take him down. Even though I was scrambling on my knees, Reid still got beat up on quite a bit. Sometimes my dad would come out, and he'd play all-time quarterback, but most of the time it was just Reid and me.

I grew up in a very sports-minded family. My mother, Mina, was very athletic. In the late 1960s she was all-state in high school track, volleyball, and basketball. If she were playing today, she'd have gotten an athletic scholarship to just about any school in the country for any of those sports. But at that time women weren't given many of those opportunities. She decided to attend Texas A&M, which had been an all-male military school. My mother was in one of the first classes of women to attend Texas A&M. It was there that she met my dad, an athlete himself who played freshman basketball.

My mom's brother, Marty Akins, was an All-American quarterback at the University of Texas. Marty was part of the Longhorns team that beat Alabama and Bear Bryant in the 1973 Cotton Bowl.

My mom's father, Ray Akins, was a Marine and served in World War II. After the war he coached high school football for thirty-eight years, winning 302 games in his career. He was a legend in the state of Texas, and best of all, he was my grandfather. He coached at Gregory-Portland High School in Portland, Texas, just outside Corpus Christi. He used to let Reid and me attend his summer two-a-day practices. From the time I was about seven years old, right around my parents' divorce, until my grandfather stopped coaching in 1988, Reid and I would stand on the sidelines and hand out this green water to the players during breaks. It was something like Gatorade—green because of the electrolytes mixed in. I always felt like my grandpa was ahead of his time with that kind of stuff. It didn't matter what Reid and I were doing—it was a thrill just to be that close to the game and the players. I never would have guessed back then that I'd be on the other side someday.

That's my lineage. We have always been a very athletic and competitive family. Our get-togethers when I was growing up were all about sports. That's what we all loved. On Thanksgiving, Christmas, Easter, the Fourth of July, or any other time we got together, we'd eat a big meal and then end up in the yard playing something. We played basketball, football, Wiffle ball, washers, you name it. At the end of the day there was always a winner and a loser. The winner went away happy and the loser was mad, and you wouldn't talk to each other for a while. That's just the way it was, and we looked forward to those get-togethers like you wouldn't believe.

When I say we were competitive, that didn't just encompass sports. For example, there were times we'd be sitting on the porch at my grandparents' house eating plums from my grandmother's plum trees. After we ate them, we would see who could spit their pit farthest into the yard. Somebody would mark the longest spit, and we'd eat more plums just so we could have another chance to beat whoever was in first place. It was crazy, but it was so much fun. I usually won, by the way!

Anything we could find for competition, we were all

over it. One of my favorites was pitching washers. Also called Texas horseshoes, this game involves two- to three-inch metal washers and PVC cups that are sunk into the ground. You pitch the washer toward the cup and get points for being closest to the cup and more points for having it actually go in. Some people play on sandpits, but my grandfather made a court out of turf. That was a big game for us as kids, and it taught me control and accuracy.

I have no doubt all those backyard games played a huge part in stoking my competitive fire. And they're also some of my best memories.

The Split

One of the most difficult things I experienced as a child was the divorce of my mom and dad. But it was that adversity that brought Reid and me so close. I was seven and Reid was about five when Mom and Dad divorced. At that age you don't quite understand how the world works. We were so young and had so many unanswered questions: *Why are Mommy and Daddy not together anymore? Was it something we did? Could we have stopped it somehow?* That is why when I met my wife, I knew divorce was not an option and I never wanted to put my children through that.

I remember seeing my parents sit down many times to talk, and I figured it was only a matter of time before we would be a family again. That is, until the day my dad sat Reid and me down on the couch to explain the situation. I remember it like it was yesterday. There are certain moments in your life you just don't forget. When he sat us down, I had no idea what was coming at first, although whenever he took off his glasses to talk to us, I knew it was not going to be good. The only time I have ever seen my dad take off his glasses, besides to clean them, is when he is about to get emotional. He made it clear that day that things would never be the same again. To this day, I still get teary-eyed when I think about how painful that moment was for all of us.

Reid and I spent many nights awake long after lights-out, hoping and praying that our parents would get back together. We cried ourselves to sleep a lot during that time. The split wasn't an amicable one, and there was bitterness between the two sides. In fact, Reid and I were caught in the middle from the time we were kids until my mom passed away in August 2009. When you're a kid, normal is whatever is happening at the time. Reid and I basically had two homes. I'd spend two days at my mom's house, then two days at my dad's house, and we'd switch off every other weekend.

My brother and I really leaned on each other during that time. Our escape from everything was to take a bucket and a net down to the creek that ran through our neighborhood in central Austin to catch minnows and crawdaddies. That same creek ran through a local nine-hole golf course about six blocks away from our duplex. Reid and I even started a business as kids by fishing out the orange and yellow golf balls from the creek, shining them up, and selling them to the golfers. We weren't going to get rich off that deal, but it was enough to buy us baseball cards and Big League Chew at the local convenience store. As good as those times with my brother were, when we got back home every evening after one of our adventures, we would have to face the reality of a broken family.

We were inseparable, best friends. We did have conflict, though. I know it was tough on Reid to have me as an older brother. As much as we both assumed our futures were aligned, we were destined to travel different roads. He excelled in sports, but he didn't want to do the exact same things I did.

He wanted to find his own way. Since he didn't play quarterback, people would ask, "Why don't you play quarterback like Drew? Why don't you follow your brother?" He heard that a lot, and it made him mentally tough—that and all the whuppings he took from me. The truth is, I always felt like Reid was tougher than me. Of course, that was my plan all along: I was preparing him.

When Reid went to college, he partied a little too hard, got a couple of tattoos, probably because he knew our parents would not approve. He was rebellious like that. It was his way of separating, becoming his own person.

We're both supercompetitive; we work really hard at things, and when we set our minds to something, we will accomplish it. I'm so proud of him for walking on to play baseball at Baylor. His goal was to earn a scholarship and help lead his team to the College World Series, and that's what he did. The funny thing is, if you'd asked either one of us our dream when we were growing up, neither of us would have mentioned anything about football. We wanted to play in the College World Series. So watching my brother play in Omaha at Rosenblatt Stadium in 2005 ranks up there as one of the proudest moments in my life. My brother was living out a childhood dream for both of us.

In a way, my brother used the pressure people put on him to excel in different areas, like baseball and business. He now lives in Denver and works in sales.

Some things in my life have made me step back and say, "Man, how did my family end up with so many problems?" But I've found that when you start talking to people, everybody's family has something they've dealt with. Every family has issues and is a little dysfunctional. It's not whether you will have problems within your family; it's how you handle those difficulties when they come your way.

Westlake High School

In spite of the divorce, I really didn't have a bad childhood. In fact, in my mind, my life was the greatest I could have asked for. Some things weren't easy to go through, but I wouldn't trade any of it. All the negative and positive mixed together to make me who I am.

For example, when I was a freshman in high school, I changed school districts. Mom felt that of all the public schools in the area, Westlake High School in Austin had the best combination of academics and athletics. She valued high academic standards as well as a good sports program, and Westlake had both.

I remember some conflict between my mom and dad about the school decision. My dad's a real easygoing guy, kind of a go-with-the-flow type, whereas my mom was super-competitive, probably overly competitive, if there is such a thing. When she and Dad would argue, she'd refuse to back down. Whenever she'd get in that bulldog mode, my dad would have no other choice than to agree with her decision.

My mom was the reason I went to St. Andrew's Episcopal School for sixth, seventh, and eighth grade. She wanted me to get a solid education as well as have a great athletic experience. Dad would say, "Why do we have to pay for private school? The public school's just fine."

But Mom wouldn't budge.

When I moved into the Westlake district, I didn't know many people. I remember the first set of two-a-days as a freshman. This was Texas 5A football. It was *Friday Night Lights*. There was a sea of guys, probably 150 to 200 kids, all ready to play. The coach said, "Okay, who thinks they can be quarterback?"

I raised my hand and looked around to see forty other hands in the air. I thought, *I am never going to see the field*. I was the new guy. All these guys had been part of the same program at the two middle schools in the district. They'd had real game preparation and full-contact experience. I'd been playing flag football the past three years because our small Christian school didn't have enough players to field a tackle football team. The season hadn't even started yet, and already I was at a disadvantage.

There was a positive side, though: playing flag football had kept me from getting hurt early on. Plus, I'd learned a lot of the fundamentals without wearing pads. Flag football is all about throwing, catching, and running as opposed to blocking and contact. The movement is very athletic and fluid, and it forces you to have a solid grasp of the basics.

I ended up as the fourth quarterback of six my freshman year. The first three went to the freshman A team, and the next three went to the freshman B team. In effect, I was the starter on the freshman B team. Not bad, but I felt lost in a swarm of players.

During my sophomore year, when I was in the middle of two-a-days, my mom picked me up from practice. She could tell something was up because I was unusually quiet. After she pulled into the garage, she turned off the car and we sat there for a minute.

I looked at her and used a word that normally didn't come out of my mouth. "Mom, I think I might want to *quit* football."

She didn't freak out. She just squinted her eyes with concern and said, "Why?"

"Because I don't feel like I'm ever going to get an opportunity to play."

Jay Rodgers was the quarterback for the varsity team, and his younger brother Johnny was the quarterback on junior varsity. This was a football family. Their middle brother was the starting center on varsity, and their dad, Randy Rodgers, was the recruiting coordinator at the University of Texas.

Johnny Rodgers was destined to be the next starting quarterback for Westlake High School, and I was sure I'd get lost in the shuffle.

"You know, my real sport is baseball," I told my mom. "I want to get a baseball scholarship. I play football because I like it, but I don't want to sit on the bench. I don't feel like I'm going to get an opportunity, and maybe I'd be better off playing fall baseball and trying to get a baseball scholarship."

My mom took a deep breath. "That's a valid point. I wouldn't want to sit the bench any more than you do. So if you don't want to play, you don't have to play. But remember this: when you least expect it, that opportunity will present itself. You never know when it's going to come, but all it takes is one play."

I sat there and thought about what she'd said. My mother was an athlete and a competitor, and I valued her opinion. Besides, with a grandfather who was a coach and an uncle who'd played for the University of Texas, I didn't want to feel like I was missing out on some experiences. *This might be something I'll regret for the rest of my life if I don't at least follow through with this year.*

"You know what?" I said. "I think I'll stick it out for a little bit longer, and we'll see how it goes. I'm not going to quit midway through two-a-days."

Mom nodded and smiled. In retrospect, I think the fact that she didn't push me one way or the other freed me up to think clearly for myself. As it turned out, her words rang true the very next week.

One JV quarterback had decided to play baseball and the other moved to defense, so I was second in line to Johnny Rodgers. It was the last scrimmage of the year against Killeen, a tough team comprised mostly of kids whose parents were in the military, stationed at nearby Fort Hood. With the season just one week away, this was the final dress rehearsal. Near the end of the game, when there was only one series left, Johnny dropped back to pass, hoping to end the scrimmage on a high note. In a split second, everything changed for me. Johnny got sacked in the backfield, and in the process he tore his ACL, putting him out for the entire year. One minute I was the guy who would ride the bench all season, and the next I was thrust into the role of starting JV quarterback.

Our JV team went 10–0 my sophomore year. In my junior year, I was the varsity starter. We were undefeated going into the third round of the playoffs.

That's when I tore *my* ACL.

An injury like that can change your life. I had no doubt about that—after all, that was the reason I was the starting quarter-back. Johnny Rodgers had returned, but he was now our start-ing free safety. I had seen other players who tore their ACLs either recover really slowly or not come back at all. I was sure this was the worst thing that could have happened to me. It was the third round of the playoffs. We were going to state, and we were going to win the championship. Suddenly my season was over.

Our team lost in the next round.

I had been getting recruiting letters from some good schools, but when I blew out my knee, all the letters stopped. No school wanted to touch me. The worst part about it was that I would also miss the entire basketball and baseball seasons. And in my mind, my number one priority was still to get a baseball scholarship. I was only a junior in high school, and it felt like my life was over.

I had a six-month rehabilitation process, and I had to make

a decision: Was I going to quit or come back stronger? I chose to come back.

It was grueling. For three or four hours every day after school, I'd go in the training room and just grind, grind, grind. The pain of the injury was intense, and every day I had to fight to regain flexibility and mobility. But in the process, I was building up my strength and resolve.

The doctor told me that my ability to recover from this injury was totally dependent on my commitment to the rehab. I was bound and determined to come back—not just to where I was before, but better. My goal has always been to take a negative and turn it into a positive. I want to be a problem solver, not a problem creator. The glass is always half full for me. Make the best of every situation.

The ACL injury was a defining moment in my life. I made a decision not to let something negative control my emotions. And the interesting thing is that decision led to another that would also follow me the rest of my life.

A FEW
GOOD MEN

MANY PEOPLE WOULD DEFINE the "good life" as one that's free of pain and hardship and heartache. But I've learned that adversity is actually an opportunity. It's a gift, though it may not look like it in the moment. The difficulties life throws at you can be a doorway to something better—something you hadn't even dreamed was possible.

After I tore my ACL on a fateful day in December 1995, I had surgery, which resulted in my having to wear a knee brace and walk with crutches for six weeks. I felt like I was at a dead end—or at least, had hit a huge roadblock. But at the same time, something unexpected was happening internally. The injury had stirred me up inside, and I was filled with questions: *Do I have a purpose? Is there a reason I'm on this earth? Do I have a destiny, or is everything just chance?*

I remember hobbling with my dad into First Baptist Church of Austin, Texas. Usually I didn't pay much attention during the sermon. I would nod off or elbow my brother or check out the girls. I had been taught from a young age that church was important, but like most sixteen-year-olds, I didn't see how it connected with real life. Church was just something you did on Sundays and maybe Wednesday nights if you didn't have practice.

For some reason the message that day wasn't normal. I had a different feeling as I listened. And this time I was really listening.

I was sitting in the pew with my crutches next to me and my knee brace on, thinking about the future. It had been about two weeks since the surgery, and I was lost in all the questions. I wasn't only thinking about my football future—I was thinking about the direction I wanted to go in life. This injury had stopped me from pursuing my sports dream, and it was this crisis that created a defining moment for the rest of my life.

As I sat there thinking about those deep, huge questions that everyone faces at some point, the pastor, Dr. Browning Ware, was preaching about what God desires us to be. As an illustration in his message, he mentioned the movie *A Few Good Men*. He said that God is looking for a few good men to carry on his teachings and to walk the walk with Christ. That's when the lightbulb came on for me. *He's talking to* me. *I want to be one of God's few good men.*

It was an epiphany. Life finally made sense—this was not some random existence here on earth. God had a plan for me, and he wanted me to be in a relationship with him. If I would cultivate that relationship, good things would spill over to others in my life. I knew I wanted to be one of God's few good men no matter what happened with my sports career.

At that point I didn't know if I would ever play quarterback again. I didn't have a clue what the future would hold. But I knew that no matter what happened, I wanted to do things the right way—to please God and live my life for him.

I didn't see a vision, and lightning bolts didn't shoot out of the ceiling. I didn't walk forward at the end of the service either. But there was something going on inside of me—something I can only explain as God moving in. A calmness came over my life because I finally understood that God had a plan for me. He was in control. I still approached every day with determination, and I tried to use the gifts and talents he had given me to be the best I could be at everything. But in the end, I knew it wasn't about my striving and clawing my way to the top. I knew God would take care of me. And I knew I had to trust that whatever path he led me down was the path I was meant to be on.

This belief immediately carried over into my daily approach to life as I was propelled into my studies and my rehab. All that pressure I used to feel started to disappear as I learned to give it my best and then commit the rest to the Lord. I couldn't escape the sense that God's plan for me was to come back stronger and lead my team again.

Coming Back

When I went down with the ACL injury, I was six feet, 170 pounds—skin and bones. I had a bum knee. I was on crutches. In other words, I looked pretty pathetic. But I began rehab, throwing myself into it every day after school.

Before I knew it, I was going into my senior year of high school, which is when colleges ask for commitments from players. But my prospects looked bleak. I was coming off the ACL injury, plus I was a little smaller than most quarterbacks—not the prototype a lot of schools are looking for. Texas A&M and the University of Texas already had their quarterbacks. Baylor said no thanks. TCU and Texas Tech were a no go. Rice ran the option, and that wasn't my strength. SMU was still struggling to recover from the "death penalty" they'd received from the NCAA ten years earlier for recruiting violations. Every school in Texas seemed closed to me.

Six months after my surgery, I was fully healed and once again starting as quarterback. Because of the weights and rigorous training, I now weighed 195 pounds. I had gained twenty-five pounds of muscle, so I was physically much stronger. But for me the real difference wasn't in my body but in my head and my heart. I had a new sense of confidence because I knew I had worked hard to fight through the injury. I'd pushed myself past limits I'd previously thought I could not go beyond. I was physically, mentally, and spiritually tougher because of what I had endured in order to get to that point.

We won every game in the regular season, and we were now in the playoffs, preparing for our fourteenth game of the year. When we were on the practice field, our offensive coordinator, Neal LaHue, approached me.

"Drew, is anybody recruiting you?"

"No, Coach."

He just looked at me with a puzzled expression on his face, as if to say, *They don't know what they're missing, kid.*

I laughed. "I'm not worried. Anyway, I'm going to get a baseball scholarship." I still had my heart set on baseball.

We won the next two games and went 16–0, winning the first 5A state championship in the history of our school. That season was a turning point for me. A year earlier, before I'd torn my ACL, I was just a high school kid whose world revolved around whatever sport was in season and who I would ask to the prom. At the time, I'd thought my ACL tear was the worst-case scenario. Now I realized that injury was really the best thing that could have happened to me. I was stronger. I was more focused. And best of all, I was starting to understand more about God and how he wanted to lead me.

I might have been young, but I knew what had gotten me to that point. And it certainly was not my own doing. It was the fact that God was with me every step of the way. I had a strong belief that no matter what happened, things were going to work out for the greater good. I didn't realize it at the time, but that was a truth I was going to need to cling to in the months and years ahead.

The Dregs of the Big Ten

After having a perfect season my senior year, a few teams started showing interest in me. But by now it was December, and most schools already had their commitments from players. I ended up being recruited by a few Ivy League schools, along with Purdue and Kentucky.

Purdue and Kentucky both had new coaching staffs, hired at the end of the 1996 season. Joe Tiller moved to Purdue from Wyoming, and Hal Mumme came from Valdosta State to Kentucky. Both coaches ran spread offenses, so they needed a quarterback who could pass it around. They had to throw together a recruiting class in a month and a half, and I was one of the few quarterbacks who hadn't signed on with other schools.

The very week after Coach LaHue had shaken his head about my not getting recruited, Purdue and Kentucky sent scouts to Westlake—to the same practice. David White, our receiver and one of my best friends in high school, leaned over and whispered, "They're here to see you."

I shrugged him off. "That's pretty cool. By the way, where's Purdue?" For all I knew, Purdue was an Ivy League school. Princeton, Purdue . . . it all sounded close enough.

The truth is, I was still thinking about a baseball scholarship. I didn't want to get too excited about football because I figured I'd focus on baseball in college and then work my way up to the major leagues. Even after I signed with Purdue, my hope was that I would get drafted really high in baseball or receive a baseball scholarship to a Texas school. After it became clear that neither of those things would happen, I figured I was truly meant to go to Purdue.

I took trips to Brown, Kentucky, and Purdue. After doing some research, I wound up choosing Purdue because of its academic reputation (some call it the Ivy League of the Midwest) and also because of the opportunity to play in the best conference in the country at the time: the Big Ten. Plus, I loved Joe Tiller and his spread offense and knew it would be a perfect fit. True, it was a basketball school . . . until *we* made it a football school.

I was part of a recruiting class that was able to sign only fifteen players. We were considered the last-place recruiting class in the Big Ten. The dregs. The bottom of the barrel. Whatever was picked over by everyone else. But instead of getting upset about the disrespect, we used that label to bring us together as a group. We said to each other, "Nobody's giving us a chance. But by the time we leave here, we're going to be Big Ten champions, and we're taking Purdue to the Rose Bowl."

The nation was going to be surprised at what could come out of West Lafayette, Indiana.

Life as a Boilermaker

Moving from high school football to the Big Ten was a big jump, although playing 5A football in Texas did help. They say adversity will either make you stronger or break you. If that's true, the Big Ten will make you tough as nails . . . or it will tear you apart.

Purdue is a proud school with strong athletics and a respected academic tradition. Nearly every building on campus is red brick, and according to legend, benefactor John Purdue insisted that since he owned the local brickyard, all future university buildings must be built with red brick. Whatever the reason, it makes for a majestic atmosphere. Some of my greatest memories from my time there are walking across campus to the athletic facility after my last class on Fridays during football season. The week of homework and tests was over, and it was almost game time. There is no better time of year than autumn in the Midwest. As I strolled through campus, I could feel the cool, crisp air and the sunshine on my face as I admired the leaves changing to beautiful shades of red, orange, and yellow. The bell tower would chime a tune just as I crossed the engineering mall and hit the homestretch to the locker room.

All the teams I played with during my four years at Purdue had great leadership and tremendous team dynamics. We knew how to work hard, but we also knew how to have fun doing it. This was due in large part to Joe Tiller and the culture and attitude he created when he came to Purdue. He ran about twenty guys off the team in the spring of 1997, a lot like the military weeds out the weak links during boot camp. Coach Tiller had a couple of very simple rules that you were expected to follow: Do what you are supposed to do, when you are supposed to do it. And do it that way every time. He also emphasized that if you do things the right way, good things will happen to you. They might not happen today or tomorrow, but eventually they will.

Oh, and then there was the "golden rule," at least Coach Tiller's version: he who has all the gold makes all the rules. As long as you acknowledged this, you would be just fine. We all knew who the boss was. If you missed class, were late to a meeting or a workout, or disrespected authority, you would pay for it with a 6 a.m. workout or a "throw-up session," as the players liked to call it. You ran so much or did so many up-downs and barrel rolls that throwing up was almost guaranteed. It was this leadership and discipline and fear of failure that allowed us to be as successful as we were those four years.

I vividly remember many exciting games from my time at Purdue, but there are a few that have left permanent marks on me. One of those was a game against Notre Dame, which I see as one of the defining moments of my college career.

I didn't start for Purdue until my sophomore year, in 1998. The first game of the year was against USC in the Pigskin Classic. We lost that game after taking a halftime lead, then won against Rice and Central Florida. The fourth game of the season had us playing at Notre Dame. In a game against the Fighting Irish, you have all the storied tradition of Notre Dame football—"Touchdown Jesus," the Golden Dome, the Gipper—and it was nationally televised on NBC. Purdue hadn't beaten Notre Dame in South Bend in almost twenty-five years. It was the biggest game of my life.

My play in the first three games had been okay, but I still hadn't convinced anyone that I was the quarterback of the future. There were questions about whether I could lead the Boilermakers to a Big Ten championship and a Rose Bowl.

Notre Dame was a highly ranked team at the time, not to mention the fact that they ended up in a Bowl Championship Series game at the end of that season. They also had an unbelievable defense. When I was a kid, I would watch games like this on TV and dream about being in that moment. Now that moment was here.

It All Comes Down to Two Minutes

For the first fifty-eight minutes of the game, I played some of the best football I ever had. Unfortunately, a game is sixty minutes long. At halftime we were winning 24–14. I had completed seventeen of twenty-one passes for more than 200 yards and two touchdowns. We were rolling.

In the second half Notre Dame came back. We were up 30–28, and we had the ball in our territory. We basically needed only one first down to run out the clock. The Fighting Irish defense stuffed the first two run plays for no gain, and then we moved back five yards on a penalty. It was third and fifteen with about 1:50 on the clock. Jim Chaney, our offensive coordinator, called a pass play where I would roll out to the left and throw the ball to a receiver running a deep in route right into my vision. It's not an easy pass—you have to time it well and stay balanced in order to deliver the ball accurately. But it was a play we'd run many times with success. If the pass was completed, we'd have a first down and the game would be over.

I rolled out, and wide receiver Randall Lane broke across the field in front of me as expected. The coverage was good, but I saw a window to complete the pass. As the ball left my hand, I could feel it come out a little high as I was attempting to elevate it over the head of a defender. Randall jumped for it, but the ball glanced off his fingertips and landed right in free safety Tony Driver's hands. He ran the interception back to the five yard line. Our defense held, but the Irish kicked a field goal and took the lead, 31–30.

I was in shock. Because of my mistake, we had gone from being one play away from victory to being behind. Even if I hadn't completed the pass, we would have punted, and our defense would have had a chance for a stop. Now we were losing. And it was my fault.

The game wasn't over yet, though. We had less than a minute to get into field goal range, and our offense had been clicking the whole game. We still had a chance. We threw a pass on first down, but it fell incomplete. Then lightning struck again. On second down, I threw the ball a little high, and it bounced off my receiver's fingertips. Another interception. Game over.

I knelt down on the field, unable to believe what had just happened. I had thrown two interceptions in the last two minutes, erasing the good play of the whole game. I headed into the locker room, still stunned, and sat at my locker. I looked around at the seniors and watched as tears ran from their eyes. We had worked so hard, and now here I was, the sophomore quarterback in his fourth start who had just lost the game for everybody. The first win on Notre Dame territory in twenty-five years had been in our grasp, and I had let everyone down. I felt awful.

I started wondering whether I was fit to play at Purdue. *Do I belong here? Can I compete at this level?* Fortunately I had friends who knew what I needed. That night I went out to eat with my two roommates, Ben Smith and Jason Loerzel. Jason was from Park Ridge, Illinois, and played linebacker. Ben was a quarterback from Nebraska who switched to free safety when he came to Purdue. We all came in during the same year and formed a bond, a brotherhood. We were from very different backgrounds and different parts of the country, but we were like glue.

Jason and Ben insisted we go to C Ray's, a local restaurant with the best chicken wings in town. "You're pretty miserable to be around right now," they said. "Let's order up some C Ray's wings, and we'll relax and let you vent."

That's what we did. Even though I was down, the wings were good. Still, I had trouble letting go of those last two minutes. I knew I was the reason we had lost. It's one thing to start well, but you have to finish—you have to follow through. You have to be able to win the big one and deliver when the game is on the line. But as we talked through the feelings, I realized that for fifty-eight minutes in the biggest game of my life, I'd played some of my best football. There was so much pressure to perform in that game. I hadn't finished well, but for fifty-eight minutes I'd showed I belonged on that field. That gave me confidence. The glass was half full. Find the positive out of every negative. That is what I always tried to do.

Jason and Ben helped get me out of my funk and focus on the next game, which was Minnesota at home. It was a misty day—foggy to the point where you almost couldn't see the field from the press box. For home games the team stayed at the hotel in the Union. We'd get up in the morning and walk about a half mile to the stadium as a team. To everybody else that day may have seemed dreary, but for me it felt like there was energy in the air. It felt like a fresh start, and the mist was bringing in a brand-new opportunity. I was going to show people what I had inside. I wasn't going to let the last two minutes of the Notre Dame game wreck my future.

That dinner at C Ray's was a proverbial fork in the road for me. I realized I could focus on my mistakes and feel sorry for myself, or I could learn from those mistakes and use them as motivation to come back stronger. Under pressure, would I fold and disappear, or would I show everyone that when bad things happen, you fight? I wanted to prove to my team that they could count on me and that I was the guy who could lead them.

In the game against Minnesota, I went thirty-one for thirty-six, with 522 yards and six touchdowns, until Coach Tiller pulled me after the third quarter. We were winning the game 56–14 at the time, and he wanted to get the young guys some action. All those stats were school records, and we could have gone for the NCAA record books if we'd wanted to, but running up the score is not how you play the game. In reality, the outcome of the Notre Dame game wasn't those two interceptions and the loss. It was the way it motivated me to play the next week—and helped me to turn a corner in my college career.

We went 9–4 that season and beat fourth-ranked Kansas State 37–34 in the Alamo Bowl. But we still hadn't made it to the Rose Bowl. That had been my ultimate goal as an incoming freshman. I knew the road to get there would not be easy, but anything worth fighting for never is.

Fixing What You Break

Two years later, I was a senior, and we were playing Ohio State. We'd had a frustrating year in 1999, going 7–5 and making it to the Outback Bowl but losing to a talented Georgia team in overtime. Now it was a new season, a new millennium, and there were great hopes that this was going to be our year.

We started out with a disappointing 3–2 record. We had two heartbreaking road losses to Penn State and Notre Dame— both by just two points. The next game was in West Lafayette against Michigan, who was ranked sixth. Then we had to go on the road against Wisconsin and Northwestern, both ranked in the top twenty. After that we'd play at home against Ohio State, another top ten team. And we hadn't beaten Michigan and Ohio State in forever, it seemed. Looking at this schedule could have been overwhelming, but that's why the philosophy always needs to be one game at a time. Never look too far ahead, or you will end up tripping over something right in front of you. We could do this. We had to do this. We had no other choice if we wanted to be called champions.

The first victim was Michigan, and it was a wild game— we won with a last-second field goal, 32–31. We then went to Northwestern and won. Next we traveled to Wisconsin and won in overtime. The team was rolling, and we were ready for the showdown: Ohio State at Purdue. We were ranked sixteen, they were twelve, and everybody was saying, "This game is for the Rose Bowl." Whoever won that game had to win only one more game to clinch the Big Ten title.

It was a late October night—a great night for football. The Purdue fans were into the game, and everyone was pumped to beat Ohio State. But we didn't start well. Going into the fourth quarter, we were losing 20–10, and I had thrown three interceptions. This was not what I'd envisioned for this game. We had moved the ball well offensively; we just kept turning it over at the worst times. But in spite of all that, in the fourth quarter we were down only two scores.

We started the fourth quarter with the ball and drove down the field. I threw a touchdown pass to wide receiver John Standeford: 20–17, Ohio State. We got the ball back, and I threw another touchdown pass, this time to wide receiver Vinny Sutherland. Now we were winning 24–20 with about six minutes left in the game. The fans were going wild. The defense stepped up, and we got the ball back with a chance to run out the clock.

We ran a few plays and watched the clock. It could not tick down fast enough. The number one priority in this situation was to take care of the football. Whatever we did, we couldn't give them a short field or any momentum with a turnover. The next play I dropped back to pass and was immediately flushed out of the pocket by a blitzing linebacker running free up the middle. I scrambled to my right and thought, *Be smart. Throw the ball away.* As I pulled the ball back to throw it away, my foot slipped and the ball fluttered in the air toward the sideline. It didn't go out-of-bounds like I'd intended—it sailed. I watched in horror as the strong safety, Mike Doss, intercepted it and ran it down the sideline. I couldn't believe this was happening. Practically on autopilot, I chased him down and knocked him out-of-bounds at the two yard line. In the process, I almost knocked myself out.

Dazed, I tried to get up onto one knee. *What did I just do?*

Ohio State celebrated around me, and our defense came out. I headed back to the sideline and watched as, a couple of plays later, the Buckeyes scored a touchdown to go up 27–24 with a little over two minutes left in the game. Some players tapped me and said, "It's okay," or "Go win the game for us." But other than that people pretty much left me alone.

As I did between most drives in the game, I got on the phone with my quarterbacks coach, Greg Olson, who was positioned up in the press box. "Shake it off. Focus on the next series. You are going to win this game for us—you watch."

It was eerie how similar this felt to that Notre Dame game two years earlier, but I had learned from that experience. Finally defensive end Warren "Ike" Moore came up to me. He was a senior, too, and a guy who really didn't get a lot of playing time. But he was a well-respected, quiet leader on the team. He put his arm around me and said something I'll never forget.

"You broke it. Now go out and fix it."

For some reason that made sense. It had been my mistake, but I had time to make up for that mistake. Instead of kicking myself or replaying the interception, I focused on the task at hand. One thing you learn quickly is that great quarterbacks must have short-term memories when it comes to things like this. Good or bad, you have to be able to finish a play, push it aside, and move on to the next one. You can never let a play from the past affect the present. Your job is to play in the moment.

Ohio State kicked off, and I went out onto the field. I was feeling the pressure, but it was that pressure that gave me an edge. I was focused and determined and maintained the philosophy of one play at a time. *Trust yourself. Trust your teammates.*

Trust the progression. I threw the first pass, but it was batted down by the defense. *Okay, shake it off. Second and ten.* Our offensive coordinator, Jim Chaney, then called a routine play—one of my favorites. In this play there are four receivers to throw the ball to. Ninety percent of the time the ball goes to the first or second receiver. The third receiver gets the ball about 10 percent of the time. And then there's the guy on the outside who runs a post route to clear out the defense. He never gets the ball, except maybe one play in a thousand.

I dropped back and went through my progression. This drill was ingrained in me. You practice it; you visualize it; you go through each receiver methodically and decide yes or no. If any receiver in the progression is open, you pull the trigger. I read the first receiver on a hitch to my left, and he was covered. The second receiver, running a seam route down the left numbers, was covered too. Next I looked at the seam route running right down the middle of the field, and the defense was all over him. All three were a no go.

Then I scanned for the fourth option—the one I never threw to. He was open—and I mean wide open! In a split second, my mind said, *Turn it loose.* The ball came out of my hand, and Seth Morales caught it for a sixty-four-yard touchdown. We won the game 31–27.

Overcome with emotion, I went down on one knee. "Thank you, Lord." My offensive linemen came over and picked me up.

The left tackle, Matt Light, who now has a great career with the New England Patriots, including three Super Bowl rings, was one of the first ones there. He grabbed me under my shoulder pads and lifted me off the ground while screaming in my face, "That is what makes you great! That is what makes you great!" What a moment. I loved my offensive line. Most of them were seniors, and we had set out on this journey together. That's what made the experience so special—being able to share it with people like them.

After four years of hard work, we finally had a chance to win the Big Ten championship and go to the Rose Bowl. We could have given up when Ohio State scored the touchdown. I could have beaten myself up over the mistake. But I was given the opportunity to make it right, to fix it.

We fixed it together.

Not long ago I talked with Coach Jim Tressel, who has coached Ohio State since 2001. He said, "I'll never forget what you did to Ohio State in that game in 2000. In fact, I might not have this job if it weren't for that play." John Cooper was the head coach at Ohio State that year, and he was let go after that season.

"I guess everything happens for a reason, doesn't it, Coach?" I said.

GIRL MEETS
IDIOT QUARTERBACK

IN HIGH SCHOOL and in college, I was the kind of guy who was friends with everybody. I dated a lot of girls, but I never found anyone I wanted to be serious with. My longest relationship up to that point had probably lasted no more than a couple of months. School and athletics consumed me. When I got to Purdue, I was even more lasered in on football and academics. I was an industrial management major with a manufacturing minor. Everyone knows Purdue is one of the top ten engineering schools in the country, but most people don't realize that the Krannert School of Management at Purdue is in the top ten among business schools at public universities. My course work upheld Purdue's reputation as the Ivy League of the Midwest.

I started off the first semester of my freshman year with a 3.5 GPA, but that fell off significantly in the spring with a 2.6 GPA, due in large part to my pledgeship responsibilities with Sigma Chi fraternity. But no excuses. I needed to suck it up.

I continued on a pretty good pace with my classes until the spring of my sophomore year, when I made a D in one of the most important management courses. This put my GPA right around a 3.2, which wasn't all bad, except that in order to be considered for Academic All-American, you have to have at least a 3.25 GPA. That was one of my goals, and I was not about to let Management 201 get the best of me.

I very easily could have moved on to the next prerequisite courses for my major, but the D did not sit well with me. That was the first and only D I'd ever made in my life. When summer school rolled around, I enrolled in the course again. It was time to seek my redemption. I needed a B to hit the 3.25 mark for Academic All-American, and when it came time for the final, I was right on the bubble. I had to get a B on the test—there was no other option. I studied and prepared as much as I could, and after the two-hour exam, I had to wait a full day for the results. I was chomping at the bit, but when the score came back, I had aced the final with a 100 percent. My final grade for the course was an A. I was able to keep up the Academic All-American title throughout my time at Purdue.

With all that was on my mind with academics and football, I didn't let myself dream of getting married and settling down yet. I was too focused on everything else. But I'll tell you the truth: the minute I saw Brittany, I told myself, *I'm going to marry that woman.* Of course, she didn't feel that way about me, because I made a fool of myself the first time I met her.

It was January 15, 1999, my twentieth birthday. I was with a bunch of players who lived at an apartment complex near school, and we were feeling pretty invincible that night, having partaken of a few adult beverages to celebrate my birthday. I'm not proud of it, but that's what we sometimes did on a night out with the fellas. I remember seeing Brittany from twenty feet away, walking across the parking lot toward the apartment. She was with a friend of hers who knew one of the guys on our team. I just stared at her and wondered, *Who is that? She's the most beautiful woman I've ever seen. And look at the way she carries herself.* It's hard to describe the feeling that came over me at that moment. My legs became weak, my mind halted, and my heart just melted. I knew right then that I wanted to marry her.

At one point during the evening I got up enough nerve to talk with her. I was acting stupid because of the alcohol, throwing out every cheesy pickup line in the book. It's humiliating to even recall it. I remember Brittany looking at me and just shaking her head before she simply walked away.

I found out later that when I left, she was thinking, *Who is this young idiot who's so full of himself?* Somebody told her I was the quarterback of the football team, to which she responded, "Then who is this young idiot football player who's so full of himself?" Turns out my cheesy pickup lines had sent her running, and the fact that I played football pretty much solidified I would never get a shot again. Football players don't have the greatest reputation for being good boyfriends, and she wanted nothing to do with me.

When I woke up the next day, my head was pounding and I was kicking myself. *I'm such a jerk. I blew it.* I figured I'd probably never see her again. Actually I hoped I wouldn't run into her because of how embarrassed I felt. I was sure I'd ruined any opportunity to get to know her.

However, for the next six months I saw Brittany everywhere. On the way to class, out to eat somewhere, at a party, in the library—wherever I went, she was there. On a campus with thirty-five thousand students, this was no small feat. I wasn't sure why this was happening, but to me it seemed like more than chance. To hear Brittany's version of things, she figured I was a full-blown stalker at that point. She thought I was creepy; I was sure it was destiny.

Every time I saw her, I watched from across the room (okay, so maybe a little creepy), thinking, *I really want to talk to her, but she thinks I'm an idiot.* I might have been confident on the football field, but I was really shy in these kinds of situations. I started scheming ways to make up for my embarrassing first impression. The truth was, even though I'd been drinking the night I first met her, I didn't go out a lot. I wasn't a big partyer. I was grateful to be at a good school, and I was focused on my education and my commitment to the football team. Now I just had to get Brittany to see that.

Six months later I was going to summer school and heading into summer training. Brittany was there for the summer too since she had a job there. On June 25, I was invited to a friend's apartment, and one of the guys from the team went with me. It was our first night back from break, just before we started our practice schedule in the Midwest heat. I was talking to some guys and having a great time but was about to call it a night because of some early commitments I had the next day. Just then Brittany walked in the door with two of her friends. This was it—my chance at redemption.

For all this time I'd been scared to talk to her. But maybe, just maybe, enough time had passed to make her forget my stupid behavior in January. As the crowd mingled, Brittany's two friends left her side long enough for me to make my move. I kind of snuck up to her and confidently said hello, pretending we were meeting for the first time.

Sure enough, she hadn't forgotten. I couldn't quite place the look on her face. Was she surprised? startled? maybe even a little scared? Regardless, I had her cornered, and she was forced to talk to me. I introduced myself and started over.

With the loud music and conversation, I knew this wasn't the best place to get to know her. I wanted to find out more about her, and I really wanted her to know I wasn't a jerk. My strategy was to get to a place where we could be alone and talk.

"Where are you guys going?" I asked Brittany and her friends. I knew they lived in an apartment complex a few miles away. Maybe I could finagle my way into driving her home and having a little more time with her.

"Oh, we're just going back to our apartment. I need to get some sleep." Little did she know that I had several friends who lived near her in the same apartment complex. I also knew that everyone was headed back there to go swimming. She was trying to get rid of me, but it wasn't working.

I looked at my watch. "Yeah, it is getting late. Well, I was going to head over anyway to go swimming with my friends. Can I catch a ride with you?"

"I don't think so," she said. "I probably shouldn't be driving."

"Well, at least I could drive you home so you don't have to come back for your car tomorrow."

She winced. "No thanks."

"Really, it's no problem. I'll drive your car back."

"It's a stick. I'm sure you don't know how to drive it," she said, feeling pretty confident that this would end the conversation and she would be rid of me.

"Oh, sure," I lied. I'd never driven a standard in my life.

She finally relented. "Okay. I guess you can drive my car and just drop us at home."

"Okay, cool."

We got to her car, which was a 1990 Toyota Celica twin turbo in two shades of red. It had been in an accident at some point, and the front left fender had been repainted a slightly different shade from the rest of the car since Brittany had to pay for the repairs herself.

We got to the car, and I put the key in. I felt as nervous at that moment as in any game against a Big Ten opponent. I knew enough to push in the clutch, but I wasn't sure what to do next. I got the car started and tried to figure out how to put it in reverse.

"Are you sure you've driven a stick before?" she said.

"Yeah, yeah. I'm just not used to how loose this clutch is. It's different."

I started sweating. *Don't ruin this. This is your one chance to make up for being such an idiot.* I got us out of the parking lot, and we began jerking down the street. I pulled to a stop sign, and we stalled. Brittany just stared at me.

"Don't worry; we're fine," I said.

It took me half an hour to drive to her apartment—a drive that should have taken only about five minutes. At one point during our whiplashed road trip, I heard Brittany's head hit the window as I gunned the car forward. I looked over hesitantly, but to my relief Brittany was laughing so hard, there were tears coming down her face. Maybe she was coming around and starting to appreciate my effort, or I had just given her a concussion and she wouldn't remember this ride home in the morning. Either scenario could work to my advantage.

Somehow, someway, I got us to her place in one piece. I handed her the keys and told her I was going to meet my friends at the pool and I'd love for her to join us. I really didn't know if she would show up or not. But a few minutes later, there she was, along with her roommate. I felt like I was slowly making progress. After we swam for a while, I asked Brittany if I could use her apartment to change into my dry clothes. She agreed, and I walked her and her roommate back to their apartment. We ended up sitting in her place and talking for hours. We watched the sun come up. And we found we had so many things in common—our love for traveling, our families, the faith and beliefs we shared, how many children we wanted, and on and on. Brittany had been raised in the Episcopal church, and with my faith having really blossomed at St. Andrew's Episcopal School, we had very similar beliefs. I hoped she was starting to see that I really wasn't this cheeseball who had hit on her six months earlier. I was a decent guy, not the "typical football player" that people have preconceived notions about.

I didn't tell her that night because I didn't want to freak her out, but I was sure of it now: I was going to marry this girl. Brittany drove me home—I guess she'd had enough of my driving—and I called my mom the next day to tell her I had met the woman of my dreams.

Neither one of us had seen this coming. Just six months earlier, Brittany had had a two-year dating relationship end badly. She had been pretty hurt and was still working through some trust issues. She was going into her senior year and had no intention of meeting anyone new, let alone starting a relationship. I was only twenty, and I had a full life with football, school, and hanging out with my friends. It was a shock for both of us to be knocked off our feet over each other. But the more time we spent together, the more we talked and shared, the more we were convinced that we were meant to be together. I remember at one point telling her about my injury in high school and how it had been a turning point in my life. She said, "That which does not kill you makes you stronger." That quote really struck a chord with me. She was right. Little did we both know it was going to be a theme in our lives.

There are so many similarities between us, but I was also intrigued by our differences. I believe God made us different so we'd be more fully one. He brought us together with our similarities, but the differences helped bond us as well. That might seem counterintuitive, but it's true.

Brittany has certain weaknesses where I have strengths, and I have weaknesses where she is strong. We complete and complement each other. For example, Brittany would admit she will eat anything with chocolate on it (while I am a pretty healthy eater), has horrible penmanship, has the mouth of a truck driver, hates to do math (even though she worked at a bank and can do it), and can't spell to save her life. She'll be texting, and in the middle of the message she'll ask me how to spell a street name or a difficult word. For me it's no problem. I was born spelling and computing.

My weak points are putting too much on my calendar (I say yes to everything and then don't have time for anything), cooking (I believe that surprising Brittany with a meal means bringing home takeout), and communication. I hate hurting people I care about, so I don't say the things that bother me until they build up and become a much bigger issue than they would have been had I just addressed it at the time. I'm also the kind of person who will spring things on Brittany and assume she knows what's going on when I haven't really talked about it until that point. Like "Hey, babe, *Sports Illustrated* is doing a photo shoot at our house today—can you clean up the house and be ready in forty-five minutes?" She *loves* when I do that to her. Those are the times flowers are soon to follow.

One of the things I admire about Brittany is the way she's in touch with her feelings and other people's too. She has an innate ability to read people and connect with them, and I try to learn from her. She has a knack for meeting someone and really understanding who they are and, a lot of times, what their intentions are.

At Purdue my coaches taught me how important progression is. I had to read the defense, find my receivers, and become the best team player I could be. I did everything I could to win, but I also needed to fight through the losses and learn from them. It was the same with Brittany.

For my final two years at Purdue, my family stayed with Brittany for every home game. She was forced to witness first-hand how divorced parents deal with having to see each other every weekend during the football season. She was thrown into the "custody battle" pretty fast and had to rotate who she sat with at the games. Then on Sundays we would get up and have breakfast with one parent and lunch with the other. It was not an option to all be at the same table together without snide comments or eye rolling. It was pretty stressful for her because it seemed that both parties were trying to get her to pick a side. I remember many nights when we would come home from a dinner with one parent or the other and she would be crying, not knowing how to handle the situation. I was used to this way of life, but it was all foreign to Brittany, who is extremely close to her immediate family as well as her extended family. I would simply ignore the fighting and let the two sides battle it out like they had always done. I was just told where to be and when once the dust settled.

The older I got, the more difficult it became for me to witness the bitterness between my parents. I felt like I needed to start making my own decisions and believed that by doing that, there would be less fighting. This coming-of-age did not go over smoothly. Although I'm sure this process of asserting independence is an issue in every parent-child relationship, unfortunately it was what began the deterioration of my relationship with my mother.

During my senior year I begged Brittany to stay in West Lafayette while I finished school. Although she had already graduated, her plans of going out into the working world were put on hold while I tried to accomplish my final goals as a student athlete. I couldn't imagine not having her there for every game and every special moment. She worked full-time as a travel agent, paying all the bills. My scholarship check was enough to get us dinner at Bruno's, a local pizza joint, once a month, and that was pretty much it.

Brittany and I leaned on each other during that time and grew up together over the next few years. But we had no idea what we were getting into. Early on we committed ourselves to each other, and we decided that no matter what happened, we were going to work through any hard times we faced. We would fight together. Quitting or giving up on each other was never an option. Without her I wouldn't be where I am today.

I didn't know how important that lesson would be until I made it to the NFL.

CHARGING AHEAD

THOSE WERE GOOD YEARS at Purdue. Just as I'd dreamed, we made it to the Rose Bowl my senior year. We fought hard and won the Big Ten, and then we finally found ourselves at the big game. We played the Washington Huskies, and it was tight almost the whole game. The Huskies scored twenty points in the second half, and we ended up losing 34–24. It was a big disappointment to the team, but we were thrilled to have left our mark on the "granddaddy" of all bowl games. Along the way I was nominated twice for the Heisman Trophy, finishing fourth in 1999 and third in 2000.

In what seemed like no time at all, I was getting ready for the NFL draft. In February 2001, I participated in the Scouting Combine, where players are poked and prodded and sized up in virtually any way you can imagine. If your knees and shoulders and ankles don't hurt when you get there, they do by the time you leave, after all the team doctors yank on your joints. They make you feel like a piece of meat.

To test physical speed and agility, players run a forty-yard dash, the 5-10-5 shuttle, and the L drill. The scouts even clock your throws with a radar gun—similar to what police officers use when they give you a speeding ticket on the highway. I wasn't breaking any speeding laws in terms of arm strength. I think my fastest throw was around 60 mph. Then you go through multiple interviews with coaches who pry into just about every subject, trying to find out how much you understand about the game as well as what your personality is like and what kind of guy you are.

A few of those interviews stick out in my mind. Dick Vermeil of the Chiefs asked me a lot of questions, none of which I remember because I was too busy staring at his Super Bowl ring. He'd won it with the Rams a few years earlier. I really wanted one of those. Meeting with offensive coordinator Norv Turner of the Chargers was another key interview. I could really feel his interest in me as a player and a person, and that sense was confirmed when Norv, Chargers head coach Mike Riley, general manager John Butler, and a few other scouts came to Purdue a few weeks later to give me a personal workout. I think I took him back when I asked what they were going to do with Ryan Leaf, whom the Chargers had drafted three years earlier with the second pick but who didn't seem like a good fit for San Diego. He told me that was none of my business, and then I watched as they released him a week later. That was when I knew they might be drafting a quarterback.

The last memorable interview came with a young quarterbacks coach from the Washington Redskins named Brian Schottenheimer. It was his first year as an NFL coach, and he was only a little older than I was. Little did I know that someday he would coach me for four years in San Diego and become one of my great friends and mentors. Funny how things work out.

It was an exhausting day, but overall I had a positive feeling about how everything had gone. I must admit, though, that I was tired of answering the same questions about my short stature and the fact that I had played in a spread offense almost exclusively in the shotgun my whole college career. Would I be able to adapt to an NFL offense where I would be under center the majority of the time? I kept reassuring them that they had no need to worry—I was pretty sure I could take a snap from under center. In all seriousness, they could watch the film, talk to my coaches, talk to those I played with and against. I tried to give them everything they needed to see and hear. Now there was only one thing left to do: wait for draft day.

On April 21, the air seemed to be filled with electricity. Brittany and I were waiting for the results in my apartment along with Tim Layden, a writer for *Sports Illustrated*, who was doing a draft profile on me. Brittany had saved up her money to surprise me by flying in my brother, Reid, to also share in the moment with us. I was frying up some fish in the deep fryer and watching the draft on ESPN.

Being a competitive person, I was really counting on going in the first round, at as high a number as possible. I knew very well that's how a player's worth is measured. If you're the number one pick, or in the top five or top ten, you're deemed one of the best prospects in the league. There's a big difference between the contract of the first pick and the seventh, between the tenth pick and the twentieth.

New England had talked with me about taking me as their sixth pick, and I knew San Diego, who held the fifth pick after a trade with Atlanta, was also interested in me, so I thought I would go pretty high. In the first round, San Diego chose LaDainian Tomlinson. I figured that was it for my chances to play for the Chargers. But I still felt fairly confident I would go as the sixth pick to New England—until they chose Richard Seymour instead.

There were about six other teams who said they might draft me if I was available in the first round. Seattle and Kansas City showed a lot of interest early but traded for Matt Hasselbeck and Trent Green, respectively, prior to the draft. Carolina and Jacksonville had draft picks in the teens and had both seen me throw lights out at my pro day in March at Purdue. Neither one was meant to be. Players like Michael Vick, Santana Moss, and Deuce McAllister, whom I would team up with later in New Orleans, were all drafted ahead of me. I listened as the names were announced all the way through the teens and into the twenties. That left Miami with the twenty-sixth pick.

I had been told by numerous sources, but most significantly Coach Tiller, who had a friend in the Dolphins organization, that if I was still available at that point, they would definitely draft me. I stood by the phone, ready for the call that would say, "Congratulations—welcome to South Florida!" But the call never came. I checked the ringer to make sure the phone was working. Sure enough, that was not meant to be either.

I was frustrated and a little hurt—not so much by the fact that I wasn't a first-round pick, but more so because I thought I had been lied to. The fact of the matter is, you can't believe a thing most teams tell you on draft day. I didn't realize at the time how much goes on behind the scenes. It looks like a pretty exact science, but it's not. Emotions are high and last-minute information is getting thrown around right up until the draft decisions are made. As the first round neared an end, it became obvious that I would not be drafted by any of the remaining teams. They didn't need a quarterback. I then saw a familiar team pop up on the draft board.

San Diego had the first pick in the second round. Little did

I know they had actually tried to trade up to get me late in the first round, but no one would trade with them. They were sure that I wouldn't be available to them in the second round. But there I was, still watching, still waiting.

Finally the phone rang. It was John Butler, general manager for the Chargers. I was going to San Diego! They chose me with the first pick of the second round, the thirty-second pick overall. Of course I would have liked to have been drafted higher, but I was happy about going to San Diego. I loved John and the coaching staff he had put together. His résumé spoke for itself. He had been with the Buffalo Bills for many years, including four consecutive trips to the Super Bowl in the early nineties. He had also brought in Doug Flutie a few weeks earlier as the starting quarterback. In my mind—and a lot of people would agree with me—Doug Flutie was a legend. I was five years old when he threw that legendary Hail Mary for Boston College to beat Miami in 1984. There was so much I could learn from this guy, and with no pressure to immediately come in as the starter, I could relax and get indoctrinated gradually. Plus, I would have the opportunity to play with some of the greatest to ever play the game—LaDainian Tomlinson, Junior Seau, and Rodney Harrison.

I hopped on a plane to San Diego to meet with head coach Mike Riley and answer questions from the media. As I tried to wrap my brain around my new reality, I realized something: I could get stuck in disappointment because I hadn't gone in the first round like I'd envisioned, or I could be thankful I'd landed in the right place. Sometimes it's not how you get to your destination that's most important. The key is ending up in the right place—on the right team, in the right situation, with the right opportunity. I felt that God had put me in San Diego for a reason. A new adventure was about to begin.

Second-String

As soon as training camp was underway, one thing was clear: I was the backup. In fact, I was competing for a spot on the team, as far as I was concerned. Dave Dickenson was making a run for the backup quarterback role, and I had my work cut out for me. Doug Flutie, the former Heisman Trophy winner and free agent who had been acquired by the Chargers, would be the starting quarterback. I played in only one game all year—when Flutie got a concussion—and even then, it was only for about half of the game. But I was watching Doug and taking notes.

Doug Flutie was a mentor to me; he did so much for my career and my development as a young player. I loved the way he played the game—with a fire and passion to win like I'd never seen before. I'm sure that's why he played professional football for so long—over twenty years in three different leagues. We were friends then, and we are to this day. He really cared about me as a person and as a player—I don't think he saw me as a threat. When I became a Charger, I wanted to help Doug and the rest of the team. My goal was to work my tail off and play as well as I could, and if I was good enough to play, great. If I wasn't good enough, then I wouldn't play. I just wanted to play my best, and I think Doug respected that.

Flutie was tough. He's a small guy—only five-nine. He'll tell you he's five-ten, but don't believe him. He's five-nine and 180 pounds. But what he lacks in height, he makes up for in heart, athletic ability, and a supercompetitive nature. Mentally he's as tough as they come, and physically he can't be kept down. You can knock him around all you want, but he's going to get back up and fight. A great example of this came during the 2002 training camp. In a freak accident during practice, someone ran into Doug on the sideline and separated his shoulder. He jumped up, brushed himself off, and didn't tell anyone about the injury until two weeks later. Meanwhile, he kept slinging the ball around as if nothing had happened. That was Doug.

Early in that season Doug revealed something interesting to me that must have come from his experience in Buffalo. He said, "I've learned to never take myself out of a game and to never let someone else take you out of a game. Do whatever you can to prevent injury, but if you do get hurt, fight through whatever you can. Never give your backup the opportunity to see the field because you might not get back out there again."

In Buffalo, Doug had experienced a divided locker room, where half the players wanted Rob Johnson as quarterback and the other half wanted Doug. There were stories of heated rivalries within the team, and when Doug came to San Diego, he wanted to be as far away from that as possible. I had heard about that situation secondhand, and although Doug and I would compete fiercely for the starting job the next year, we could not have been better friends during our four years together.

In the 2000 season, the year before I arrived, San Diego had a 1–15 record—about as bad as you can get. The year I joined the team, Flutie led the team to a 5–2 start before losing the last nine games of the season. It was disappointing to all of us, but it was still an improvement. The next year Mike Riley was let go as head coach, and Marty Schottenheimer was hired. My world was about to change.

Valentine's Day Amour

The past several years had been a whirlwind for Brittany and me. Between finishing school, getting drafted, and playing my first season in the NFL, it seemed like we'd barely had time to catch our breath, let alone spend much quality time together. We decided to take our first big trip as a couple, and we settled on Europe: London, Italy, Normandy, and Paris. We started making the plans together, but what Brittany didn't know was that I was also making plans to propose.

I made sure we were in Paris on Valentine's Day. I'd practiced my proposal speech over and over—I knew exactly what I was going to say. And I was going to say it in French. I wish I could tell you what I said because I am quite proud of my memorization, but it was for her ears only. Although Brittany had taken six years of French classes in high school and college, I wasn't sure she'd be able to understand my pronunciation. But I figured once I got down on one knee, she'd catch on pretty quickly.

I had done research and talked to the concierge to find the perfect restaurant. It made me nervous having never been there before. I'm a visual person, and I like to see all the factors so I can anticipate what's going to happen. I tried to imagine the restaurant's layout and the setting for the proposal, but there were still some unknowns.

When we arrived at Le Petit Bofinger, we were seated at a table for two. I had the ring in my coat pocket. I took off my coat and placed it on the back of the bench where she was sitting. We relived the highlights from the day—our tour of Notre Dame Cathedral and some of our favorite painters and sculptors from the stroll through the Louvre. I was waiting for the right time. Finally I said, "Hey, babe, reach into my coat pocket and grab the map. Let's figure out where we're going tomorrow."

She reached in and suddenly pulled her hand back out as if she'd found something crawling in there. "The map's not in there," she said.

"Are you sure? Check one more time." I knew full well the ring box was waiting for her in that pocket. Again she insisted the map was not in that pocket and began to check the other pockets in my coat.

"Check that pocket again, sweetie."

"It's not there." She shoved the coat my way for me to find the map.

"Baby, just pull out what's in there."

She was kind of flustered at that point, but she reached in and pulled out the box. While she was concentrating on that, I slipped onto one knee next to her. I took out the ring and put it on her finger, proposing in my best Texas French. She was wiping away the tears. I was crying too. It was a good thing I'd practiced so much—somehow the words came out perfectly.

What we didn't know at the time was that a couple from Canada was sitting behind us to our right. Brittany and I were so oblivious, we had no idea there was a single other person in the restaurant. The husband saw me go down on my knee, and he must have been a Boy Scout—always prepared—because he pulled out his camera and took a picture.

Six months later I got the picture in the mail. There would be many more good snapshots to come.

A New Coach, a New Season

When I got back from the trip, I was introduced to our new coach, Marty Schottenheimer. I loved the guy from the start. I'd still run through a wall for him. But when I started out, I was a young quarterback who needed to learn, grow, mature, and develop. He was a hard-nosed football coach who knew only one way. He helped toughen me up mentally and emotionally. He talked about the great quarterbacks he had coached in the past—guys like Bernie Kosar, Joe Montana, and Rich Gannon. I just hoped he would be talking about me like that someday.

Marty was passionate about coaching. He always wore his emotions on his sleeve. If he was talking about somebody he cared about, he'd get choked up. He'd cry at half the team meetings too—that was just his personality. And if you were sitting in the front row, your chances of catching some of his saliva on your forehead from the speech he was giving were pretty good. Behind that passion was always a very articulate and specific message. Marty was a great communicator and motivator, and he had an old-school mentality of taking pride in being tough. That was one of the things we loved about him. "We're gonna pound the ball! We're gonna play great defense! And we're gonna hit 'em in the mouth." That was saying it nicely.

At training camp in the summer of 2002, Marty introduced a new set of coaches: Cam Cameron, Brian Schottenheimer, and Pete Carmichael. Marty sized up the quarterback situation and said, "Competition's open, Drew and Doug. And whoever wins this job will have earned it—I can promise you that."

Doug and I battled it out that preseason. Doug was a fierce competitor, and his desire to keep the job made me better. Competition seems to bring out the best in everyone. By the time regular season began, I was named starting quarterback. To be perfectly honest, I think it was dead even between me and Doug. But the fact was, he was forty years old and I was twenty-three. Marty seemed to like the upside of the young buck, although he could certainly appreciate the fight the old dog still had in him. I started every game that year.

Then came a pivotal moment in a matchup against Buffalo, the fourteenth game of the season. We had gotten off to a blistering start that year, winning six of our first seven games, but now we were stalled. After a tough few weeks, we had an 8–5 record and still had a good shot at making the playoffs. We were losing to the Bills at Orchard Park, New York. Nobody on our team was playing well. I know I wasn't. In the fourth quarter Marty came up to me on the sideline and said, "I'm going to pull you, and I'm going to put Flutie in."

I knew Doug had some loaded history with the Bills after his time playing there. He was pretty pumped up for the game, and I could understand that. But I couldn't believe that Marty would take me out. So I voiced my displeasure.

"We just need a spark right now," Marty said. "I think Doug can do that for us."

I could understand it from a coaching perspective, but I also remembered what Doug had told me about not letting your backup see the field. This was the first time anybody had pulled me out of a game like that. Coaches had taken me out because we were up by four touchdowns, more of a "Hey, great job—you're done for the day" kind of thing. But this wasn't a reward; this was pulling me for somebody else. And I wasn't about to let that happen.

"No, I'm not coming out," I said.

Marty recognized the fire in me and said, "You're still the starter. It's just for this game."

I was angry and hurt, and I kept pushing. "No, you can't do this. This is my team. I'm not coming out."

He said, "Oh yes, you are. Doug is in."

I fought Marty really hard, but there's a point when you finally have to relent to the head coach. There was nothing I could say or do to change his mind. I realized I had to accept his decision and support the team.

We wound up losing our last four games and went 8–8 that year. Once again we missed the playoffs. But as we assessed the past few seasons, we could see a gradual improvement in the team. We had gone from winning one game to five games to eight games. That progression gave us hope for the next year. Our talent level was off the charts, and so were our expectations.

A Low Point in My Career

But in 2003, things didn't work out as planned. Looking back, I can see how the adversity of that season helped prepare me for better things down the road, but it was excruciating at the time. I was still a young player, with much to learn about playing in the big leagues. Going into that season, we were as talented a team as I'd ever known, and the expectation was playoffs or bust. Unfortunately, it ended up being a huge bust. Injuries plagued us all season long, but the real problem was our youth, inexperience, and lack of leadership. When things started going downhill early in the season with a 0–5 start, the finger-pointing began.

No one wanted to admit they were at fault, so instead, players went around blaming everyone else. Cliques began forming on the team, and people would either bash the coaches or talk about the other guys behind their backs. The negativity became like a disease that spread throughout our team and infected us all to the point that we were completely dysfunctional. There was so much distrust in each other and in the system that the young guys didn't know who to follow.

The fact is, we were all to blame. Especially me, because it's my job as a quarterback to squash that kind of stuff the minute it rears its ugly head. But I was young and probably not equipped to handle it at the time. Still, you live and learn. Sometimes you have to go through some deep valleys in order to climb the next mountain.

The lowest point of that season came in the eighth game of the year. We were 1–6 and playing at Chicago. The minute I got into the game, I began putting intense pressure on myself. I desperately wanted things to turn around with this game. I knew I needed to relax and just play, but I couldn't loosen up. This led to forced throws, and I played terribly for the first three quarters.

Near the end of the third quarter, we were down 13–0. Chicago had just kicked a field goal, putting us behind by two scores. If we were going to win, I knew we needed a big momentum shift. And it was up to me to create it.

After playing poorly the whole game, I saw this as my opportunity to come in and fix things, just like I'd done in college many times before. Cam Cameron, our offensive coordinator, called the play—a pass to wide receiver Tim Dwight—and I hesitated. I was lacking a bit of confidence, so I didn't turn the ball loose and fire it in there like I should have. The throw was late, and the ball got knocked down. Incomplete.

On second down, another pass play was called, so I went through my read and threw it out in the flat. LaDainian Tomlinson got pushed out-of-bounds almost immediately for a short three-yard gain. So now we were third and seven, in Chicago territory. We called a pass play, and I felt confident we would get the first down. Tim Dwight ran the route again, and like most routes in an NFL offense, it required trust and timing for it to work—neither of which I had at that moment. Tim ran a nine-yard stop route, a pass I normally could complete in my sleep. He was open, and I threw it, but again my lack of confidence caused me to airmail the ball high and behind him. I was so afraid of making a mistake or making a bad throw that ironically, that's what inevitably happened. When you think negative thoughts, negative things usually happen. On the flip side, when you think positively and visualize success, that's usually what you get. It's amazing how that works. Tim tried to recover to make the catch, but the ball slipped through his fingers. Incomplete again. Fourth down.

As I jogged off the field, reality set in. *That was my opportunity to save my job, and I blew it.* I realized I was about to get benched.

I got to the sideline, and sure enough Marty Schottenheimer came up to me. "I'm pulling you. Doug's in." I could see in Marty's eyes that he was ready for a fight. He was remembering that game in Buffalo and the fire I'd shown him. He was expecting me to get in his face and refuse to come out of the game.

But by that point I was defeated mentally and emotionally. In my entire professional career, I'd never been this low. So instead of fighting with him, I just took off my helmet. "I understand."

As I headed to the bench, I thought about my quarterbacks coach from Purdue, Greg Olson, who was now the quarterbacks coach for the Bears. He was a mentor to me, not only in my growth as a quarterback, but also in my maturity as a person. He'd been key in helping me approach the game professionally and develop a strong work ethic. We'd spent countless hours at Purdue studying film, with Coach Olson guiding me through each play, each mistake, so I could learn from it.

Knowing my former coach was across the field had been added incentive for me to play well that game. I wanted to impress him and show him that all his hard work was for a purpose. And now, instead of excelling, I'd just been benched.

We ended up losing to Chicago 20–7. Doug Flutie finished out the game at quarterback and led us on a scoring drive capped off by a LaDainian Tomlinson touchdown, but it was too little, too late. It was a devastating loss, bringing our record to 1–7. After the game, I was more disheartened than I'd ever been. The little confidence I'd had left seemed to have dried up. I walked across the field and found Greg. I saw the hurt in his eyes. *He's hurting for* me.

"Hey, things are going to be okay," Greg said, putting his arm around me. He continued to try to console me as I nodded to acknowledge his efforts.

I was fighting back tears. I felt lost. Suddenly something came over me—sort of a courageous feeling. I stepped back and looked him dead in the eyes. With my chin still quivering a bit, I choked out, "I'm going to be a great player in this league someday."

It was kind of a funny thing to say at that moment, after such a miserable performance. But my hope was returning. I knew the kind of person I was—I knew I was capable of playing well. Something inside was telling me I was not going to go out like that. I had gotten this far; I was not about to give up now.

Greg looked at me, and I noticed there was a mist in his eyes too. "I know you are."

Marty benched me for the next five games. I had let my backup see the field . . . and now I was the backup.

On the Bench

I could have looked at this benching as a huge negative, but gradually I started moving beyond the disappointment and seeing it as something that could help me. I wanted to use this obstacle to help me become a better player, a better man. The truth is, you don't learn much from winning, but losing can make you a lot stronger. Some say experience is what you gain when you don't get what you want. In that case, I was gaining a lot of experience on the bench. I can look back on that time now and say it was exactly what I needed.

I couldn't have made it through that season without Brittany's support. We had been married only nine months then, and already she was getting dragged along on this roller-coaster ride. When I returned to San Diego after the game in Chicago, I was lower than I'd ever been. I lugged all my bags into the house and couldn't believe what I saw.

There were sticky notes and signs everywhere! In the living room, in the kitchen, in the hallway, on the stairs—they were all over. *You're the greatest! You're the best! Best husband ever! The best quarterback! You can't keep a good man down!* I went to our bathroom and saw that she'd taped pictures of me on the mirror—shots of all the great moments of my athletic career, from high school to the pros. Her support helped me bounce back after the big hit I'd taken. I am so blessed to have her in my life.

Marty's goal was for me to gain perspective while I was on the bench, and for those weeks that's exactly what I tried to do. Being on the sideline gives you an advantage you don't have when you're playing: you get to observe like a spectator. When a fan watches the game on TV or in the stands, things seem so obvious. "Man, how did he not see that guy? He was wide open." I was the Monday morning quarterback for a change.

It was this perspective that helped me simplify the game and learn from what I saw. The last couple of games I had operated in a haze because of the pressure I was putting on myself. I realized I was making the game so much more complicated than it really needed to be. Before that point in my career, I'd felt invincible. I thought I could make every play. That meant that every time I stepped onto the field, I *had* to make every play. When you go into a game with that mind-set, you put undue pressure on yourself. And you're destined to fail.

That period of warming the bench also gave me a chance to evaluate my attitude toward my teammates and my coaches. Human nature tells me to be angry and resentful and defensive when things don't go my way—to seek revenge. I always have to fight that. The more positive approach is to step back and look at reality. *This is not what I anticipated. But how can I make the most of it? What's the silver lining? This door may be closed, but there has to be an open window somewhere.* Anyone can see the adversity in a difficult situation, but it takes a stronger person to see the opportunity.

From the sideline I heard the play called. Flutie went into the huddle, then came to the line of scrimmage. I looked at the defense and immediately sized up the play: *Our best matchup is the single receiver to our left. He should throw it there.* Sure enough, Doug dropped back and threw it to the left. *That was easy.* Another play came in, and it was evident right away that we should check from the run to a pass because of the blitz look on defense. It was all coming back—the reasons I loved this game, the reasons I'd dedicated my life to it. This is what I was meant to do. If I was given another opportunity, I knew I'd be ready. I would go back out there and show them what I could do.

Back in the Game

Doug started five games, and then Marty approached me again. "Okay, it's time to put you back in."

I was ready.

Game fourteen of the 2003 season was against the Green Bay Packers. I would get the chance to face off against Brett Favre, one of the great quarterbacks of all time, in front of our home crowd. They ended up beating us, but it was clear that this was the beginning of a new era for me. I turned some balls loose, the kind you can throw only when you have complete confidence and trust in what you're doing. No hesitation, no doubt, no fear of making a mistake. On that Sunday, I made progress as a starting quarterback in the league. Sitting on the bench had helped me develop a stiff upper lip. I was tougher now.

After that we traveled to Pittsburgh—our next-to-last game of the season. The Steelers scored on their first three possessions. The game had barely begun, and already they were beating us 21–0. But then our offense started to click. We scored two touchdowns and a field goal, bringing the tally to 21–17. It was now the third quarter, and we had the ball with a chance to take the lead. *Maybe this is our chance for a turnaround,* I thought. *This could be the spark!*

I fumbled.

On the next possession I threw an interception.

Those two mistakes led to ten more points on the scoreboard for the Steelers. Later in the fourth quarter, I threw a pass underneath to LaDainian Tomlinson, but he was blocked by the official. As he came to the other side of the referee, he reached back for the ball and tipped it off his hand. Deshea Townsend intercepted it and ran it back. Touchdown.

Suddenly we were down sixteen points with four minutes left in the game. We'd had a chance at the lead, and then bang, bang, bang—three critical turnovers in a matter of a few minutes. By then the game was out of reach.

When I got to the sideline, I was more frustrated than I'd ever been. Marty came over and said, "You're out."

I don't know how to describe what I felt in that moment. The fire inside had returned, and I wasn't going down without a fight. "I am not leaving this game. I deserve to be in there. Don't give up on me."

We went at it for a while on the sideline. If you watch the footage of the game, you'll see two people who want to win with two different ideas about how to make it happen. In the end, it was his decision—he was the head coach. He pulled me and I sat. Actually, pacing was more like it. I walked up and down the sideline, trying to keep my head from exploding.

We ended up losing 40–24. As the team headed to the locker room after the game, Marty and I went at it again in the hallway. We didn't call each other names or tear each other down; we were just two passionate guys who each believed he was right. I didn't feel like I deserved to get pulled, and he felt like he was doing what was best for the team—and for me.

"Listen," Marty finally said. "You're still our starter, and you're going to start next week. But you need to realize how you win and how you lose in this league. You were playing well, and then all of a sudden you turned it over three times. I don't care how the turnovers happened. The fact is, you turned the ball over three times. And when that happens, I'm pulling your a—— out of the game."

The next game, our final game of the year, we played the Oakland Raiders at home. The wildfires in California had messed up our practice and game schedule earlier in the year, and it was good to be back at Qualcomm. I started the game, and we won 21–14.

When the smoke cleared for the season, our record was a dismal 4–12. What a waste of talent and expectations. The only good thing about it all was that because we had the worst record in the NFL, we now got the first pick in the draft—a draft that incidentally would end up having a big influence on my future as a Charger. But despite our record, the 2003 season hadn't been a waste. I felt like I'd learned a lot from all of it— the losses, the disappointments, even the benching. My faith was also strengthened during this time, as was as my relationship with our team chaplain, Pastor Shawn Mitchell. He would pull me aside regularly to pray for me at our team facility, and he even prayed for me on the phone one time as I was driving down the highway. He was full of God's Spirit and was always looking to pass on that grace and mercy to me.

I couldn't wait to get back on the field in 2004.

However, there were now questions from the front office. "Is Drew the guy? He was benched two times. The team went 4–12. Maybe it's time to go another direction."

We were working under new management. John Butler, who had drafted me out of Purdue, had lost his nine-month battle with cancer in April 2003. The new general manager, A. J. Smith, hadn't drafted me, and he certainly wasn't convinced that my play deserved another season. He was determined to do whatever it took not to go 4–12 again. And despite the fact that he still had Flutie and me on the roster, it seemed as if he wanted to look on the outside to find the future of the franchise.

Going into that off-season, Cam Cameron asked me to come into his office. He closed the door and looked straight at me. "Drew, I'm just letting you know . . . I don't think they would want me to tell you this, but I owe it to you: they are going to bring somebody in."

"Another quarterback?"

He nodded. "It's going to be a free agent or maybe a high draft pick. Now, I can promise you this: you will have the opportunity to compete. But you need to be prepared."

I thanked him for telling me. "That's all I want—just let me have a chance."

"I'll be honest with you. At the other side of the building, they don't believe in you. Marty has confidence in you; I have confidence in you; Brian has confidence in you. But you have to be ready to compete for this job. Basically you're going to have to win your job back."

I was up for a fight. But I needed a plan to give me an edge on my competition.

CREATING
THE EDGE
CHAPTER FIVE

WITH THE KNOWLEDGE that another quarterback would be vying for my position in 2004, I was looking for an advantage, a way to rise above the competition. It seemed like in the past I was always the one chasing someone in front of me. Now, instead of being the hunter, it would be very easy to feel like the hunted. Someone was coming after my job. But that was not the approach I took. I always wanted to be striving to be better, to push myself past my limits, to be willing to try new things. If I kept that attitude, I would always be the hunter. I wanted to be a great player in the NFL, and I knew I wasn't there yet. Somehow I had to find a way to get from where I was to where I wanted to be. I was the quarterback of the future, and *nobody* was going to take my job.

Cam Cameron knew I was determined to do whatever was necessary to keep my spot as starter. "I think I have someone who can help you," he told me.

Tom House is a well-known pitching coach, now on staff

at USC. He has quite a coaching history in Major League
Baseball, including a stint as Nolan Ryan's pitching coach
with the Texas Rangers. He played professional baseball himself for eight years, pitching for Atlanta, Boston, and Seattle.
One of his claims to fame was catching Hank Aaron's record-
setting 715th home run in the bullpen at Fulton County
Stadium.

Tom House has a doctorate in psychology, and when I met
him, he was conducting baseball camps, working with individual athletes to get them into peak physical condition. But
he didn't just deal with the physical; he worked on the whole
person—the mental and emotional components as well. He
tackled everything from sleep patterns and diet to attitude and
awareness.

I was open to any approach that would help me achieve
my goals. I had the will, I had the desire, and I wasn't afraid
of hard work. I just needed a method—and someone to help
me map it out.

I sat down with Tom, and he understood immediately what
I wanted to do. "Hey, I'd love to work with you. Meet me at
the gym at five o'clock tomorrow morning."

That was the beginning of a four-month process of getting
up early each morning to work out and learn things I never
knew about the mechanics of the quarterback position as well
as the mental and emotional aspects of playing the game. Tom
immediately started diagnosing the weak areas that needed to
be developed.

"In order to be a great quarterback, what do you think you
need strength-wise?" he asked.

"I guess I need a strong arm. And strong legs for power,"
I said.

He smiled and broke it down for me. "I can tell by looking
at you that you lack some back-side shoulder strength. We're

going to need to work on that. You're very front-loaded—
you have more muscle in the front of your shoulders than in
the back. That's creating an imbalance. So if the front of your
shoulder is strong enough to throw a hundred miles an hour
but the back of your shoulder is only strong enough to throw
eighty miles an hour, then—guess what?—you're only going
to throw eighty miles an hour. You're only as strong as your
weakest link." Pretty amazing that the guy could identify that
just by looking at my posture.

That was the theme throughout the process: *you're only as
strong as your weakest link*. He listed all of my body's deficiencies.
Then he came up with a plan to bring those areas up to speed.
He showed me joint integrity exercises for building up the
muscles around my shoulder joint, especially the back side of
my shoulder, and I worked on them every day. Strength equal-
ity in your shoulders will not only help you throw with more
velocity and consistency but will also prevent injury since the
muscles around the joint protect it.

We spent time strengthening my core. I had never heard
much about working my core or what role it played in my
movements. As it turns out, your core is the focal point for
your body's operations. All the muscles in the rest of your body
can't make up for a weak core. It all starts there. And with
the help of Tom and his exercises, soon enough I was gaining strength and balance. That was vital for me, because the
quarterback position is all about balance: keeping steady in
the pocket; being able to slide, move, and then still be stable
enough to deliver the ball accurately and with velocity.

We also discussed diet. At the time I thought I ate well. I
didn't get a lot of fast food. But Tom House took things a step
further. "Have you ever had a food allergy test?"

I'd never even considered it before. But I didn't question
him. Brittany and I flew to Portland together to see a specialist,

and she took the tests with me. I figured she would have all the allergies because she couldn't drink milk and had frequent stomachaches after meals. My stomach, on the other hand, was made of iron. I could eat anything. Or so I thought.

As it turned out, I was the one with the problem. The tests revealed that I was allergic to a lot of the things I ate every day. Dr. Richard Heitsch explained what that meant.

"When you eat these foods you're allergic to, your body fights against them instead of repairing muscles and fighting off the free radicals in your body that cause sickness and disease. If you keep eating this way, you'll feel fatigued, you won't recover as fast, and you'll get sick more often. And you won't sleep as well. Everything works together—either for or against your body."

I discovered I was allergic to nuts, dairy, wheat, gluten, and eggs. I had jars of cashews, pistachios, and peanuts that I would take handfuls from throughout the day, and the other foods were staples in my daily meals. It was time to change my diet, find alternatives, and make some drastic adjustments. Tom also said I shouldn't eat the same things over and over again. Anything in excess isn't good for you. The body can take only so much of one thing, so it's better to space it out. For example, if you eat red meat regularly, he said, the body will eventually decide it's had enough and will start fighting against it.

When I began this process, I wasn't feeling bad. But I had no baseline to know what feeling good was like. Up to that point it was normal for me not to be 100 percent, but I didn't know any different. When I changed my diet and stuck with it, I found I recovered faster, saw improvements in my strength training, slept better, and actually needed less sleep. I had more energy.

But I didn't stop with strength training and diet. To get me to the next level, Tom referred me to a friend to start working on visualization techniques. I'm a visual person anyway, and I believe if you can picture what success looks like—if you can put yourself in the moment, prepare for it, and play that scenario over in your mind—then when you actually get there, what you visualized can happen. You don't have to think about it; you just react because you've done it so many times in your head.

On my first day of visualization and focus training, the instructor had me sit down across from him. We talked for a minute or so, and then he asked me to close my eyes. I'll admit, it felt weird at first.

"What am I wearing?" he said.

I had no idea, but I guessed. A brown jacket? Blue jeans?

"What does the writing on my shirt say? And be specific."

"I don't know."

"There's a sign in the workout room over the watercooler. What does it say? What shape is the sign?"

He wasn't teaching me to memorize details. He was training me to go deeper into the moment and use all my senses. Here's how it applies: just because I couldn't see didn't mean I had lost vision. There's a big difference between sight and vision. There is a direct correlation between being aware of your surroundings and standing in the pocket as a quarterback. As a quarterback, you can't always see your receivers or spot the rush coming at you or see defenders in coverage, but you have to be able to feel those things. You need to have the confidence to turn the ball loose and trust that your receivers will be where they are supposed to be to make the catch. There were times before a game when I would spend an hour with my eyes closed, visualizing all seventy of the plays we were going to run that day. I would picture every detail of the situation—the down, the distance, what hash mark we were on, everything.

This really helped me play with confidence, feeling like I knew what was going to happen before it happened.

Finally, Tom suggested I do what he called a "star profile," which is basically a personality test tweaked for athletes. The questions reveal a lot about what makes you tick as an athlete and a person and the way you approach life—and where you might need some improvement.

I saw myself as an outgoing, assertive person. The profile revealed the opposite. So my first task was to get my perception in line with reality, to learn the truth about myself. And if I didn't like what I saw, I needed to take steps to change that. Everyone needed to see me as I saw myself. As the tests indicated, though I'm outgoing and can make friends with anybody, there are times I can be reserved and shy and keep to myself. If I was going to be a good leader, I needed to know when it was time to come out of my shell and leave my comfort zone. Cam Cameron used to say, "You need to learn to be comfortable when you are uncomfortable." In other words, as a starting quarterback in this league, I would no doubt find myself in many tough situations along the way, so I'd better learn to like the pressure.

Tom showed me how other athletes had scored on certain questions. Michael Jordan was off the charts in one area. Nolan Ryan was low in another area. He referenced great players, great leaders, and champions and showed me how I was in line with them in some ways but how I was not where I thought I was in other areas.

That fired me up. I wanted to be a great leader. And I wanted others to see what I knew deep down about myself so they would follow me.

As I headed to training camp for that season, I wasn't going to show up as the same player. I was coming back stronger and better than ever.

Let the Competition Begin

San Diego didn't sign a quarterback when free agency opened in 2004. I felt good about that and hoped management had changed their minds about me. But the draft was still ahead, and San Diego had the number one pick.

A day or two before, I stopped upstairs after my workout to talk with Brian Schottenheimer, our quarterbacks coach. "What does it look like?" I said. "Are we going to draft an offensive lineman?" I had almost convinced myself that the inevitable was not going to happen.

Brian looked right at me. "Drew, you know we're going to draft a quarterback."

I stared him dead in the eye and said, "That will be the biggest mistake this organization ever makes."

There was quite a bit of drama in the draft world that off-season. Eli Manning, the projected number one pick, had publicly said, "I don't want to go to San Diego." Some said it was because of the state of the Chargers organization, while others said it was because he would be a better fit with the New York Giants, who held the fourth pick. Our management chose him anyway, knowing that the Giants wanted Manning badly and confident that they would be able to work a trade and still get the player they wanted. It was a shrewd business move. The Giants chose quarterback Philip Rivers from North Carolina State, but the negotiations for a trade with San Diego had already begun. About an hour later, San Diego traded Manning to the Giants and received Rivers and three draft picks, including a first-round pick for the following year.

Immediately following the trade, I specifically remember storming into my garage and jumping on the treadmill. Maybe it was partly to continue to build my edge and partly just to blow off some steam. Regardless, I knew that right then I was working and the guy they'd just drafted was probably sipping champagne somewhere. The phone rang in the middle of my workout—Marty Schottenheimer. "We've traded for Philip Rivers. Let the competition begin."

It didn't matter who the new quarterback was. I wanted my boss and my team to know that I was their quarterback for the future. *Nobody you bring here is going to take my job.* After the previous disappointing season, I was already motivated to play better. But the draft lit a fire under me and gave me even more incentive to make this my best year yet.

At some point in life, every person—no matter how successful—is told he isn't talented enough, big enough, strong enough, fast enough, or smart enough. When that happens, it's easy to spend all our energy trying to prove those people wrong. We can spend our whole lives trying to debunk the naysayers.

But I'm convinced that's not the best way. At the beginning of that season, when so many people were doubting me, I made a choice: instead of being spurred on by those who doubted me, I'd be motivated by those who had faith in me. These were the people who mentored me, supported me, and believed in me. To this day, when I walk from the locker room to our tunnel on Sundays, I'm overcome with emotion thinking of all the people in my life who have had a positive impact on me—everyone from my parents to my teachers, coaches, mentors, teammates, and now the city of New Orleans. Whatever success I achieve is directly related to those who have stood behind me. I get emotional thinking, *This is for them.*

Forget all the doubters. Forget all the critics. Is there satisfaction in proving them wrong? Sure, but I don't want to give those people the gratification of even dwelling on their words that long. There's a motivator much more powerful than doubt. I play in honor of those who believe in me.

Earning My Nickname

Competition can bring out the best in a player. If the Chargers hadn't drafted Philip Rivers in 2004, would I have been as successful that season? There's no way to know. But the fact is, I knew I needed to bring my best that year—not only to fulfill the commitment I'd made to myself after the Chicago game, but also to win my job back.

Training camp came, and I was ready for a showdown. Despite our competitive rivalry from the start of his rookie year, Philip and I were friends. I respected him as a player and as a teammate, and now as a father to his five children. But San Diego had drafted him to take my job. And I wasn't going to let that happen.

From day one, I needed to make sure that everyone on my team knew I was going to lead them. I asked Marty at the end of the first team meeting at training camp to take the other coaches and leave the room to give me a few moments to talk to my teammates. This was unusual, especially on the first day of camp, and especially from a guy who was supposed to lose his job that year. And that was what I loved about it. I didn't care—I talked to my team about leadership, about commitment, and about fighting through adversity. I read them a few motivational quotes I had picked up in the off-season. We then set our goals together as a team. Most important, I looked every last one of those guys in the eye and didn't flinch. In my heart I was telling them that they hadn't seen anything yet and that I was ready to lead them. I believe they got the message.

In week one against the Houston Texans, I was named the starter, and Philip began the season as my second backup, behind Doug Flutie.

Winning on the road in the NFL is no easy task. We were playing in Reliant Stadium and were tied 20–20 in the fourth quarter. We drove into Texan territory and scored on a pass to Eric Parker. There was a power outage in the stadium on our next drive, and then we were forced to punt. A couple of plays later, though, we recovered a fumble and got a few first downs to run out the clock. By the time we hit the locker room, I had gone seventeen of twenty-four, for 209 yards and two touchdowns. It was a solid victory for us and a good start to the season for me.

The next game we faced the Jets, but this time it was a different story. I threw a couple of interceptions, which were bad enough blows to the ego. Then in the third quarter I suffered a blow to the head. It was an all-out blitz—Jon McGraw and Jonathan Vilma came untouched up the middle, and after I let go of the ball, they each took turns hitting me in the head like a pinball machine. Then my head smacked the ground. The first thing I remember after my vision cleared was staring at the ground and seeing everything spinning. I spat what felt like gravel out of my mouth. Three of my teeth were chipped.

At that point I didn't know I had a concussion, so I stayed in the game. The play came into my headset, but I could barely comprehend the words. I felt like I was underwater. I handed off to LaDainian Tomlinson, and he went in for a touchdown. We celebrated, but I was out of it. I almost ran to the wrong sideline.

By the time I reached our sideline, everything was spinning. The doctors came over to look at me and did the normal routine for a potential head injury. They said three unrelated words—something like "Dog. Banana. Bicycle." Then they asked me how I felt and checked me out. A couple of minutes later they asked, "What were those three words we said to you earlier?"

"What are you talking about?" I said.

At that point they knew there was a problem. They conferred and kept an eye on me, but when our offense went back on the field, I went with them. Now my head was really pounding, and I wasn't thinking straight. I had to concentrate hard on the play calls, but in some strange way the injury actually relaxed me. I played two possessions after taking that blow to the head, and on the second one I threw a thirty-three-yard touchdown pass.

When I returned to the sideline, Cam Cameron approached me. "Listen, I know you got dinged. How are you feeling? What percentage are you?"

"I don't know. Seventy? Sixty? I'm not all here, but I'm fine."

"You are not going back in this game," Cam said. "I can't risk it."

"There's no way I'm coming out."

"If you go back in and you take another shot, you could really get hurt, Drew." Studies have shown how serious hits like these can be. Cam knew better. He had his wits about him, and I didn't.

Physically things progressed from bad to worse for me. My head was pounding something awful. Marty put Flutie in, since he was technically my backup. Later I heard that management was upset—they wanted to get Philip in the game. He hadn't taken a snap yet.

The Jets ended up beating us 34–28. The next week we played the Broncos in Denver, which had been a tough venue for us in the past. I had come back from the concussion, but I didn't play well. We lost 23–13. We were sitting at 1–2 with the Tennessee Titans coming to town. That week Marty came to me with an announcement: he was upgrading Philip to the backup position.

"So what?"

"Just wanted you to know," Marty said.

I heard the underlying message—I was on a short leash. If I didn't play well, I would be pulled. Philip would be going in. I gave Marty a look that said, *I don't care who the backup quarterback is because he's never going to see the field.*

It was during this time that I had a conversation with Lorenzo Neal I'll never forget. Lorenzo was our fullback—one of the best blocking fullbacks in the league—and in my book he deserves to be in the Hall of Fame. He told me, "This is the moment you need to decide something. Are you going to be a great player in this league or a career backup? Take this challenge and turn it into motivation. I know you're going to be a Pro Bowl player. You're going to be a championship quarterback." He didn't see me as a backup. He saw me as championship material. Sometimes when you feel like you have been beaten down so much, all you need is for someone to show that they believe in you.

The Tennessee game was a pivotal one in the season. Whatever happened, we didn't want to go 1–3. But things didn't start out well. I just couldn't seem to find the rhythm I wanted. On a third-down play in the second quarter, I went back for a pass and got thrown to the ground like a slingshot by Rien Long. My body landed hard and in an awkward position. Immediately I felt a sharp pain in my left arm. Either I'd broken my collarbone or I had just separated my shoulder. As I walked to the sideline, my arm felt like a dead weight.

The doctors checked it and said I'd separated my AC joint, probably a grade two or grade three separation. Philip Rivers began to warm up on the sideline. I thought about what Lorenzo Neal had said. *Do I want to be a career backup? If I come out of the game right now, even for one play, that may be my destiny. Who knows if I'll ever get an opportunity again.*

Just then Lorenzo walked over to me. During training camp he had given me a nickname: PB, for Pro Bowler. I hadn't thought much about the Pro Bowl before. I was just trying to win back my job as starting quarterback. Making it to the Pro Bowl was the furthest thing from my mind.

Lorenzo saw the doctors examining me. "Come on, PB, we need you. This is your time. Right here. Right now. Show them what you got."

I knew then that no matter what happened, I had to tough out the injury and find a way to get back out on the field. The team needed me, and I had something to prove.

I told the coaches I was good to go. The look on Marty's face said it all. "You have one more series," he said. In other words, if I didn't get something done right then, I would be pulled.

We went out and drove down the field. I threw an eleven-yard pass to Antonio Gates to put us up 14–7. We scored another touchdown on the next series and ended up winning the game 38–17. With a separated left shoulder, going on nothing but adrenaline and painkillers, I threw three touchdowns, with no interceptions. It was one of my better performances in the NFL so far. And even more significantly, I didn't let my backup see the field.

That year we went 12–4 and won our division. We made it to the playoffs but lost a heartbreaker to the New York Jets in overtime, 20–17. It was my best season to that point, and I won NFL Comeback Player of the Year.

And on top of that, I ended up making the Pro Bowl. Lorenzo Neal called it.

INSULT
AND INJURY
CHAPTER SIX

THINGS LOOKED GOOD for the Chargers going into the 2005 season. We had almost every starter returning from the previous year, as well as some talented newcomers like Shawne Merriman, our outside linebacker, who made a huge impact on defense and was named Rookie of the Year. We had some games where everything came together and we played well, but in others we just couldn't get things to click. We lost a lot of close games that year, including one against Dallas on a goal line stand. We also fell to Denver and Pittsburgh on last-second field goals. We had another heart-breaker at Philadelphia, where they blocked one of our field goals and ran it back for a touchdown with about two and a half minutes left. We then drove down to their twenty yard line with a chance to win only to fumble the ball and lose the game. It was just that kind of year. We finished with a 9–7 record and wound up third in our division behind Denver and Kansas City.

To anyone watching, our last game of the season, against Denver, was pretty meaningless. We had no shot at the play-offs. But it mattered to me—I didn't want to be off the field in *any* game. Besides, I didn't have a contract after that season, and there was a lot of speculation from the press and from management about what next year would hold. "Is it time to go in a different direction with Philip Rivers?" Others were saying, "How can you let go of a guy like Drew Brees after he took you to the playoffs the year before?"

Difficult decisions were looming for the team—and for me. And by the end of the game against Denver, those decisions would have even higher stakes.

Shredding My Shoulder

It took only one play to change the course of my life and my career in the last game of the season on the last day of the year in 2005. It was late in the second quarter and we had been shut out up to that point. We needed someone to make a play, and that someone needed to be me. As I reared back to throw just inside our own end zone, I felt a presence at my back side. It was Denver free safety John Lynch, and he laid a hit on me that knocked the ball out of my hand and onto the ground, spinning to a stop at the one yard line. It was a live ball, but in my eyes it was my ball, and I had to get it back. With no regard for my own safety or future, I committed the cardinal sin for a quarterback. I jumped into the pile for a loose ball. It wasn't a rational decision—it was the only way I knew how to play the game. Unfortunately I didn't get the ball, and even worse, after the dust had settled, my right shoulder was out of socket. My arm stuck out to the side as if I were resting it on a fence post.

As I walked off the field on December 31, 2005, my arm

numb and motionless, I was staring at the one thing I feared the most: that I might never wear a Chargers uniform again. I wouldn't know for sure until I heard what the surgeon said, but I'd been around football long enough to know that this injury had the potential to shatter not just my shoulder but also my dreams for the next season . . . or possibly even my entire career.

I refused to let myself dwell on it, though. And I certainly wasn't going to admit that possibility to anyone else. My faith was being tested, but I stood firm, knowing even then that God had a plan. I tried to downplay the injury and make sure everyone knew I would be back in 2006. Some would call it foolish; others would consider it impossible. But this was the hope I held on to: I would put on my blue and gold again. And I would come back stronger than ever.

I had never heard many positive words from the Chargers general manager, A. J. Smith. He had drafted Philip Rivers two years earlier, and it was clear he thought Philip was the future of the franchise. However, before I left for Alabama to see a specialist, A. J. reached out to me. "Drew, don't worry about this. We're going to extend you a long-term contract. Just go and take care of your arm, and we'll be here for you when you get out of surgery. I just want to put your mind at ease."

His words did put me at ease. I believed him.

San Diego had put the franchise player tag on me for 2005, which meant I had a one-year deal and my pay was based on the average salary of the top five quarterbacks in the NFL. In 2006 I would be available for free agency, but the Chargers could choose to franchise me again—or give me a more permanent contract. When I was drafted by San Diego in 2001, I looked up to players like Troy Aikman, John Elway, and Dan Marino, who had played their entire careers with one team. That was my hope and plan from day one with the Chargers.

I wanted to be the one-team quarterback who led San Diego to their first championship, so I committed my entire career to that organization and that city. A long-term contract would put me on track to do just that.

But for now, the contract wasn't my biggest concern. I was on my way to Birmingham to see if I even had a future in football. After all, a football contract doesn't do you much good if you can't throw a ball.

Between dealing with my parents' split, my injury in high school, and the threat of replacement and benching in the NFL, I thought I'd faced a decent share of adversity so far in my life. I considered myself to be pretty tough mentally. But that was all child's play compared to what lay ahead. I was about to face the most defining moment of my life.

Under the Knife

As soon as I left the locker room after the fateful game against Denver, I called Dr. James Andrews of Birmingham, Alabama, to talk about my injury. He's known as one of the best orthopedic surgeons in the country, especially when it comes to knees, elbows, and shoulders. There was no question about where I would go.

"Yeah, yeah, I figured you'd be calling me," Dr. Andrews said in his Southern drawl. "I saw the play live on TV."

Brittany and I flew to Alabama and stayed with her parents, Pete and Kathie Dudchenko, who happened to live in Birmingham at the time. If you ask Brittany, she thought my initial exam with Dr. Andrews would do more damage than the hit had done. He pulled, pushed, and rotated my arm every possible direction. From the corner of my eye I could see her cringing as if she were in physical pain herself. Dr. Andrews took a look at the results from the MRI, and his face was grim. "I'll be honest. It's a tough injury. It looks like your labrum's torn pretty bad. I'm not quite sure about the full extent. There's some rotator cuff damage too. I'm going to need to get in there and see."

I swallowed hard. Was this the end of everything I'd worked so hard for? Then he added in his quiet, confident way, "But you came to the right place. Once I get in there, I'll fix it all."

"Are you going to be able to do this with just a scope?" I asked. If he used arthroscopic surgery, there was a possibility I could recover in eight months or so. On that schedule, if I pushed myself hard, I might make it back for training camp in July. If he had to cut, I would need another two months of rehab at the very least to rebuild the shoulder muscles that would be sliced through during surgery. Best-case scenario, I might be able to return midseason. Worst-case scenario . . . well, I wasn't even going to go there.

"I hope so," Dr. Andrews said. "But if you have significant cuff damage, I might have to cut."

When he said the word *cut*, it was like taking another hit, just as powerful as the physical one that had landed me here. My mind raced with anxious thoughts. *Will I ever throw again? And if I do, will I throw in the NFL?*

"I'll fix you up," Dr. Andrews said. "But the surgery is just the beginning. The real question is how committed you are to the rehab. If you're even going to have a chance at coming back, that's what will get you there."

The thought of the long road ahead was overwhelming, so I tried not to think beyond the surgery. That was priority number one.

Brittany sat with me before I went into surgery, and we prayed together. It was all we could do—this was out of our hands. Later she told me that as she sat in the waiting room with her parents, Dr. Andrews had her paged to the nurses' station three times to let her know everything was going well. She said her heart sank each time because she thought he was going to tell her something had gone wrong.

As I was coming out of the anesthesia after surgery, a nurse came to check on me. Still groggy, the first thing I said was "Did he cut? How's my rotator cuff?"

"Let me look at the chart," she said. An infinitely long pause. "Yes. He had to repair the rotator cuff."

"Oh no . . ." My heart sank. I pictured the doctor slicing through the muscle of my shoulder—my livelihood. Things were worse than I'd feared.

I was wheeled back to my room still in shock. Brittany and her parents came in. I tried to put on a brave face, but I was barely holding it together. Brittany gave me a kiss, and with tears in her eyes, she told me they didn't have to cut. Being pretty out of it still from the drugs, I told her she was wrong and also that I thought someone had punched me because my eye was swollen. She laughed and tried to explain that it was probably from being on my side during the surgery, but I couldn't make sense of anything. I was convinced this was the beginning of the end.

Dr. Andrews walked in and shook hands with everyone. Then he came to my bed and just stood there with a smile on his face.

"So you had to cut," I said, wishing he'd stop smiling.

"Nope!"

I was shocked. "The nurse told me you had to repair the rotator cuff."

"Well, I did, but I was able to scope it all. It took seven scope holes and eleven anchors in your shoulder, but we got it done."

He explained that a normal labrum tear might require three

or four arthroscopic holes and four or five anchors at most. In other words, my injury was highly devastating compared to most. But in that moment the doctor gave me a precious gift: hope. With God's help, there was a chance I might make it back. I was ecstatic. So relieved. If I could have jumped up and kissed Dr. Andrews on the mouth right then, I would have.

Dr. Andrews beamed at me. The words he said next were a cup of cold water to a thirsty man.

"If I had to do that surgery a hundred times, I couldn't have done it as well as I just did."

Relief flooded over me. There are no better words you could ask to hear from someone who has just put you under the knife.

He tapped me on the chest. "Now it's up to you, Drew."

I spent the next two nights in the hospital with Brittany on a reclining chair beside me. She tells me I single-handedly prepared her for having babies after the way she had to take care of me postsurgery. I had always believed I was fairly ambidextrous, but it turns out I needed help with everything from putting in my contacts to brushing my teeth and bathing. And let's just say there was a bedpan or two involved as well.

Working My Way out of the Sling

I was told at the beginning of rehab that if everything went smoothly, it would be eight months before I could play again. And I wouldn't feel totally "normal" for two years. Except for my ACL tear in high school, I had barely gone a day of my life without football—I couldn't even imagine eight months. But I knew I couldn't focus on that huge obstacle right now. As it was, getting through each day was going to require a minor miracle. A good friend of mine once told me that each morning when you wake up, think about winning the day. Don't worry about a week from now or a month from now—just think about one day at a time. If you are worried about the mountain in the distance, you might trip over the molehill right in front of you. Win the day! That was great advice to remember at a time like this. For the next eight months, I'd need all the endurance I could muster to face each grueling nine-hour rehab routine.

Each morning at 7:30 my father-in-law drove me to rehab. My sessions always consisted of a lot of stretching, range-of-motion exercises, manual resistance exercises, and eventually some light weights as I progressed. Even now, almost five years later, I still do a lot of the same exercises for my shoulder as I did back then. Only now, instead of rehab, it is "prehab." I use the exercises to prevent injury and maintain strength for all the little muscles in my shoulders and back. Those exercises would pay big dividends for me in the future.

After my morning session, I would eat lunch with the physical therapists and the other guys who were there for rehab, or Brittany would come down to eat with me on special occasions. Then I was at it again for my afternoon session, which didn't end until 5:00. Brittany or my father-in-law would pick me up; then my mother-in-law would cook me dinner and I'd collapse into the La-Z-Boy. The great thing about the home-cooked meals was that Brittany and her mom made sure all my food allergies were taken into consideration. Whereas I tended to let that slip from time to time, they were like drill instructors, making sure I was taking my vitamins and only putting things in front of me that would agree with my body and help me recover the fastest.

I still needed help with even the most basic tasks. I was starting to get better at brushing my teeth and putting in my contacts, but Brittany cut up my food, helped me bathe, got me dressed, and changed the ice in a machine that was strapped to my arm. I felt like a child again—I couldn't drive and I couldn't button my own shirt, let alone toss a football. As someone with a fierce independent streak, I had a hard time relying on other people to do everything for me. But it was the only way I would recover.

The first two months were excruciating. On top of the constant pain, I barely slept. I couldn't roll over on my right side. Brittany would sleep with her hand on my arm because I twitched so much that she was convinced I was going to throw my arm around in my sleep and tear out my anchors. A lot of nights the only way I could get comfortable was to scrunch up in a chair in the living room. La-Z-Boys may be great for watching TV, but sleeping in one for a couple of months gets old fast.

I have always been a very goal-oriented person, but looking ahead to an eight-month rehab was daunting. It was overwhelming to think it would be so long until I was healthy again. I was afraid the days would become monotonous and I would drive myself crazy. I had to find a way to conquer this by setting short-term goals that would eventually lead up to the ultimate objective. Each smaller accomplishment gave me confidence and momentum on my way to the next challenge. Before I knew it, I would be on the field again.

I remember walking in to rehab the first day after surgery, feeling spry and ready to take on the world.

"Okay, Doc, I'm in this sling. How long until I can get out of it?"

He looked at me for a moment. "Four weeks, I'd say."

"All right, I'm going to beat that."

Once I'd zeroed in on that goal, I wouldn't let my attention be diverted to anything else. Two and a half weeks later, I took off the sling.

I had started stretching and doing exercises the day after surgery. I was just as determined to heal as I'd ever been to win a game, but I also knew how important it is to find balance when you're in rehab. I needed to push myself and do as much as I possibly could, but at the same time I had to listen to my body and realize I had been through a traumatic injury. If I pushed too hard too fast, I could pop an anchor, and I'd be worse off than before.

After the surgery, Dr. Andrews handed me over to one of the best physical therapists in sports medicine: Kevin Wilk. God gets the ultimate credit for healing my body, but as far as human beings go, Kevin deserves the kudos for my comeback. Kevin and I were pretty much locked at the hip for six months. At every stage of my recovery, he was able to read the situation, and he knew exactly how far to push me. He knew what I could and couldn't do, and if it was too soon or just the right time for the next step. I applaud him because he was dealing with a patient who wanted to push the envelope as far as possible. Somehow he figured out a way to balance my desires with a dose of realism.

The day after surgery, Kevin showed me basic pendulum swings. This is where you bend forward and let your arm hang and then move it slightly in a circular motion. It seems hard to believe now, but even that small exercise was painful and felt very awkward.

Most days I was able to stay positive and cling to the hope of suiting up in my Chargers uniform again. But other days I wasn't so sure. There was no guarantee the surgery would work, and even if it did, no one knew if I'd be able to play at that level again. In January I watched the playoffs on TV, like any other spectator. I was miserable. It wasn't just the pain in my shoulder and my arm or the confinement of my La-Z-Boy prison; it was the mental anguish of watching those guys live out their dream while I was questioning whether I'd ever be out on the field again.

It was a lonely time—away from home, far from my team-mates, miles from Qualcomm Stadium. There was an upside to the loneliness, though. In the midst of this sequestering, there were no distractions. I was forced to focus all my energy and attention on getting myself back to being the best I could be.

I read my Bible often during this time and explored my faith at a deeper level. God was up to something in my life. I wasn't sure what it was yet, but I trusted him and believed that better days were ahead. I believed that when you give it your best and commit the rest to him, he will work wonders in your life. And right then, I needed a miracle. As long as I continued to do things the right way, good things would happen. I firmly believed that.

Before I knew it, I was ready to tackle my next goal. The moment I got out of the sling, I said, "So what's next?"

"Well, the next thing we'll work on is full range of motion. That will take you about nine weeks."

"Okay, I'm going to beat it."

I had full range of motion in six weeks.

I was starting to feel more like myself. "Now when can I start throwing?"

"Well, that's at four months. We can't fudge that one. You gotta let it heal."

I told him I understood. But I still beat that by about three and a half weeks. I'd always been competitive—why stop now?

Every Wednesday I met with Dr. Andrews. It became my goal to have him look at me and say, "You're ahead of schedule." But he was always careful to add, "But you're not *healed* yet." That was his classic line. He knew how much I was chomping at the bit. He said I would get to a point when I felt like I could go out and do anything—and that was the most dangerous time. My body was still in the critical stages of healing, and if I got reinjured, I'd be back to square one . . . but with even more scar tissue.

Looking for Someone to Believe in Me

In February, a little over a month after my surgery, negotiations began for the next season. I was waiting for the Chargers to make me a long-term offer, as A. J. Smith had promised. Dr. Andrews gave the Chargers his report. After several weeks of therapy, I was hitting my short-term goals and feeling pretty good about next season. I still had a long way to go, but I was making progress and was way ahead of schedule.

Through my agent, I finally got the news I'd been waiting to hear: "We're going to offer you a long-term deal." But as the terms of the contract unfolded, I grew more and more disappointed. The deal they were presenting was basically equivalent to a backup quarterback's salary. There were incentives in the deal to put me at a starter's salary, but who was to say I was going to even get an opportunity to compete for the job? It wasn't about the money; what hurt the most was the underlying message. They were saying, *Yeah, we'll sign you; we'll bring you back. But you're no longer our guy. We've moved on to Philip Rivers.*

I know that football is a business, so I try to never take negotiations personally. But it was obvious to me from the get-go what their vision was. And it hurt a lot. Yes, the Chargers had offered me a long-term contract. But it wasn't a contract that told me they wanted me to stay. Now, I'm a pretty confident guy. I have a strong belief system and a solid faith. But when you play a team sport, you need others to believe in you too. And I wasn't feeling that support from San Diego right then, at the moment I needed it most.

I knew Coach Schottenheimer believed in me. Brian and

Cam and a lot of the guys on the team believed in me. Many of the fans believed in me too. I had downplayed the injury to the media and tried to paint the picture that it might have been a tough break, but I was a tough guy. I wanted everyone to know that I was one of those people who might get knocked down but comes back stronger. Still, management and ownership had their doubts. They might have respected my work ethic and the way I approached the game, but when it came to the question "Who can lead us to a championship?" they didn't feel like I was their guy. That feeling was worse than any hit I've ever taken in a football game.

The worst part was there was only so much I could do to get them to see the truth about me. I could point to the 2004 and 2005 seasons. I could remind them that I was still a young player with my best years ahead of me. I could tell them I wasn't a quitter—that I was going to take the adversity and turn it into an opportunity to come back better, for my sake and the team's. But it was tough to convince them of this when my arm had just gotten out of the sling and my shoulder was held together with steel anchors.

The minute I got that first offer, I knew I wasn't going back. Negotiations went back and forth for the next two or three weeks and my agent did his best, but deep down I knew that my era with San Diego was ending. It was a difficult truth to accept—it was hard to let that dream die.

I wasn't the only one who struggled when things ended with the Chargers. Brittany was really hurt by the process, especially knowing how much I had given to the organization. She probably took it twice as hard as I did. She cared about me, and she knew what this was doing inside me. Her protective instincts kicked in, and she wanted to do whatever she could to defend my honor and encourage me.

That's one thing I love about her—she is as fierce as a

lioness protecting her cubs when it comes to the people she loves. If the Chargers didn't want us, fine. We'd go someplace where someone did. What meant the most to her was not where we lived but being with people who believed in me as much as she did. When something major happens to a player—like an injury or a tough loss or a move to another team—people tend to focus on how it affects him and his team. But the truth is, the player's family is impacted even more. We as athletes are somewhat immune to the drama because we see it all the time, but our families aren't used to it and always take it the hardest.

Brittany and I had planned on starting a family during that off-season, but when I got hurt and the Chargers' offer didn't come through as we'd hoped, there were suddenly a lot of unknowns. Where would we wind up? Where would we live? Would I get a long-term deal so we could settle down somewhere, or would it be a temporary situation where we couldn't put down roots? How far would we be from family and friends? We knew God had a plan, and this felt like a sign that we needed to put our dreams for children on hold for a little longer.

As a football player who had experienced all different levels of the game, from flag football to the NFL, I was pretty well equipped to handle what was happening. Even if I hadn't experienced an injury or a letdown to this extent before, I'd at least seen it happen to other guys. But it was hard for Brittany to see me in physical pain—and even worse, to try to understand why the team didn't believe in me.

Through it all, with the strength of her faith in God and in me, she was able to trust me during that time of hurt and uncertainty about where we would wind up. She assured me she'd follow me anywhere, that we were a package deal. This bump in the road was just that—a bump. Brittany had grown up in the Midwest, so she could handle any weather situation. She had also moved around a lot as a child, so the idea of packing up again didn't affect her much. She always says, "Home is not necessarily where you were born—you had no control of that. Home is where you make it." She told me, "Don't worry about me. You just concentrate on getting your shoulder better." God knew I needed her then. Now we can see how the Lord used that time to deepen our love and to help us become more committed to each other than ever.

This experience really showed us the people in our lives who were with us through good times and bad. There were those I thought would have been there for sure, and they weren't. There were also a lot of people I never thought would be there for me, and yet there they were. You can't help but make a mental list and remember those people. When I was at my lowest—when I didn't know if I'd ever play football again—I discovered the people who were truly there for me. At that point you realize family doesn't only include blood. I have friends who are like brothers—the guys who stick around even when you're not all smiles and good times. It turns out that family really means the people in your life who are always there, even when you are at your weakest.

Not Backup Material

When negotiations with the Chargers broke down, it was clear that free agency was my next step. At the beginning of that process, a lot of teams tend to throw their hats into the ring. In my case, as many as eight teams expressed an interest. At best, they were offering the same deal as the Chargers . . . meaning they wanted me to be their backup. In essence, their offers were saying, *We like you, but we're just not sure if you're going to recover from this injury. We don't want to make a big investment. If* it worked out, great. If I didn't come back, at least they hadn't put too much on the line.

As I was going through my rehab, fighting to make my way back, I didn't have my sights set on a backup position. That was not even an option in my eyes. I understood that I was considered a big risk after such a serious injury. But I believed God wasn't finished with me in the NFL yet, and I was going to return better than before. I wanted somebody to share that vision—someone who would take a chance on me. So far, no team had done that.

In the midst of fielding offers, I continued the grueling rehab. In the end it came down to two teams: the Miami Dolphins and the New Orleans Saints. Over the past few years some people have speculated about what really happened during this process. Why did I choose one team over the other? Well, it wasn't exactly a straight path east, all the way to New Orleans—there were some twists and turns along the way. I was perhaps more surprised than anyone about the way things turned out.

MIAMI VS. NEW ORLEANS

FOOTBALL IS ALL ABOUT TIMING. There's the timing of the snap count. The speed and depth of the receiver running his route. The pause of the running back before he explodes toward the line.

When I was lying on a gurney in the training room during the last game of 2005, my shoulder shredded and my career in jeopardy, I couldn't imagine how anything good could come out of something so awful. But as I would soon learn, sometimes the way God works is all about timing too. I had to wait. I had to work. But in the end, he had a clear purpose in everything that happened.

I'll admit, his timing often felt slow—especially while I was going through rehab. *When will I feel back to normal? When will I be able to play again? When will the right opportunity come my way?* But no one ever said the Christian faith is about living according to your own terms or timetable. It's about dropping anchor even when you're in an unpredictable place. It's about *knowing* that though things may not make sense on paper, you have to trust God to see the bigger picture. You have to choose to live from the heart and trust what you cannot see.

Less than a year after my shoulder injury, I was already starting to experience the unexpected good that can come out of adversity. That event took me to new places in my faith, as I knew God was sharpening me for a significant task down the road. It marked a new place of vulnerability and openness in my relationship with Brittany. It was a time of growing closer to her parents while I lived with them in Alabama during rehab. And in terms of my career, this incident allowed me to discover the people who were really on my team. In a strange way, I'm grateful for it, because it was a catalyst to change that needed to happen.

One of the most significant lessons I learned during that dark period of injury and rehab is this: if God leads you to it, he will lead you through it. Everything happens for a reason, and everything is part of his master plan. If you let adversity do its work in you, it will make you stronger. When you come out on the other side, you just may be amazed at the things God has allowed you to accomplish—things you might not have believed were possible.

God's refining process is never easy. It's kind of like a blacksmith creating a sword. The metal is strengthened when it is repeatedly put in the fire and then pounded with a hammer. But the end result is perfection. All the heat and pounding create a strength and beauty, not only on the outside, but especially on the inside. God sometimes puts us in the fire, and it's going to hurt, but it will mold and shape us into the people he intends for us to be. When I went through that fire, I didn't know what was ahead for me, and I didn't know what the end result would be. I had to trust and believe that there was a purpose for all this and take things one day at a time.

The Obvious Choice

I've been asked on a number of occasions what happened between head coach Nick Saban, the Dolphins, and me. To the outside observer, it must have seemed really obvious what my choice would be when it came down to Miami or New Orleans. But there were other factors at play besides geography and football.

I met with Tom Condon, my agent, after things fell through on my contract with San Diego. Once the dust settled in the days prior to the start of free agency in early March 2006, it was clear that there were only two contenders who saw me as a starting quarterback in the NFL: the Dolphins and the Saints. Tom and I sat together and talked through the pros and cons of each.

"Here's how I see it," Tom said. "For New Orleans, you have to factor in that the city has just been through the biggest natural disaster in the history of the country. More than 80 percent of the city was underwater. I don't know how many good places there are to live. The whole city was devastated—it still is." That was no exaggeration. At the time, the team had been relocated to San Antonio, Texas, and there had been talk of moving the team permanently. Plans had even been made to tear down the Superdome. The previous season had been played entirely on the road—San Antonio, Baton Rouge, even New Jersey. Tom went on, "Now, they have a brand-new coaching staff—but there are a lot of unknowns." It was true: a lot of good things were being said about Sean Payton, but he had never been a head coach before. Then there was the clincher: "Drew, the overall reputation of the organization is not good. The team has been pretty dysfunctional for a long time. I like the general manager, Mickey Loomis, but he is going to have a hard time attracting talented players to come down there."

If you would have asked me in 2004, before Hurricane Katrina, "What one team in the league would you *least* want to play for?" I probably would have said the New Orleans Saints. That's not a knock against the city. I had been through New Orleans once before, for a wedding, and the only thing I saw aside from the ceremony was Bourbon Street since our hotel was right there. That was my concept of the city.

My impression of the team wasn't much better. I didn't know many of the players personally, but I'd heard about the team's reputation from other players in the league and observed it from afar. Most people viewed the Saints as a dead-end organization at the time. When you thought of New Orleans, you just didn't think of a great atmosphere conducive to winning and building a championship-caliber team. So before we even started talking, I had an overwhelmingly negative view of the club.

After a successful 2000 season, in which the Saints won their first playoff game in franchise history, they followed it up with four consecutive mediocre seasons from 2001 to 2004. The Saints had a lot of talent, but they couldn't figure out how to win consistently. They were streaky and unpredictable. They then went 3–13 in 2005, the Katrina year. Now here they were knocking on my door in 2006. Tom was trying to go through the pros and cons of New Orleans with me, but it was hard to see anything but the cons. The assignment was fraught with challenges and downsides—the rebuilding needed in the city, the uncertainty about the future of keeping the organization in New Orleans, and the fact that this was not where I had imagined starting a family. Besides, from a football perspective, it just didn't seem like a great prospect.

"Then there's Miami," Tom said. "First of all, there's the obvious advantage: you'd get to live in Miami. It's a great city, a great climate." He had a point. Plus, there was no rebuilding needed there. "Second, there's an unbelievable tradition with the Dolphins. They've won Super Bowls. They have a great ownership structure. And Nick Saban has a reputation as a winner." Saban was a young head coach with a lot of energy and ideas, and he had turned the team around the previous season, his first as an NFL head coach. They were 9–7 in 2005, and every indication was that they were going to win more. Tom went on, "Saban is an extremely talented defensive coach, so you know he's going to take care of that side of the ball. And you've also got superb coaches on the offensive side. Mike Mularkey, the offensive coordinator, has head coaching experience and is running the same offense you did in San Diego. Jason Garrett is one of the best up-and-coming young offensive minds in the league, plus the O line coach is your old O line coach from San Diego, Hudson Houck. You've got familiarity there."

On paper, the obvious choice was Miami. It was an organization on the rise. They wanted to win. And they were coming after me.

Daunte Culpepper was another highly regarded quarterback looking for a new team that year. He had torn up his knee in 2005. (Incidentally, Dr. Andrews had operated on both of us.) The consensus around the league was that one of us would play for Miami and the other would play for New Orleans. The question was "Who will go where?"

In reality, the Saints really weren't interested in Culpepper, and I knew it. Rumor had it they would be drafting a quarterback with a high pick in the first round if they didn't get me. I also knew that the Dolphins preferred me over Culpepper, in part because in order to get Culpepper, they would have to trade a high draft pick to Minnesota, whereas getting me was free. However, both teams were going to negotiate hard and use the fact that Culpepper was out there to their advantage.

I figured it was a matter of trying to get the deal done and making it work financially that would move the negotiations with the Dolphins forward.

I had all but made up my mind by the time I talked with Saints head coach Sean Payton. He had a tough sell—you're not going to attract sought-after free agents with "Hey, come to our city that was destroyed six months ago." The organization had just moved back into the facility that had been taken over by the National Guard for several months. There was no guarantee that the Superdome would be playable by the time the season started. They were hoping it would be ready by the third game, but no one knew for sure yet.

I had never spoken with Sean Payton before, and I knew I needed to have a conversation with him before making any decision about New Orleans. Our first conversation occurred while I was going through the Arby's drive-through in Birmingham, and I realized right away that I liked his personality. I appreciated what he had to say about the team and the direction they were going. The business side of me said it made sense to use a New Orleans visit as leverage against Miami. But the loyalist side of me, the more powerful side, was reminding me that the Saints were the first team to throw their hat in the ring. I could feel that they truly wanted me and would very much appreciate a chance. (I found out later that they were somewhat shocked I decided to make the visit, under the circumstances.) So instead of jumping for Miami, which was my first inclination, I decided I owed it to myself to take a trip to New Orleans and at least see it with my own eyes. I had no idea what I was going to see when I touched down at Louis Armstrong International.

Tom and I agreed that I would take a trip to both New Orleans and Miami and then make the call. I still felt pretty confident I'd ultimately end up in South Florida, but I wanted to give each team a fair shot. Apparently the Dolphins also thought the idea of my playing for the Saints was pretty far-fetched. Who in their right mind would pick New Orleans over Miami?

They believed they were in the driver's seat.

Big Trip to the Big Easy

The Saints booked a visit for me in early March, and I committed to going there first. As soon as the Dolphins heard about it, they called and asked me to fly to Miami before that. I told them I was a man of my word and I'd make the trip to Miami after my visit to New Orleans. On the night before I left for New Orleans, Miami called again. They said they wanted to fly in and have breakfast in Birmingham before I visited the Saints.

Obviously New Orleans was not thrilled with that, but I wanted to get as much time as I could with each team. Here was an opportunity to sit and talk with Miami right on my doorstep, so why not? Brittany and I drove to a little pancake house close to the Five Points area of Birmingham. Nick Saban, the head coach, and Randy Mueller, the general manager, met us there.

Nick was up-front with me. He told me straight out that he was interested in having me play for the Dolphins. His personality is not real warm, and you struggle to ever get a smile out of him. He's a hard-nosed, stoic kind of guy, and he did most of the talking at the breakfast, as I recall. He wasn't trying to sell me on his team—he just explained things. "We have a great owner, a great staff, a great team, and a great organization behind us. We also have great facilities." He then focused on Brittany. "And we have great communities and great places to raise a family. I have a house on the

Intracoastal Waterway and a boat. When you visit, we'll get you both out on the water and show you around." Like any good recruiter, he directed those statements right at my wife. If you can win over the woman in the player's life, you've won the recruiting battle.

Nothing really eventful happened at that breakfast other than getting the chance to meet both men in person. We talked. We ate. It was primarily an opportunity for them to get in front of me and let me think about Miami as I talked with New Orleans. I think that was part of the game. After breakfast Brittany and I left for the airport and headed to New Orleans.

I remember flying into New Orleans that day. It's a flight I love now, soaring over the bayou and the swamp, with the beautiful cypress trees and the waterways below. But that day I stared dismally out the window. It was crummy weather—rainy and drizzly—and as we got under the thick clouds, I caught my first glimpse of the area. Most of the trees looked like they'd been chopped off at the top, beheaded by Katrina.

Oh, boy, I thought. *This is going to be interesting.*

As soon as we landed, we were in a limo on our way to the team facility. Mickey and Sean seemed to be making sure Brittany and I were constantly talking so there was as little looking out the window as possible. I also recall that the limo had the darkest tint on the windows I had ever seen. We could barely see out. I'm pretty sure that was the point—to prevent us from being scared off by all the devastation.

For dinner that night we went to Emeril's restaurant. That's one thing about New Orleans: no matter how bleak things seem, you can always count on a great meal and good people. We sat at the chef's table, which was actually in the kitchen. Sean and his wife, Beth, were there, along with Mickey and Melanie, now his wife. We were joined by some other members of the coaching staff, including quarterbacks coach Pete

Carmichael, who was the quality control coach in San Diego the entire time I was there. I had a great relationship with Pete. He was one of the people I knew believed in me.

Part of their philosophy was to treat Brittany and me like family. The discussion at dinner didn't turn to free agency or the contract—we just enjoyed the evening and got to know each other. They promised to show us some neighborhoods they thought would be conducive to raising a family. Brittany fell in love with Beth and Mel.

Brittany and I spent the night at the Loews Hotel downtown. Some people from the community had sent flowers and gift baskets to welcome us. That night Brittany pulled me into the bathroom and ran the shower while we talked. She was convinced there could be listening devices in the room, and she wanted to make sure the sound of the water would drown out what we said. Okay, so maybe we'd been watching too many spy movies lately. The truth is, we were welcomed there with open arms.

The next day I met with Sean to discuss the offense. He and the crew had put together a highlight video with some of my best plays from the past couple of years. We talked about the specifics of the offense and how I saw myself fitting in. Everything he said to me seemed to communicate one central message: *We want you here. We believe in you, and we are as confident in your ability to come back and lead this team to a championship as you are.*

"I'm going to take everything you like and everything you're good at, and we're going to install it," Sean said. "We're going to put it in our offense. We're going to develop this thing together. I want to put you in the best position to lead this offense by executing what you are comfortable with and have confidence running. I'll have the final say, but you're going to have a lot of input."

A lot of coaches would come in and tell you to listen up while they spelled out the offensive scheme—a "my way or the highway" approach. But Sean was different. He wanted me to be part of the process; he valued my input. Nobody had ever given me that opportunity before. No coach had ever expressed so much belief in me—really a blind faith at this point. This was the first time we had shaken hands with each other. I was blown away.

Meanwhile, Brittany was being entertained by Doug Marrone, the offensive coordinator, although I don't know who was entertaining whom because I'm sure Brittany was doing most of the talking. They ate peanut butter pretzels and talked while watching film. It was right up Brittany's alley— very relaxed and informal. Doug's wife, Helen, would end up being one of Brittany's closest friends in the Saints family.

Later, as we drove around to look at neighborhoods, they tried to help me overcome my misconception that the entire city was uninhabitable. The coaches all lived in different areas, and we drove to a development called English Turn and then to Uptown. We immediately fell in love with the Uptown area. There was a big, beautiful park and lots of historic homes with wraparound porches, plus Loyola and Tulane universities and the world-renowned St. Charles Avenue. After the devastation we had seen on the flight in, I was surprised to find these areas in such good shape.

Then we drove to the North Shore, where Sean Payton's home was being built. As beautiful as it was, I knew we couldn't live in that area—the bridge across Lake Pontchartrain is twenty-four miles long! I was sure I would fall asleep making the forty-five-minute drive back and forth to the facility every day. But still, I was starting to think this might not be such a bad place to live after all.

It was on the way back I was about to see a different side of New Orleans.

Lost . . . and Found

Brittany and I were in the car with Sean having a great conversation. We got off the bridge, and he took an exit into New Orleans proper. I had no idea where we were, but he seemed confident that he did. We were headed back to the facility, where I would be talking with Tom Benson, the owner, as well as Mickey Loomis. Then they were taking us to the airport to catch our flight to Miami. By that point we'd seen everything in New Orleans, it seemed, except the hurricane damage.

Sean was driving and talking, looking at street signs, and it seemed to be taking quite a while to get back. It wasn't a big deal because we had some time to spare. I relaxed and just took in the scenery. But gradually that scenery started taking a turn for the worse. We drove into neighborhoods where the houses were off their foundations. There were boats in yards and cars halfway into living rooms. It was unbelievable. We'd seen images like these on the news months earlier, but no amount of TV can prepare you for the reality of seeing it with your own eyes.

I looked back at Brittany, and she was just as sobered as I was. (She had gone from almost falling asleep to wearing a look of pure shock.) Both of us glanced at Sean, who was trying to play it cool. We didn't realize it at the time, but he had no idea where we were. We were making our way through Metairie and Lakeview, two areas that were hit really hard by Katrina. Later I took friends to this area to see the devastation and the progress—or the lack thereof. There's no way words can describe the scope of the wreckage we saw that day.

Sean finally pulled out his phone and called Mickey Loomis. He tried to be discreet, but we heard him ask Mickey where we were and how to get back to the facility. He was really embarrassed. "I'm sorry. I'm new here too. I've only been in town a month and a half."

We wound our way through those neighborhoods for about forty-five minutes. At first we were just taking it all in—there was so much to process. We saw the giant X's spray-painted on doors where the police and National Guard had checked homes for bodies, noting the number of survivors—and victims—they had found. Yards were cluttered with debris, broken windows, and overturned cars. Some houses were gone altogether, with nothing left but a slab of concrete. The people who had lived in those homes were now scattered to the wind.

There's something you learn quickly about New Orleans when you visit: people there have a clear sense of home. Many families have lived in New Orleans for countless generations. They will never leave, and they don't want to go anywhere else. They love life. They love living here. But a huge part of the population had been lost. Displaced.

There was a moment when we were driving, trying to find our way back to the facility, when I felt myself going into information overload. During the first part of the visit, I was focused exclusively on meeting Sean and the other coaches, talking to the owner and the general manager, discussing the offense. I had thought about where we might live and about the future of the club. All that was swirling in my brain when suddenly I was hit with a dose of reality. All that devastation really put things in perspective for me. By the time we reached the facility, I honestly felt like I needed to lie down.

I quickly met with Mickey and Mr. Benson, and then it was off to the airport. We were an hour behind schedule already, and I could sense that Mickey wanted to do everything in his power to prevent me from getting on that plane. You see, typically on a recruiting visit, the last stop is where a player signs. Mickey figured if I got on that plane, I was never coming back.

But I had given my word that I would make the trip to Miami before I made any decisions. I needed perspective, but more than anything, I needed time to let what I had seen in New Orleans sink in. It was heavy stuff, and I needed to find a way to compartmentalize it for a while so I could give my attention to the opportunity in Miami.

The Dolphins picked us up in owner Wayne Huizenga's customized 747. It was huge and impressive. They had flown in several coaches and their wives for the flight back to Miami. We immediately started talking team and offensive philosophy and all the other pertinent details of Dolphins football.

Wayne Huizenga, Nick Saban, the other coaches, and their wives took us to dinner that night, and we had a very nice time. At the outset, our visit looked a lot like what we'd received in New Orleans. However, that was about to change. When I woke up the next morning, the first thing planned was an appointment with the Dolphins team doctor at his office. There they required me to go through extensive physicals on my shoulder. They hadn't prepared me for this, and my agent had no idea it was coming either. But I had nothing to hide, so I agreed to let them examine me all they wanted.

I saw a neurologist to determine if I had any nerve damage. He stuck a bunch of big needles in my arm and tried to make sure that my nerve endings were firing properly and that I was going to get all the feeling back from the top of my shoulder down to my fingertips. I was only two months out of surgery at this point, and I wondered what Dr. Andrews would say about this. I was fairly certain he wouldn't like all the prodding and poking on my still-sensitive shoulder, and I was concerned this could potentially set us back from the progress we'd made.

Then they did an MRI with contrast, where I was injected with a solution that shows more detail than a normal MRI would. It was a two-hour process—and quite painful. After the injection, which caused my arm to swell, I had to lie in the MRI tube. I'm not claustrophobic, but after a while you start wondering if you'll ever make it out of there.

I literally spent six hours with various medical staff, trying to convince them that I was going to come back okay. Most of my time in Miami was consumed by people jerking, poking, and prodding me in different ways. I felt like I was at a cattle show—or, at the very least, at the draft combine again. And all through the process, from the moment I stepped on the plane until we drove back to the airport, I got the feeling that the Dolphins were looking at me with a sense of doubt. Was I supposed to be selling myself to them? It sure felt like it.

Sure, they had everything in place in Miami. They had top-notch coaches. They looked like they were headed in the right direction as an organization. South Florida was a gorgeous place to live, a wonderful place to raise a family. There were so many pluses to the equation, but I couldn't shake the sense that they doubted me. It almost felt like I'd be stepping into the same situation I had just exited in San Diego.

The responses to my rehab highlight reel seemed to illustrate the striking difference between the two organizations. I had a DVD Dr. Andrews had made of the actual surgery and a DVD that offered a detailed look at all I'd been doing in my rehab and how I was improving. I gave them to both teams when we met. At the time I was three weeks ahead of schedule and proud of the accomplishments I'd made so far. I wanted them to look me in the eye and see how serious I was about making a complete comeback. I wanted to show them I was on my way to coming back stronger.

In New Orleans I got a nod, a pat on the back, and the feeling *That's what we like to hear.* They communicated warmth, encouragement, and confidence.

In Miami they took the DVD and shrugged. *Okay, we'll see.*

I felt like I had a hole I needed to dig myself out of right from the beginning. The vibe I was getting from them was doubt and mistrust. *You should feel lucky we're considering you.*

Brittany and I returned to Birmingham utterly exhausted. We had been up late in New Orleans and in Miami. Plus it had been an emotionally taxing few days. But as tired as we were, that first night back we stayed up and talked, just like we had the night of our first date. We had a lot of the same reactions about what we'd seen. If leaving New Orleans had been information and emotion overload, leaving Miami was pure frustration. I was so disappointed. I had been hoping for so much more from Miami. But as Brittany and I reflected on all that had happened in the past week, we had to admit there was something special about New Orleans. At one point we sat on the bed and just stared at each other. The revelation seemed to hit us at the same time. We couldn't quite explain it, but it was almost like New Orleans was calling to us. We prayed together that night as we do every night, and we asked God to continue to show us what direction we should go and allow us to sense his purpose.

Miami had seemed to be such an obvious choice. We hadn't been expecting this, and we certainly weren't looking for it. But we couldn't ignore the irresistible feeling—a sense of spiritual calling, even—that God wanted us in New Orleans. Maybe it was because we could approach the city from a different angle than perhaps anybody else. Where some people might look at the city and see disaster, we saw opportunity. Where some people might be deterred by the devastation, we were drawn to it. We saw the adversity as a chance to build something special from the ground up. Before the hurricane, New Orleans had had its fair share of problems, just like every major city does. Up to that point most of those problems had been ignored, accepted as the norm, or patched with duct tape for the time being. After Katrina, the city now had a clean slate, an opportunity to start over and rebuild the right way. This was a chance to fill in the voids that had been missing for some time now, in everything from politics to crime to the education system to infrastructure. What if God wanted us in New Orleans for such a time as this?

Am I being called to New Orleans? Pastors and missionaries might get a calling from God to do something . . . but football players? Do they get that kind of tug from the Almighty?

I wasn't sure, but I was about to find out where I *wasn't* being called.

The Call

The night we arrived back in Birmingham, I talked with Tom, my agent. When I told him about what I'd seen in New Orleans, I felt like a young Marine who had just witnessed his first day of combat. I still needed to process a lot of what I'd seen and felt while I was there. But Tom could already tell which direction I was leaning.

The money was almost identical from both teams, so that really wasn't a huge factor. New Orleans was ready to sign a deal if I wanted it. The Dolphins were studying the MRI and the physicals I had been through while I was in Miami. I was confident the results would come back great and perhaps I'd get some of the affirmation I'd been hoping for during my visit. My heart was definitely being tugged toward New Orleans, but I hadn't closed the door on the possibility of Miami at that point. The decision was coming down to this: *What organization do I want to be part of? What city do I want to call home? What community will Brittany and I raise our future children in? Who really believes in me?*

Tom had a different take on Miami's approach. "I've seen this before," he said. "Here's what's going to happen: Miami will call tomorrow. They're going to say that the physical didn't turn out as well as they had hoped. They're going to threaten to pull the offer."

"You know this?"

"Not only do I know it, but I can pretty much guarantee it."

Sure enough, the next day the phone rang. It was Miami. They gave Tom the runaround about the deal and said there were problems with my physical. Tom had nailed it.

As the discussion continued with Miami, I kept feeling this steady pull toward New Orleans. The calling didn't hit me all at once—it was more like a progression of realizing how God was directing us. In some ways, it paralleled my experience with Brittany at Purdue. I continued to see her over and over after our first encounter on my twentieth birthday. It was like God kept allowing our paths to cross. I couldn't forget about her. Now I had to wonder if it wasn't just a mistake that we took that wrong turn and saw those sights in New Orleans. I couldn't escape the nagging feeling that maybe I belonged in New Orleans, that God was opening doors there for a purpose.

I didn't understand it all, I didn't have it figured out, but I knew in my gut that there was an opportunity presenting itself. I was trying to rebuild my shoulder and my career, the organization was rebuilding its reputation and reestablishing itself, and the city was restoring not only the homes but also the lives of its people. Why not do this together and lean on each other in the process? We were all going through the same struggles and battling the same doubts. The vision was starting to crystallize as Brittany and I weighed both sides.

What I kept coming back to when I processed all the issues was the fact that the Saints wanted me. That was what I'd struggled with over the past five years with the Chargers. I didn't have their respect. I hadn't felt supported or fully appreciated.

But here was a community and an organization welcoming me with open arms, saying that I was their guy. They wanted me to be part of their team. They thought I could come back and play as well as, if not better than, before. They believed in me.

I called Tom Condon, and we discussed the options some more. "It sounds like you want to do the deal with New Orleans," he said. "You want me to get it done now?"

"I do, but I have to make one call first."

This probably seemed pretty odd to Tom, but he knows me well enough to understand what I was about to do.

Before I made my final decision, I had to know where Miami stood. I had heard what they'd told my agent. But that could have been a bargaining strategy. What was going through Nick Saban's brain in Miami? Would he pick up the phone and say, "I don't care what the doctors say—you're a winner, and we want you here"? In my heart I needed to know exactly how Saban was feeling. Then, when I walked away from this, I'd have closure. I wanted to have that measure of peace with my decision, leaving nothing to chance. This way I'd never have to look back and wonder what might have been.

I hung up and dialed Nick's office. His secretary answered, and my call was directed to his office.

"Coach, it's Drew Brees. I had a conversation with my agent, and I have a question for you."

"Sure, Drew."

Deep breath. "I heard that my medical reports came back and your doctors didn't like what they saw."

"Right. Well, you know, our doctors have given you a 25 percent chance of coming back and playing. I don't know what else to trust or look at other than what our medical people tell us. They're professionals, and they know what they're doing and how to interpret those tests. We'd still love to have you, but . . . that number we talked about earlier might have to change."

I understood that he was in a tough spot. He was facing the restrictions of their salary cap while still trying to put together a championship team. The doctors had given him the reports, and he had to trust them.

"You have to understand our situation. If we sign you for this amount of money and all of a sudden you can't play, it puts us in a really difficult position down the road. That's a lot of money going to a guy who's not contributing to the team. And then I won't be able to pay other players to fill that void."

Another breath. "Coach, I know what your doctors believe about me. My question is, what do *you* believe? Do you believe that I can come back and be better than I was before and lead your team to a championship?"

I already knew how New Orleans had answered that question. Now I needed to hear what Miami had to say.

Nick Saban paused.

That was really all I needed to hear. His pause told me everything.

"Well, Drew," he said, "I would still love to have you, but I have to trust what our medical people are saying. . . ."

He went on from there, basically repeating what he had said before, like he was reading from a script. But I was starting to tune out. By then I had all the information I needed. I had made my decision. Now the only question was how I was going to deliver it.

When Nick finished, I said, "You know what, Coach Saban, thank you very much for your time. I appreciate your interest. I appreciate the visit and the invitation to come down there. I'm going to New Orleans."

Click.

I knew I wasn't supposed to do that. In the world of negotiating, that type of reveal is verboten for someone in my position. I knew the organization was trying to get me for as little money as possible. They thought they had me. Now I'd flat out told them I was going to New Orleans. But in that moment I couldn't resist the honest disclosure.

As soon as I hung up, I knew what would happen on the other end. Coach Saban would call their general manager and tell him to do the deal with Daunte Culpepper. But the minute I was off the table, they had no bargaining leverage. I had just thrown a wrench in their negotiations.

Immediately I called my agent. "Tom, do the deal with New Orleans."

THE COMEBACK

CHAPTER EIGHT

FROM THE VERY BEGINNING in New Orleans, there was a warmth from the people that confirmed this was where we were supposed to be. When we ate in the chef's kitchen at Emeril's restaurant, he left a cookbook for me at the table. I opened the front cover and saw he had signed it.

> *To Drew: You sign with the Saints, and I'll be cooking your first meal for you in your house here in New Orleans.*
> *Emeril Lagasse*

As we walked through the restaurant and down the street, I was amazed by how many people randomly came up to us. "Hey, I've been a fan of yours since college. We'd love to have you in our city."

I had anticipated the feeling that this was a city on its way out, but that's not what we discovered at all. Instead, we found a tight-knit, welcoming community filled with people who are deeply rooted in the city they love. When they realized Brittany and I were considering making that area our home, they opened their arms to us. Their energy and optimism for their community showed us what could be done in New Orleans. Despite the tragedy of the hurricane and the devastation and mismanagement that followed, there was hope. There was life. And no matter how desolate things might have appeared on the outside, if you went deeper, you could feel a strong heartbeat in the city.

I had no doubt when I signed the contract with New Orleans that this was the right place for us. But at the same time, I felt a sense of fear and angst because there was such a big job ahead. Just rehabbing my shoulder felt at times like I was giving every ounce that I had. To rebuild a team and organization, then a stadium, and then an entire city—those were huge tasks beyond the scope of human capability. When I looked at the challenges before us, it was overwhelming, and I hoped I could fulfill my role and do my part.

However, I clung to the belief that if God calls you to it, he will give you the power to walk through it. He will give you the tools required to accomplish the task. He will give you the heart, the resolve, and the fortitude you need. In one sense, I'm glad the task was so much bigger than any person or team could achieve. It forced me to rely on God and other people in new ways—this wasn't something I could try to pull off by myself. And if we had any success, everyone would know we couldn't have achieved it by human effort alone. There was something—Someone—bigger involved.

I compare the feeling I had right then with the butterflies I get before a game. There's an excitement, a nervousness, that comes prior to any big event, and no matter how much you prepare, no matter how confident you are, you still have a bit of fear and anxiety mixed with anticipation. At the core of that is a feeling of responsibility. *I have a task to complete, and I want to bring my best today.*

The Bible says, "To whom much is given . . . much will be required." I know I have been given a lot throughout my life. I've been blessed with a ton of tremendous opportunities. I've been surrounded by unbelievable people—family, mentors, coaches, teachers, friends, my wife and soul mate. These people have supported me and helped mold me into who I am. They've given me the confidence to attempt some things that are too big for me to handle on my own. Every time I walk onto the field or stand in front of a group to raise awareness for our foundation or pick up a hammer to work on rebuilding a house in the Lower Ninth Ward, I feel this sense of responsibility on my shoulders. I want to give back a little of what has been given to me and in some way pay it forward to those who otherwise might not have as many opportunities as I've been given.

But before I could really dig in to the rebuilding process in New Orleans, I had to move further down my own long road to recovery. And I wasn't prepared for how long or painful it would be.

My Throwing Arm

Ever since I was little, whether I was playing baseball or football, I've always had a strong arm. It didn't matter if I was tossing the ball in the yard with my brother, Reid; playing a pickup game on the playground; or participating in organized ball—there was a certain feeling I had when I could zing the ball to a friend and hit him right in the chest. There was nothing like the sound of a fastball popping a catcher's mitt or the thump of a football hitting your target in the chest. Sometimes my teammates got upset with me back then. "Why are you throwing so hard, Drew?" I wasn't doing it on purpose. Well, not all the time, anyway. But that throwing arm has always had fire in it. It is my gift.

As I grew up, it was like the football became an extension of me. Pitchers talk about the almost-magical feel of the baseball in their hands, and quarterbacks over the years have tried to describe the sensation that comes over them when they're holding a football. I can't quite explain it, except to say it feels like there's an energy source there. When a player picks up the ball, it's as if it comes to life in his hands.

I have a certain comfort level when I'm holding a football. It gives me a sense of strength but also responsibility. It clears my head and allows me to focus. When you have the ball, you feel like you are holding the sword of King Leonidas of Sparta, leading your team into battle. When you're in control of this thing in your hands, you have the power to do great things and ultimately determine if your team wins or loses.

For someone like me who had lived all of my conscious life with a ball in my hands, it was excruciating to suddenly be stripped of a football. This wasn't just my job or my hobby; it was my love. And to add to the pressure, now I had a new team that was counting on me—in a city still recovering from a major disaster. The people were excited. The coaches were ready. Mentally and emotionally I was primed. But my doctors said my body wasn't there yet. I wanted to turn the dogs loose, but they were holding me back, telling me to pace myself. They knew that at this point my biggest threat for reinjury was myself.

I kept pushing Dr. Andrews to let me throw. After all, I had gotten out of the sling a week early. I had full range of motion about three weeks earlier than he'd predicted. I was continuing to progress further and further ahead of schedule. Call it the magic of God's healing along with the commitment and desire he gave me. The other big motivator for me was fear of failure—fear that I wouldn't be able to come back at all or that I would let down those who had invested so much in me. Every day I was confident I could come back even better, but there was still that sliver of anxiety in the back of my mind that gave me a drive to push myself each day. But Dr. Andrews just smiled and reminded me about the importance of letting the shoulder heal. "Remember, it's not healed yet. Let the shoulder rehab take its course. No throwing for four months." He wouldn't budge on that one.

The throwing motion he was concerned about was the shoulder's external/internal rotation. Also, as I release the ball over my head when I'm throwing, my arm is put in a similar position to where it was when it dislocated. There were plenty of precautions to be taken, but that's why we had worked so hard to gain range of motion and strength back in my shoulder. The biggest concern was that I would push my shoulder too far in the rehab process and accidentally pop an anchor, which would require another surgery and put me right back to square one. I could not afford any setbacks.

At certain times during my rehab exercises, I would feel something stretching in my shoulder like rubber bands. It would actually make a squeaking sound, like the Tin Man from *The Wizard of Oz* or nails on a chalkboard. It's a weird feeling to have something foreign inside your body holding you together, and it's even stranger to be able to feel it working. But it *was* working, so I couldn't complain. Without those anchors, I wouldn't have had a chance.

Kevin Wilk saw the progress I was making, and he knew it was time for me to pick up a ball again. There's no test that can tell you it's time to begin throwing, so he judged it all by feel. Shortly before the fourth month, ahead of schedule, Dr. Andrews gave me the go-ahead. I was finally ready to throw again!

Transitions off the Field

Things weren't just coasting from that point on, though. I had my good days of rehab and throwing and those days when my arm would ache and fatigue very quickly. It was obvious that my shoulder still needed a lot of work. Because of my injury, Brittany and I had made the hard decision to put off having children for now. Brittany's main objective was to take care of me and nurse me back to health. She stayed with me the whole time in Birmingham and would jokingly say, "I'm not ready to take care of two babies." It was tough to put that dream on hold, though.

Adding to our stress level was a move to a new city. We'd felt displaced for some time already after living with Brittany's parents in Birmingham for the rehab. We felt a little like we were being tossed around on the waves, and we wanted to get settled, to find a place that felt like home.

We did find a house to call home in New Orleans, and we loved it. But like most older homes there, it was going to take a lot of work and TLC. The house was in the Uptown neighborhood, a little north of the Mississippi River and one block off St. Charles, next to Audubon Park and Tulane University. Many of the homes there were built in the 1800s and are listed in the National Register of Historic Places. We chose that area because it was in the heart of the city, right in the thick of things. We wanted to embrace this community the way it had embraced us, so we decided to immerse ourselves in a neighborhood full of the culture and charm of the city.

The home we bought had about $50,000 worth of roof damage from Katrina that the owner had fixed before we arrived. The floodwaters had stopped about six blocks away, but almost all the houses in the area—even those that didn't have flood damage—were affected by the Category 5 hurricane.

With any older home in the historical district, you have to deal with certain issues. Ours had been built in the late 1890s or early 1900s. It had suffered some damage from the storm, but there were also general repairs and renovations needed simply because of its age. We had a lot to accomplish to bring this house to life.

This wasn't just a dream for Brittany and me. Yes, we wanted to put down roots in this place. But we also were hoping to show the community that we were committed to the rebuilding process. Whether you live there or are just passing through, people see these old homes as part of the fabric of New Orleans. We wanted to get our hands dirty and let everyone know we were on board with the restoration, doing our part to bring the city back better than it had ever been before. When you move into a historical district like the Garden District or Uptown or Old Metairie or the French Quarter, you feel a sense of responsibility to be a great steward of the community and to leave whatever you touch better than the way you found it.

We had planned for the renovation to take about eight months, which would have mirrored my projected comeback. Unfortunately, eight months stretched into eighteen—and then went even longer. We ended up spending two years on construction and rebuilding, and it was a long, grueling process. But we considered ourselves lucky. It was certainly nothing compared to what the folks whose homes had been destroyed went through. Many people had to evacuate the city they loved and were living elsewhere or were still living in temporary trailers the size of a closet. At least we had a roof over our heads and running water, despite the plastic coverings on the walls and the construction dust in the air. We actually spent the first six months in the house with no furniture—we slept on a mattress on the floor and ate dinner off TV trays while sitting in beach chairs. But with each new project we poured ourselves into, Brittany and I bonded more with this city. We were building something beautiful, one nail at a time.

Throwing Again

In the first several months of my rehab, I had been incredibly antsy to pick up the ball and toss it around. I knew I couldn't do that, but it was a great temptation. Now that it was finally time for me to start throwing again, I knew I wasn't going to simply pick up the ball one day and have everything back to normal. I had to start over. Completely. From the mechanics to the muscle memory, I needed to relearn how to throw a football. That might sound funny coming from a guy who had a football at the end of his arm most of his life, but it was true. Throwing the football, and even holding it, felt foreign to me at first.

Throughout my rehab, I had tackled all my goals with enthusiasm and a positive mind-set. With the accomplishment of each short-term goal, I gained the confidence and strength I needed to pursue the next challenge. I had worked my way out of the sling, I had gained the full range of motion in my shoulder, and I had pushed myself as hard as I could without reinjuring my arm. I had followed all of Dr. Andrews's advice, spurred on by Kevin Wilk's tenacity to get me ready.

The fear of failure was always in the rearview mirror chasing after me, forcing me to push myself further than I had ever gone before. I wore my Saints shirt to rehab at the start of every week as motivation—a reminder of how much New Orleans had invested in me. I could not let them down.

My first toss was not with a full throwing motion. Nobody on the medical staff would let me do that—they knew better. My first pass was more of a pushing motion, like a shot put. I held the ball in front of me with both hands, like I was in my set position and ready to throw, and then I just pushed it to Kevin. Simple. Sort of like when you are throwing a ball to a little kid, very gently. It wasn't strenuous at all. The feeling of throwing again was exhilarating, but at the same time the fear that tiny bit of motion brought was overwhelming.

Oh, man, I need to be so careful, I thought. *I'd better not hurt myself.*

Though my mind was strong and the rest of my body was in good shape, that little push let me know how weak I truly was. It confirmed how much damage had been done to my shoulder. Dr. Andrews was right—it wasn't healed yet.

Kevin and I would work for eight or nine hours each day going through different strengthening exercises. Looking back, I think he used the football as a carrot. If I successfully went through all the rigors of my exercises, we would head outside, where there was a small patch of grass about as big as a dining room carpet. It was a rather humbling experience to have people watching as they walked in and out of the building. Here I was, an NFL quarterback, tossing a football back and forth toddler style. Kevin would underhand a pass to me, and I'd push it back to him. Some people knew who I was and had heard what I was going through. Still, I'm sure they had no idea how difficult that little push with the football was for me. It looked like something a baby could do, but it took everything I had right then.

That was such a picture of where I was compared with where I wanted to be. My desire was to walk back into a huge stadium with one hundred yards of turf, but I was on a tiny patch of grass on the lawn of a hospital building. Still, I was seeing progress. *One small step at a time,* I reminded myself. *Trust the process.*

I remember standing on the lawn of the rehab clinic one day, looking down at that little patch of grass. I'd played in the

Rose Bowl. I'd been to the Pro Bowl. I was a quarterback in the NFL. And yet in that moment I couldn't have been more thrilled about throwing a football five yards. It might not have made sense to anyone else, but to me it was exhilarating. I finally had the ball back in my hands again.

Gradually I moved from just shot-putting the ball to lifting the ball up to my right side and then pushing it. Occasionally Kevin would let me throw the ball a few times, and I would start to feel really good. I would think, *Man, the shoulder is really coming back. This is great!* That's when I'd try to stretch it out a little and take the ball back a bit farther. Suddenly I would feel it—this pain deep in the tissue. It screamed out, *Not yet!* I had to listen to that voice many times and fight the urge to rush the recovery process.

Anyone who has played sports at any level will tell you that you can't focus on the bad things that might happen in a game or you won't be able to function properly when you are in the moment. When you climb into a NASCAR vehicle or strap on a helmet in a hockey game, you can't worry about crashing or getting hurt. You must be able to relax and compete aggressively while approaching the game with great confidence. It is the fear of failure that drives you, but it is visualizing success that gives you the positive mind-set and confidence to feel like you can accomplish anything. In the end, when you know you have given everything you have and poured out your heart for the cause, then you can relax and let God take over. All God wants is for you to utilize the talents and abilities he has given you—to be the best you can be and to reach your full potential. All you have to do is give him the credit in return.

Early in my rehab, the threat of reinjury was real, and I had to be careful. Something as simple as slipping in the shower or accidentally twitching while I slept could potentially damage the repair. Even when I began the throwing process, I had to take it one step at a time and gradually ramp up the throwing motion so I wouldn't shock the shoulder too much. There was a balance to it all. As my physical therapist, Kevin helped me learn to listen to my body and figure out the difference between good pain and bad pain. There is the good pain of stretching and gradually breaking up the scar tissue from the surgery, and then there is the bad pain of your body telling you not to go any further or you will get hurt again. It takes wisdom and experience to know the difference. Kevin had that, and I was gradually catching on.

At that stage of the rehab, when I was ready to relearn the mechanics of properly throwing the ball, I was really cautious. I would constantly ask Kevin, "How far can I take it back? How hard can I throw?"

He was infinitely patient with me. When we began, he said, "We're going to throw ten balls at five yards." It was a meager start, but it felt so good to be able to have a tangible goal for the day, to hold the ball in my hands again.

Before we went out to the little patch of grass in front of the building, I visualized everything about those short passes. I would picture my mechanics, the proper way to throw, what position I wanted the ball in, my stance, my release point. Slowly all those things that were once automatic started to come back.

"Okay, today we're going to throw twenty balls at five yards," he said the next week. The progress felt good, even though someone walking by might not notice the improvement.

Dr. Andrews had been right about recovery taking time. I learned some valuable lessons about the healing process during rehab. It's not an overnight proposition—take a pill, do a few exercises, and everything will be fine. Even though I was able to accelerate the process a little by working hard, there was no substitute for time. There are no shortcuts to healing. You can't rush it.

Whether you're talking in terms of the physical, the emotional, or the spiritual, healing has its own timetable. When there is tragedy in your life—perhaps a health crisis or the death of a family member or something else that upends your world—there's a mourning period you have to go through in order to cope with it and come out on the other side healthy and mentally whole. You have to work through the emotions and deal with the fallout. God has designed our bodies and hearts to need rest and recovery when we've been wounded, and you can't rush that. In a way, it's like the agonizing wait of pregnancy. In order for there to be proper growth for the child inside, you have to give it time. There's no way around it.

The city of New Orleans learned that lesson in the days and weeks following Katrina. One of the worst things you can do when you've been laid low is to try to come back too quickly. You have to see the truth about your situation and accept it in order to heal right and then return stronger. You need to learn the lessons while you're still down in order to put yourself in the position to make a comeback.

Everything in me wanted to rush through my rehab, and I do think my motivation helped me to get on track as quickly as possible. But I'm thankful there were people who knew more than I did about the healing process. They taught me that you have to embrace the pain in order for it to have the desired effect. The painful things we go through have a way of teaching us things we can't learn any other way. Pain is a gift I sure didn't want, but I believe God used it for a purpose in my life.

Quicker and Stronger

The last part of the rehab process focused on being able to take the ball back and extend my arm as far as necessary to throw

This is my grandpa Ray Akins holding me up. I hold my son, Baylen, like this now.

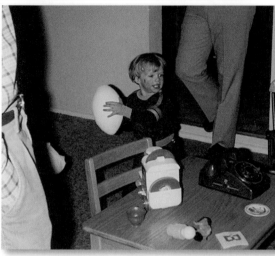

For as long as I can remember, I have had a football in my hands and that same look in my eye.

My little brother, Reid, and I always had a special bond growing up. We were best friends.

One of my favorite memories from Purdue was the day we beat Indiana 41–13 to win a trip to the Rose Bowl in 2000. I had dreamed of this from the moment I set foot on campus.

Hoisting the MVP trophy after beating #4 Kansas State in the Alamo Bowl in 1998

Brittany and I outside the Le Petit Bofinger restaurant in Paris right after we got engaged

On the beach in Okinawa, Japan, in March 2008. This is the actual beach where my grandfather Ray Akins stormed in as a 19-year-old Marine, April 1, 1945. It was a very emotional day.

Christmas 2008: Brit was 8½ months pregnant with Baylen at the time.

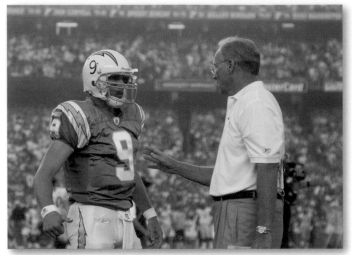

Me and Marty
Schottenheimer
during a Monday
night game against
the Steelers in 2005

Brit and I before
the Raiders game at
Qualcomm Stadium
in 2002

Two of my all-time
favorite teammates,
Lorenzo Neal (#41)
and LaDainian
Tomlinson

Dr. David Chao helping me off the field after I dislocated my shoulder against Denver on December 31, 2005

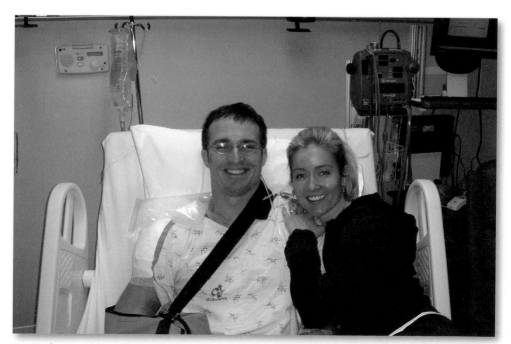

Dr. Andrews told me that if he had to do the surgery over again 100 times, he couldn't do it as well as he just did. Now *that* is what you want to hear!

St. Bernard Parish deputy sheriff Jerry Reyes uses his boat to rescue residents after Hurricane Katrina completely flooded the Ninth Ward.

The National Guard hauls a truck bed full of newly displaced residents through waist-high floodwaters to the Superdome, where thousands of post-Katrina refugees took up residence for days following the disaster.

Floodwaters from Hurricane Katrina fill the streets near downtown New Orleans (August 30, 2005).

September 25, 2006—Our first home game back in the Superdome following Katrina. We beat the Falcons 23–3 in a sold-out Monday night game.

Celebrating a Monday night victory over the Patriots with Coach Sean Payton in 2009

Leading the team in our now-famous pregame chant

Dropping back
to pass against
the Redskins on
December 6, 2009

After being down 21 points, this touchdown gave us the lead in the
fourth quarter against the Dolphins in 2009—and we never looked back.

The New Orleans fans are some of the most loyal fans in the league.

My buddy Micah's courageous battle against Hodgkin's lymphoma gave us the strength to accomplish all we did in the 2009 season.

On the 2007 "Brees on the Seas" fishing event with some of the kids from Children's Hospital of New Orleans

Getting the kids pumped up before the 2005 Brees Gridiron Classic at Qualcomm Stadium

I really appreciate the opportunity to support the men and women of our armed forces. Here I am on my third USO trip (2008) with my two former teammates, Donnie Edwards of the Chargers (fourth from left) and Billy Miller of the Saints (far right).

Brittany, two-month-old Baylen, and me in Maui in 2009

Baylen's first Christmas (2009)

Swinging with Dad in Audubon Park in New Orleans, 2009

We love this little guy!

Teaching Baylen how to putt like a pro (2010)

Pro Bowl offensive tackle
Jon Stinchcomb holding off
the pass rush like he did so well
all season so I could throw a pass
against a tough Colts defense

I have been
waiting a long
time to hold
this trophy.

An emotional moment
with my son

Celebrating with Brittany and Baylen

Riding through New Orleans in the Super Bowl parade

We did it, little boy. We did it.

it with full velocity. Of course I wasn't throwing the ball that hard then, but just getting the shoulder in that position was a large feat in itself.

Here's a glimpse of the throwing action in slow motion: after your arm pushes the ball backward away from the body into what I call the loading position, it then takes great strength and force to bring your hips and shoulders around to throw the ball. This requires a lot of external rotation in the shoulder as well as torque on the arm as it goes back and comes forward. Then, after you release the ball, the arm decelerates quickly, which requires a very strong group of muscles on the back side of the shoulder to slow the arm down. If you lack strength in the back side of the shoulder, it really limits how hard you can throw the ball. Your back-side shoulder strength must match up with your front shoulder strength, or you have created an imbalance.

The problem with an imbalance is that you are only as strong as your weakest link. If the muscles in the front of your shoulder say you can throw one hundred balls but the muscles in the back of your shoulder will only allow you to throw fifty balls, you will only be able to throw fifty balls. On top of that, the imbalance makes you more susceptible to injuries down the road. Picture the muscles as a wall of protection for the shoulder. You have already built a strong wall in the front of your shoulder, but all you have is a picket fence of muscles protecting the back. That's why so much of the focus of my rehab involved regaining strength in the most neglected areas and the muscles that atrophy the quickest, like the back side of the shoulder.

In the beginning of the rehab process, I was hardly bringing my arm back at all. After throwing just ten balls five yards, my arm was exhausted. But with each day, each throw, I started gaining strength and momentum. There was a surprising silver lining that came in the midst of this. In relearning how to throw the ball, I was able to tighten up my mechanics by shortening my release. This allowed me to get rid of the ball quicker and with more velocity than I had before the injury. My windup became more compact. I could hit a target more quickly. And in the NFL, that kind of timing can be the difference between a pass that threads the needle and one that gets intercepted.

As I continued to work with Kevin, we graduated from the patch of grass in front of the building to the parking lot. We threw for longer distances, and I increased the velocity. The risk of reinjury was slowly dissipating, but I had to continually remind myself to focus on the correct mechanics of the throw rather than the length of the throw. It really felt good to be able to extend my arm and get more rotation in my shoulder.

I wasn't all the way there yet, but I was on my way back.

Put to the Test in Jackson

By the time summer came, I could tell my legs were in good shape, my core was where it needed to be, and my mind was as focused and tough as it had ever been. But I still wasn't sure about the arm and shoulder. Will Demps, a safety for the Giants at the time, was coming off an ACL injury, and he would throw with me at the rehab facility. On the weekends, when the rehab place was closed, Brittany and I would go outside her parents' home, and I'd throw to her or have her help stretch my arm to keep it loose. I was amazed by the team of medical staff, family, and friends who rallied around me and helped me get to where I needed to be by the time training camp rolled around.

I was excited—I couldn't wait for my first training camp

with the Saints. But I was more anxious than I'd ever been. Would I be able to perform? In training camp you throw so much that even a healthy arm gets fatigued. What would happen to an arm with a bunch of anchors in it—an arm that was still in recovery mode?

In July 2006, six months after my surgery, I headed to Jackson, Mississippi, for training camp. It wasn't just a first for me—this was Sean Payton's first training camp with the Saints too. More than that, it was his first training camp as a head coach. He warned the team beforehand about how hard it would be. "You'd better come to camp with your mind right and ready to work harder than you have ever worked in your life," he said. It was just like boot camp, where they tear you down as an individual before building you back up as a team— a unit that can never be broken. Later some of the guys said the 2006 training camp took years off their lives. I was there, and I believe it.

Every training camp I've ever been part of, from high school to college to the pros, has been about survival. It's always intense. But Sean wanted to make it exceptionally tough to show he was going to expect the very best from us. He wanted us to blow past the perceived limits of history and set new standards for what we could accomplish. Couple that determination from the head coach with the humidity of a Mississippi summer, heat indexes over 110 degrees, and full pads, and you have a recipe for sweat, fatigue, and plenty of sore muscles.

We had a lot of consecutive two-a-days, which tends to be rare for teams in the NFL now. For five weeks we were outside in the sun every day, and there was no respite from the other trials that plagued us. Mosquitoes. Muscle cramps. Dehydration. Fifteen or twenty guys would get IVs after practice to replace the fluids they'd lost. It was physical, hot, and brutal.

As a quarterback in training camp, you aren't taking quite the same pounding on your body that the other positions have to deal with. Your legs get sore from all the footwork drills and drops in the pocket, and your arm might be sore from throwing so much, but the rest of your joints are spared from the constant banging that players in other positions endure on the field. The grind for a quarterback is more mental than it is physical. You have to study to make sure you know what every person on both offense and defense is doing. On top of that, I was adjusting to playing football again, getting acquainted with a new team, and getting used to a new coach, a new system, and a new playbook. It was the first time I'd had any physical contact since I'd shredded my shoulder. And it was the first time I'd sported a Saints fleur-de-lis on my helmet.

During the past six months of recovery, I had convinced myself to take it slow and trust the process of healing. But I knew coming into training camp that my arm was not 100 percent; I was probably closer to 70 percent at the time. I told myself that as long as I could creep up a percent or so each day and continue to get stronger, by the time the regular season started, I would be ready.

Sean and the other coaches understood I had to ease into things, but I really wanted to show them I was close. The first day went pretty well. It was good to be back on the field after spending all that time stuck in a La-Z-Boy and tossing the ball around on a patch of grass. It was rejuvenating to be with teammates who welcomed me and were ready for a new start, a new season. As you can imagine, it was hard to attract free agents and other young talent to the Saints that year. Many of the core players from our 2009 Super Bowl team were "castaways" from other teams, brought in for the 2006 season. We had either traded for them or signed them in free agency when few other teams wanted them. It's not a knock on those guys—

it's just the truth. This mentality that nobody else wanted us put a chip on our shoulders and united us and made New Orleans our safe haven. With so many people doubting my return as a starting quarterback in the league, I felt like one of those castaways myself.

That year we acquired our center Jeff Faine in a draft day trade with Cleveland, as well as our noseguard Hollis Thomas from Philadelphia. In fact, our entire starting linebacker core was acquired that year. Scott Fujita was a free agent from Dallas, Mark Simoneau came in a trade with Philadelphia, and we got Scott Shanle in a trade with Dallas. To a lot of people's surprise, these guys who had been written off by the rest of the league played a critical role in our success in 2006.

We had a throw count during training camp—like a pitch count in baseball—that consisted of the number of balls I threw to receivers each day. That first day I threw about eighty balls. I threw during the entire morning practice and then rested my arm in the afternoon. Going back to the dorm that night, I felt pretty good. *Not a bad start to a new era,* I thought. I had every reason to believe the next day would be even better.

I went out the second morning of training camp and began to stretch my arm. It didn't take long to realize how sore it was from throwing the first day. I tried to ignore it, and I certainly wasn't going to let on to anyone that I had a sore arm after that first stinking day of practice. I got past the long walk-through and stretching time and the ball-handling period with the running backs, and then the horn blew for our traditional "routes on air." This consists of quarterbacks throwing routes to the receivers with no defense. It's an opportunity to work on timing and technique and to visualize the play as you execute the route. Sean Payton was a quarterback and had played at all levels—in high school, at Eastern Illinois University, and professionally in the World League in England. He was also the starting quarterback for three games with the Chicago Bears during the 1987 players' strike. Plus, he had been quarterbacks coach for the Philadelphia Eagles, offensive coordinator for the New York Giants, and passing game coordinator for the Dallas Cowboys before coming to New Orleans. So he knew what goes into being a quarterback and how to coach guys at my position.

Sean was standing about five feet behind me as we began these routes on air in the first practice of the second day. It was just quarterbacks and receivers on the field. The offensive coaches were around, and everyone was anxious to see the improvement of the team from day one to day two. I have probably thrown thousands of balls in thousands of routes on air periods, but the butterflies inside me wouldn't go away that day. This was my chance to prove that the rehab had worked. I needed to impress these guys—my teammates and my coaches. I was the new quarterback and one of the main building blocks of the new team. There was a lot resting on my right arm.

My sore right arm.

We would start off with short routes to get loose and then gradually progress to throws deeper down the field. As Joe Horn, the receiver to my right, stepped up to the line, I began to stress about the weakness in my arm I had not been able to shake. I stepped up to take the snap and thought, *This should be interesting.* I took the first snap and dropped back to pass. It was a simple three-step drop to throw a slant to the receiver—the simplest route in football. I have thrown this route a million times and could do it with my eyes closed and one arm tied behind my back.

The ball thumped into the dirt at Joe's feet.

I stared at the ball still rolling on the ground as Joe returned to the line. When I released that pass, I had been sure it was heading for Joe's face mask. If anything, I actually thought it might be a little high. I couldn't believe how short I was. The velocity was terrible. I had no accuracy. I could feel the coaches staring at me.

Okay, I thought. *Still getting loose. No worries. I'm okay.*

I took the next snap, dropped back three steps, and threw to another receiver. I don't even remember who it was now because I was so concerned about sending that first pass into the ground. I put a little more oomph into this pass.

It hit the ground in the exact same spot.

Immediately my thoughts started combusting. My new head coach was behind me, watching every move I made, and it was very quiet back there. But through the thick, humid air, I could feel what he was thinking. *Did we make the right decision by bringing him here? Is this guy going to be ready for opening day?*

I didn't even want to look at Sean. It was bad enough that my body had failed me—now I'd failed him too. For the past six months I had been telling myself over and over, *You're going to be ready. Don't worry. Don't get frustrated. Don't get down on yourself. It just takes time.* I had visualized what those first passes in training camp were going to be like—what they would feel like, what they would look like, how the receivers would catch the ball, how the coaches would respond. Now that the moment was here, I wanted the instant gratification of making that completion and showing them I was back. Right then, from day one. But I couldn't even throw a simple slant route.

At that point, I expected Sean to bark at me. He could have kicked himself for choosing me and second-guessed himself, me, Dr. Andrews, and Kevin. Instead, he said three words that epitomize his personality.

"Use your legs," Sean said.

It was as simple as that. *Use your legs.*

There was a lot wrapped up in those three words. He was

saying to me, *I know your arm is not where it needs to be yet. Since your arm is still weak, you need to use the rest of your body to compensate. Your legs are strong. They're 100 percent. So use your legs.*

There was also a little humor in those words. Sean has a unique way of saying things that are funny and seem like casual conversation or simple coaching points but in reality are ways to challenge you mentally and physically as a football player.

Since Sean's background is in the quarterback position, he was able to give me those types of tips during training camp, and this continued as my arm grew stronger. If I threw a ball that sailed over a guy's head, he would usually say, "You're overstriding." When I would miss a throw behind a receiver to my left, I knew what was coming out of his mouth next. "Get your hips open" or "Get your foot in front of the target." He knew the mechanics of the position so well that he could tell immediately what went wrong. "Step into it," he would say if you threw one in the dirt, or "Slow yourself down" if he saw me with happy feet in the pocket. Whenever I was struggling with something, he had advice to help me work through it.

It's similar to what happens to a golfer when he has a shot that goes astray. It helps to have someone watching his swing who can tell if the timing is off, if he opened up the club too soon, or if he didn't keep his head down. Same thing with a baseball pitcher. A good coach can tell if his body position was off in his windup or if he needed to adjust his release point. For a quarterback, so much of your success depends on mechanics. Especially when a game gets tight and the pressure mounts, it becomes even more critical that you have those basic fundamentals to lean on. You can't be thinking about your throwing motion or your feet when you have to convert a fourth-down play to win the game. Those things have to be ingrained in you through repetition and muscle memory. I had been so worried about getting my arm back to throwing 120 balls a day that I'd lost track of the fundamentals. Quality over quantity. As soon as Sean said, "Use your legs," it clicked. Back to the basics.

A Dose of Preseason Optimism

My arm got stronger and stronger as training camp progressed, and five days into camp, my pitch count had increased to 120 balls a day, allowing me to take every rep with the first team in both practices each day. Two weeks later we were into the preseason games. Despite my optimism, things didn't start out so well for me. Our first possession of the preseason ended with a throw right in the dirt in front of Chris Horn on third down and three. Getting back on the field after an injury feels a lot like having live bullets flying at you. Next we played Dallas. I became flustered early in the first quarter because of my lack of success, and we got smoked. Then we faced Indianapolis in Jackson. The final score of that game was 27–14, Colts. Not much to be proud of based on the scoreboard. But something happened in that game that gave me hope.

It had been about four weeks since training camp, when I had thrown that first pass into the dirt. I was playing more than I normally would in a preseason game. Sean had told the starters we were probably going to play three quarters of that game. But we knew from previous experience that if things don't transpire as planned throughout the course of the game and he doesn't like what he sees, then you'll stay in and work. When we hadn't scored by the middle of the third quarter, he said we needed to get the ball in the end zone before we would come out. It was now a matter of pride for us. We didn't want to walk out of that game with a zero by our name.

By almost all counts it was a forgettable game. But there was one moment I'll never forget. In the first quarter, Coach called the play—a twenty-yard route run by the receiver across the field. In order to complete the throw, you end up having to throw the ball about forty yards in the air. I took the snap, reading the defense on my way back. The cornerback covering my primary receiver was playing soft, therefore allowing us to throw the deep out. As I hit the last step in my drop, I hitched up, cocked the ball back, and let it fly.

There's a feeling unlike any other when the ball leaves your hand just right. You know immediately that it's a good throw, and there's a thrill as you watch it spiral downfield into the hands of your receiver. That pass was a good forty yards as it made its way across the field into the hands of Donté Stallworth on the left sideline. He actually dropped it, but I didn't care. It came out at just the right velocity, perfectly timed with the stride of the receiver, right into his arms. It was just like the old days, before the injury.

That is what I've been waiting for, I thought. *I'm back!* Whatever you want to call it—the magic, the mojo—it was coming to life again. I had the velocity. I had the accuracy. The ball came off my fingertips, and the second it did, I knew that was the exact throw I wanted. Until that game, I knew I was getting better each day, and I could feel the strength coming back to my arm. I had tried to build on the small successes from the previous day. I'd followed the throw count; I'd done my rehabilitation routine consistently; I'd done my stretching—I'd done everything I was supposed to do. I trusted that as long as I did things the right way, good things would happen, and eventually I would be where I needed to be. But it wasn't until that one throw that my confidence returned. It wasn't until that moment, when the ball left my hands, that I felt deep down, *This is it. This is what I've been waiting for.* True, it was the only pass out of thirty in that game that felt right. But this proved it was possible. *Now I just need a bunch of those to come in a row.*

Sean must have thought I was crazy when I approached him after the game, completely excited. I had played poorly, and so had the whole team. The third preseason game is supposed to be a dress rehearsal for the regular season, because generally the starters see the most action in this game prior to the season opener and might not even play in the fourth preseason game.

I walked into Sean's office after the game with a grin on my face. Scott Fujita has been known to give me a hard time for being "annoyingly optimistic," and that day was a case in point. There was no reason anyone should have been encouraged by the game we had just played. But I was.

Sean looked at me with a concerned but hopeful expression as I closed his office door and sat down. "Coach, I know things didn't go the way we wanted them to today." I couldn't quench my optimism, but I did understand his frustration. Ever since training camp he had been working hard to pull us together as a team. Despite all his efforts, our offense just wasn't in sync. We were trying hard and there were occasional bright spots, but for the most part we kept coming up empty.

We needed something good to happen—and soon. When you've been beaten down for so long, it doesn't matter how hard you work; it can feel like the next thing around the bend is going to be another blow. Whether it's in football or in a job or in a relationship or with finances, it often seems like bad things compound on each other. Pretty soon you start to wonder if you can ever get out from under them. On the verge of the new season beginning, we were finding it difficult to believe—not just in ourselves, but in the process.

My philosophy has always been that it takes only one good thing to break the seal on what lies ahead. Just one positive turn of events can build your confidence and help you get the momentum going in the other direction. Once that happens, one good thing leads to another and then another. Pretty soon you find yourself riding a wave of good things.

Our team wasn't anywhere close to playing like we could play, and we all knew it. As Sean and I sat in his office, he looked dejected, which was unusual for him. He has the same positive-attitude DNA as I do. I felt bad about my performance. I felt bad about how we'd played as a team. But the one good moment—my autopilot throw—overshadowed those negative feelings. For all I knew, that well-thrown ball could be our turning point.

"Coach, we're going to be all right," I said. "I'm coming back. I felt it tonight. This game was a milestone for me. I know it."

He looked at me with a mixture of incomprehension and concern.

"Seriously," I continued. "I'm going to be all right. *We're* going to be all right. I know that sounds crazy right now, coming off a game like this, but I think we're on the verge of something good."

And it was true—things did start to improve. The next practice, I threw two passes that felt as true as they have ever felt. The day after that I threw three more, and the next day, four. It seemed like each time out on the field resulted in yet another pass that would come flying out of my hands like a gunslinger. Little by little, the confidence was building and the throws were becoming automatic. Let the season begin.

Believe

You hear a lot of players talk about "believing," and there are several different layers to that. There's the surface-level type of believing, where you acknowledge that something is true. Then there's a deeper kind of belief—the type that gets inside you and actually changes you. It's the kind of belief that changes your behavior, your attitude, and your outlook on life, and the people around you can't help but notice.

The way I see it, belief isn't enough on its own. Once you know the truth, you have to act on it. That's where real faith gets legs. Other people can tell you the truth, but until you own it, it's not worth much. It's only when you move on your belief and exercise faith that real change can come. It's only then that you'll yield concrete results.

In football, it's not enough to believe you have a great football team. I knew we had some great talent in 2006, and that was a start. But until we stepped on the field and put that belief into action, it was hollow. We had to go to work and act on that belief.

Put another way, belief is represented by the football. It's an objective thing that exists outside of me. If I hold on to it and do nothing else with it, I can't lead the team. However, if I have the guts to make the throw to my teammate, I am exercising faith—in myself, in my receiver, and in the coaching staff who put the play together. Faith in action is perfectly carried out on the field.

I had to trust the process when it came to my recovery, too. It wouldn't have been enough to simply believe what my doctors were telling me about my arm, to intellectually assent to it being true. I could have agreed with Dr. Andrews that it was up to me to work hard and then retreated to the La-Z-Boy. But I needed something more than a "belief" about my comeback. I had to translate that belief into action and actually do the things they told me to do.

Over the years I've come to realize that living out your faith in God isn't all that different from living out what you believe when you're playing a sport. You can't just talk about it—

you've got to prove it with your actions. Following God is a day-by-day process, something you have to keep focusing on and practicing. It's not some detached or compartmentalized thing that only affects your Sunday mornings. Whether I'm on top of the world with a win or stinging from a bad loss or an injury, I know that God is there and that he has a plan. To me, God is more than just "the Man Upstairs" who looks down on us all. He's concerned about us as individuals. He cares about the people of New Orleans. He wants to be near those living in FEMA trailers. He has compassion for the people who lost their homes and were scattered across the country. He allowed some of these things to happen in our lives so he could shape us and mold us and give us the opportunity to come back stronger. Without the adversity, there would be no opportunity.

Faith is a gift from God, but it's also a responsibility. It's not enough to have it. You've got to live it out, even when times are tough. One of my favorite quotes is "Your actions speak so loudly I can't hear what you're saying." In other words, don't just say it; be it.

F-A-I-T-H

When I came to New Orleans in 2006, I saw a lot of T-shirts that had the word *Faith* on the front. It was a buzzword for the people of the region, signifying that they believed in the city, that it was possible to rebuild. A lot of people took that word and applied it to our team that year too. In many ways people saw the Saints as an extension of the city and everything the community was going through. We were working together in faith, believing that things were going to come back even better than they were before. We kept on believing, even when the results were a long time coming.

As a way to motivate my teammates and give us focus for

the season ahead, I often came up with a slogan or phrase to share with the team. That year, my first season with the Saints, I wanted to simplify things and get our minds and hearts in the right place as we started the regular season. I had been thinking a lot about the concept of faith for the past several months, and I decided to break down the word into an acrostic. Each letter of the word held personal meaning for me:

Fortitude
Attitude
Integrity
Trust
Humility

For the first game of the season, we were traveling to the Dawg Pound in Cleveland to play the Browns. The Wednesday before the game we had our first team meeting. I asked Coach Payton if I could have fifteen minutes at the beginning of that meeting to say a few things to the team.

I'd printed out a bunch of sheets with the word *FAITH* written on them, and I handed them to the guys. Then I put the same thing on the overhead projector and explained my hopes for the year ahead.

"The dictionary defines *faith* a lot of different ways," I said. "Some of it has to do with religion. Other aspects of the definition talk about allegiance and duty or loyalty. I want you to know what the word means to me, and I also want you to write down what it means to you."

All the guys came up with their own working definitions of *faith* and wrote them down. I encouraged them to put their papers in the front of their playbooks. "When you're having one of those rough days, take a look at it and remember why you're here and what we're working toward.

"Now I want to tell you what faith means to me," I said. "Fortitude. Attitude. Integrity. Trust. Humility." I put the dictionary definitions of all those words on the screen.

"This is what the dictionary says about these words. But you know what? The way a book defines something can be different from how you view it and apply it in your life.

"When I think about fortitude, what comes to mind isn't the dictionary definition. I think of it as toughness and courage. Fighting for something you know is there but you might not be able to see yet.

"Attitude. To me, attitude speaks to the way you approach life. You can't always determine your circumstances, but you can always determine your attitude. Attitude is approaching each day with a positive mind-set, a glass-half-full mentality, knowing that as long as we do things the right way together, good things are going to happen. I have confidence that I can do my job, whatever it is, and I have confidence that the guy next to me is going to do his job. And as we grow together, there's no team that can stop what we're becoming.

"Integrity. A person with integrity does what he says he's going to do. So if you tell me you're going to show up at 6 a.m. to work out, then show up at 6 a.m. to work out. If you say you're going to watch extra film after practice with your teammates, then make sure you're there. We can hold each other accountable to be true to our principles, and that integrity can spread from one person to the next.

"Trust. My last coach, Marty Schottenheimer, used to say, 'Trust is the cornerstone of every meaningful relationship.' You have to be able to trust your teammate. Your teammate has to be able to trust you, and you have to earn that trust and respect every day. And so in everything you do, you have to build that relationship, that trust. You have to give your teammate a reason to believe in you, so make sure you're doing what you're supposed to be doing. And make sure you're doing it the right way.

"And finally, humility. This really sums up the meaning of teamwork. President Harry Truman said, 'It is amazing how much you can accomplish in life if you don't mind who gets the credit.' Guys, if we approach this game and this season with a selfless mentality—doing whatever it takes to help this team, fulfilling the roles we've been given, completing our tasks without worrying about who gets the glory in the end— then we will truly be winners. And we will accomplish great things as a team."

We left that meeting fired up about the season and the team. In the days that followed, one of our team mottoes became "Keep the faith." Faith in each other, faith in the process, faith in our fans, faith in our coaches. And for some of us, faith in the God who had made all of this possible in the first place. The Bible puts it this way: "Faith is being sure of what we hope for and certain of what we do not see" (Hebrews 11:1, NIV).

Just One Game

For lack of better terminology, we'd gotten our tails kicked in preseason. We'd managed to win the first game, but we'd lost the other three. Basically we had been whupped up one side and down the other.

As we headed into the 2006 season, most critics wondered if we'd win even a handful of games. Pundits said our team would probably improve from 2005's 3–13 record but that with a rookie coach like Sean Payton and a quarterback barely off the injured list, things didn't look too promising. The Carolina Panthers were the favorite to win our division, and no one had much hope of us finishing anywhere but the cellar of the

NFC South. Honestly, in the locker room, we were all looking at each other and saying, "Let's just try to win one game, all right? Then we'll worry about the rest. Just one game."

Still, we were on the lookout for something good to happen. Those commentators hadn't really seen us yet. They didn't know what we were capable of doing. We had a passion for the game, we had worked hard, and we genuinely cared about each other. We might not have been expecting a Super Bowl ring, but we were serious about winning, and we wanted to do whatever it took to make our goals become reality. And we knew you can't reach a goal if you don't set one.

One of our goals was to return to our home field with pride. For the first time since Hurricane Katrina hit, we'd be playing at the Superdome again. We committed to do everything in our power to win that first game back there—and every home game, if possible. We were going to stand our ground at the Dome. No one was going to come into our house and push us around.

Our offense set goals about being balanced with the run game and the pass game and taking care of the football. Our defense set goals for being aggressive and taking the ball away. We had team goals and individual goals—concrete ideas about how to move forward and put our beliefs and faith into action. We were motivated to win and give it our best. But inside each of us was a question: how long would it take to win just one game? And inside of me another question burned: how well would my shoulder hold up?

We were about to find answers to those questions in Cleveland.

THE
AINTS

CHAPTER NINE

THERE WAS ANOTHER BLESSING in disguise that came out of being forced to slow down during my recovery. In the midst of getting my arm back into shape, I also had time to learn more about the history and people of New Orleans. I suppose it's possible to play for a team and not have their story impact you, but that's not the kind of person I am. I like to immerse myself in the team's history and culture and put everything happening now into context. When it comes to football, whether it's for better or for worse, there's no team with richer history than the New Orleans Saints.

The Saints were organized in 1967. Since music is a big part of the city's ethos, it made sense to name the team after the well-known jazz song "When the Saints Go Marching In." Ironically, the team was formed on November 1, 1966, which also happens to be All Saints' Day. In the four decades following, the team had a reputation around the league of being hard workers but not being able to put together many wins. They didn't have any Super Bowl appearances, despite the talented players and coaches who had been part of the franchise over the years. But to me, out of all the players in the club's history, the one name that rose above the others was Archie Manning.

Archie played with the Saints for ten full seasons after getting drafted out of Ole Miss in 1971. Sadly, his teams didn't win a lot of games. In fact, during Archie's best season with the Saints, the team only went 8–8. Despite that, he went to the Pro Bowl twice and garnered many awards for his outstanding play.

But Archie Manning is more than a football player. He's an outstanding citizen of New Orleans and an exemplary humanitarian. Archie has made his home here and has supported the team over the years. I was told early on that none of the Saints players since Archie have ever lived in the Garden District or Uptown, where we bought our home. He and his wife, Olivia, welcomed us to town with open arms.

"Hey, anything you need, let us know," Archie said.

He was true to his word. If I needed to know where to take Brittany for a nice night out, Archie gave me guidance. He and Olivia are such classy people, and as soon as we arrived in the city, they extended us an invitation to dinner at their house. They were role models to us in reaching out to the community, as they were integral to New Orleans's rebuilding efforts after Katrina. Their presence alone gives people hope and a sense of pride in their city. They raised three sons who grew up cheering for the Saints and have deep roots in this area.

For most of the history of the franchise, it wasn't easy to be a Saints fan. They never even made it to the playoffs in the first twenty years of their existence. Some may remember difficult years when fans would come to games with paper bags on their heads. The team was affectionately (or not so affectionately) referred to as the Aints.

There were high points, of course. The first regular-season play in Saints history was John Gilliam's ninety-four-yard kick-off return for a touchdown in Tulane Stadium. Then in 1970 Tom Dempsey set an NFL record with his sixty-three-yard field goal, a record that was tied by Jason Elam but still stands today. But in spite of those few shining moments, disappointment and frustration seemed to plague the team year after year. That frustration spilled over to the fans. They desperately wanted to will the Saints to victory, but every season they seemed to be inching closer, another setback hit.

In the late 1980s, under Jim Mora, the Saints put together some good seasons. In 1987 they finally made it to the playoffs but lost their first NFC wild card game to Minnesota. Three years later they made it back to the wild card game and lost to Chicago. It was the first of three consecutive playoff appearances—and wild card game losses—in the 1990s. It looked like they had a chance to win their first ever playoff game in 1992, but the Philadelphia Eagles came back in the fourth quarter and buried the hopes of the fans and players.

This was a city that had hosted the Super Bowl seven times in twenty-one years but had never gotten close to playing in one. No matter how hard they played, no matter how frenzied the fans got, at the end of the year they always went home unhappy.

The frustration built as the years passed. In 1996, after a loss to the Carolina Panthers, head coach Jim Mora summed up the disappointment of not just that game but all the years of coming close and not being able to overcome. "We couldn't make a first down. We couldn't run the ball. We didn't try to run the ball. We couldn't complete a pass. We couldn't stop the run. . . . I'm totally embarrassed and totally ashamed. Coaching did a horrible job. The players did a horrible job. . . . It stunk."

The next day Jim Mora resigned. In 1997 NFL Hall of Famer

Mike Ditka was hired to coach the team, but his efforts were also unsuccessful. The team desperately needed something good to happen.

In 2000 the curse was finally broken. The Saints finally won their first playoff game in a thriller against the St. Louis Rams. But the next game and the next few years proved to be disappointing. In 2004 there was talk that the team might move away from New Orleans. San Antonio, Los Angeles, and Albuquerque were mentioned. Some thought that moving from the Crescent City would give the team a fresh start. Leave the past behind.

Those sentiments intensified later in 2005, but this time it was because of a meteorological phenomenon, not a football catastrophe. At the beginning of that season, a Category 5 hurricane hit, convincing most people that relocation was the only answer. No one knew for sure at that point, but the way things were going, it looked like the Saints would be marching out.

From Superdome to Ground Zero

As I was getting ready for the 2005 season in San Diego, news reports trickled in about a big storm heading toward the Gulf Coast. On Friday, August 26, the Saints played a preseason game against the Baltimore Ravens at the Superdome, and they were now looking ahead to their season opener at Carolina. Just two days later, Katrina hit land. The fallout from that storm resulted in the loss of hundreds of lives and billions of dollars worth of damage. It was the costliest natural disaster in the history of the United States, and people are still trying to recover. It's impossible to overstate the tragedy, not just by financial standards, but also in terms of personal loss. The trauma experienced by individuals, families, churches, and communities is incalculable.

When the storm hit, the team and everyone associated with it felt the devastation. Everyone was displaced—players, coaches, people in the front office, hot dog vendors, those who sold T-shirts. The Superdome was ground zero for those who were unable to evacuate from the city. The horrific reports of dead bodies and criminal activity there in the days following the disaster turned out to be largely unfounded. But the human misery experienced at the Superdome and the Ernest N. Morial Convention Center was palpable. People were hungry and thirsty, and the living conditions quickly became unbearable. These people had just lived through the loss of their homes and belongings, and now they found themselves in another appalling situation.

Not that a tragedy like this was totally unexpected. This type of storm was something residents had feared for years. As history had proven, hurricanes that push through this area of the country tend to pick up steam because of the warm water in the Gulf of Mexico. Since much of New Orleans and many of the outlying areas are below sea level, a series of levees, canals, and dams had been constructed so storms wouldn't overwhelm the area.

There is a misconception that when the storm hit, it simply overcame the levees, causing everything to flood. But you have to understand the intricacies of the waterways in the New Orleans area. The Mississippi River winds around the city in the shape of a crescent. New Orleans is bordered by Lake Pontchartrain to the north and the Mississippi River to the south, and that water eventually flows out into the Gulf. But there are also canals that run from Pontchartrain down into the city. Within those canals a system of pumps helps alleviate high water. When it rains hard in New Orleans—and it can rain really hard here in the spring and the fall—city streets flood, and there is standing water on the roads. The pumping stations take that excess water and dump it back into the canals and Lake Pontchartrain.

When people were ordered to evacuate before Katrina hit, the pumping stations were also evacuated. There were inevitably going to be floodwaters because of the magnitude of the storm. However, if the pumping stations had remained functional, the flooding might have ended much more quickly. Of course, that didn't happen, and what the people of New Orleans experienced was a massive loss of lives and property.

Another misconception is that Lake Pontchartrain and the Mississippi River overflowed. The truth is, the water got pushed down the canals, and the pressure of all that canal water is what caused the levees to break. When that happened, the flooding was almost instantaneous. There were some places where a wall of water came into a community and homes were literally lifted off their foundations and washed away. The people who had stayed behind were overwhelmed in a heartbeat. I can't imagine what it must have been like to see a towering wave heading straight toward you.

In the Ninth Ward, there were even more complications. The Industrial Canal runs into the Ninth Ward, and some bigger cargo ships were there when the hurricane hit. A barge came loose from its mooring and rammed into a levee wall. The wall was breached, causing unprecedented flooding in the Ninth Ward and Lower Ninth Ward.

The entire city had been dealt a crushing blow. Hundreds of thousands of people in and around New Orleans were displaced. The roof of the Superdome was damaged, making it impossible to play there, and the Saints were forced to relocate to San Antonio, Texas. From there, the team traveled around like a vagabond group, playing home games at various stadiums. The guys who returned in 2006 told me it was the worst experience of their lives. They were forced to adapt to an unfamiliar place quickly while the worry about their homes and city was still fresh in their hearts. Living away from home and practicing at subpar facilities all year made many of the guys feel like they had been forgotten.

The first game for the Saints in 2005, played at Carolina, was a heroic effort. Deuce McAllister scored two touchdowns, and John Carney hit a forty-seven-yard field goal with seven seconds left to secure the win. The next game was to be their home opener against the New York Giants. The team hoped to play in San Antonio or Baton Rouge, which would at least be close to their still-reeling New Orleans. Either city seemed an appropriate place for a charity game to support victims of the storm. But the NFL made the decision to hold that Monday night game at the Meadowlands in New Jersey, aka Giants Stadium. It was a Saints "home" game in their opponent's stadium. That location decision upset a lot of the Saints players, and the team lost 27–10.

Perhaps the low moment of that early season came in Green Bay, when Deuce McAllister took a pass in the third quarter and his foot got caught in the turf at Lambeau Field. He tore his ACL and was out for the remainder of the year. The Saints lost that game in humiliating fashion, 52–3.

Football players like the structure of an NFL schedule and feed on that. But there was anything but structure to their lives that season. They woke up in hotel rooms each morning, practiced at high school fields, and tried to get into a regimen in unfamiliar weight rooms. Some players were reeling over damage to their homes, and others had friends and family members who had been completely displaced. With so much upheaval, it was difficult to focus, and the team went 3–13 that year. Coach Jim Haslett was fired at the end of the season.

On all levels 2006 was a year of rebuilding for the city. Renovation began on the Superdome that eventually cost millions. The people in the community returned and began reconstructing their lives as best they could. And it was into that rebuilding mind-set that Sean Payton was hired. In the midst of all the upheaval, the 2006 Saints held a special place in people's hearts. You could take them away from their homes, uproot them from their neighborhoods, and dunk their city under twelve feet of water, but you couldn't take away the love they had for their team. It was a bond that couldn't be broken. Those fans gave us the love and motivation we needed for what we hoped to accomplish that year.

The Season Begins

On September 10, 2006, we played our opening game at the Cleveland Browns Stadium. Like the Saints, the Browns have a storied tradition in the NFL. With names like Paul Brown, Jim Brown, Bernie Kosar, and others, Cleveland has given their fans something to cheer about over the years. Unfortunately they, too, had fallen on hard times and in recent years had a streak of teams that put out extreme effort but earned few wins.

That season Cleveland and New Orleans were viewed as two of the teams at the bottom of the league. The year before, the Browns had won six to our three. After such a rough preseason, our goal was to just figure out how to win one game. We focused on Cleveland and scratched and clawed the entire contest, with John Carney kicking four field goals. Our rookie running back, Reggie Bush, had 141 all-purpose yards and helped us control the ball. Our defense helped us out with a solid game, and we ended up eking out a 19–14 win.

It wasn't pretty; we basically had to grind out the win. But it was a victory all the same, and beating them on their home field gave us a measure of confidence. The locker room afterward was a happy place—we had achieved our goal of winning that first game. But we knew we had our work cut out for us the next week.

Next Sunday we were on the road again to face the Packers. Lambeau Field is always a difficult place to play—we knew their fans would be out in force. The memory of the Packers embarrassing our team the year before with a 52–3 win gave us that extra edge to motivate us. I don't live in the past, but we certainly wanted to use what had happened the previous October to spur us on. We wanted to send the message that this was 2006, and we were a different team.

Beating Cleveland was definitely a start, a stepping stone. Take care of the first game and then you can move on to the second. It would take a lot more to face Green Bay at their place against Brett Favre. If we could somehow pull off a victory against the Packers, it would carry a lot more weight.

We knew we were underdogs, and in the first quarter we played like it. On our first three possessions, I had three turnovers, giving up two fumbles and throwing an interception. Both fumbles occurred on sacks in the pocket when a defensive end hit my arm as I was throwing. Hits like these can cause shoulder injuries even to healthy arms, but thankfully I came away from both plays feeling durable. Unfortunately, that didn't change the fact that Green Bay walked away with the ball in their hands—twice. The Packers scored thirteen unanswered points, and from all objective viewpoints, it looked like they were on their way to a blowout, just like the previous year. That was not the way I had envisioned my first-quarter performance, and human nature was telling me it was time to get really frustrated and start berating myself. *You blew it! Are you sure you belong here?*

But I hadn't come that far to quit. And we hadn't come that far as a team to quit either. We could have lamented our misfortune, packed up, and headed home. But something was brewing. Something was going on that the fans at Lambeau and the people watching on television couldn't see. They had no idea how hard we had worked to get where we were. They had no idea of the desire burning in the belly of each player on our team. And they had no idea how much the people of New Orleans meant to us. We were playing for them. So instead of listening to that voice of defeat, I kept visualizing doing things the right way and focusing on what I'd been coached to do.

The tide turned in the second quarter. We scored two touchdowns, one on a Deuce McAllister run and another on a twenty-six-yard pass to Devery Henderson. That brought us into the lead at the half, 14–13. In the third quarter we added two John Carney field goals, but the Packers came back with a touchdown on the second play of the fourth quarter and tied it 20–20.

An underdog team is not supposed to win in Green Bay. But we weren't concerned about that particular Packer tradition. Six and a half minutes into the fourth quarter, we scored a touchdown. Less than thirty seconds later, we scored another. By the time Brett Favre got his offense rolling, the game was over. We won 34–27.

That win was a watershed moment for us. We had faced adversity, and we hadn't let it get us down. After the game we talked about what was different for the Saints now. That was a game the Saints probably would have lost in previous years—not necessarily because the team wasn't as talented but because they didn't have the positive mentality and belief we exhibited. We really believed we could overcome any situation we found ourselves in. We knew how hard we had worked to get to this point, and we felt confident that the team across the field couldn't have put in that much sweat and effort. No matter what kind of hole we'd dug for ourselves, we still believed we could go out there and win.

There have been times in my life when I've worked hard,

when I'm doing things the right way, and I'm just not getting the opportunities. The people of New Orleans experienced that during the rebuilding after Katrina. People who have been hit hard by the economy feel that way. You don't know why, but things are really tough. In that moment, there's a temptation to give up. When you've been beaten down and beaten down some more, human nature tells you that it's not worth it to try to get up again. You might as well stay down, because if you struggle to your feet, you're just going to get whacked. And when the next bad thing comes along, you shrug and say, "See, there it is. That figures."

You have to fight that mentality with everything in you. You have to look around and believe that the negative stuff is there to strengthen you and can eventually lead to a big break. But you have to be on the lookout for it, and you have to keep believing that God can work in the midst of even the most trying circumstances. Adversity equals opportunity. The only way to believe that is to lift yourself up from the ground. Getting up is always the first step.

After our hard-fought win against Cleveland and then surprising everyone by beating Green Bay in their house, we were gaining momentum at a rapid pace. We had played some inspired football and put two wins together, and with that we believed we could do anything. We could beat anybody who came along.

Those two wins set up a huge game for my career—and all our careers, for that matter. It was time to come home.

Homecoming

For the first time since December 26, 2004, the New Orleans Saints were playing a regular-season home game in the Louisiana Superdome. The city was ready. The support of the fans still sends chills down my spine. Many thought that this moment might never happen again, with talk after the storm of the Saints moving to another city and the Superdome being torn down because of all the damage. But on September 25, 2006, there we were. We were up against our division rival the Atlanta Falcons, returning home to the Superdome after a twenty-one-month hiatus. It doesn't get much better than that.

In 2005 the season ticket sales for the Saints were somewhere around 32,000 out of the 70,000 seats in the Superdome. In 2006 it would have been understandable if barely any of the seats were filled. After all, people were living out of FEMA trailers, doing battle with insurance companies, short on funds, and trying to find work after so many businesses had been wiped out. On top of that, the Superdome was still in bad shape, and prognosticators warned of a lackluster season at best for us. But when we walked into the stadium for that first home game, we were shocked to see that the people of New Orleans had come out in full force. The seats were filled—in fact, the 2006 season tickets sold out months in advance.

With so many people barely making ends meet financially as they worked to rebuild their homes and their lives, it was incredible how many had found a way to buy season tickets. We knew there could be only one reason. They looked to our team as a symbol of hope, as something to lift their spirits during those trying times. Our team represented the struggles everyone from New Orleans was going through, and if we could win, then maybe they, too, could overcome the suffering Katrina had caused. An even stronger bond was beginning to form between the fans and the team, and it would carry us all to a place we had only dreamed we could be.

There was palpable electricity in the air that night. Not only was it a battle for the NFC South, but there was also the historic rivalry between the two teams. Ask anybody walking down the street in New Orleans about the Atlanta Falcons, and chances are you'll hear some saucy language. Even if we'd both been 0–2, it would have been a contest. But as it was, we were both unbeaten going in.

What made that night so memorable, though, was not the rivalry. It was what the game symbolized. Over the past year the city had put up with rumors, snide remarks, put-downs, and conjecture that New Orleans was dead. With a city that's below sea level and a levee system in need of being completely revamped, there was the very real threat of hurricanes coming through the Gulf each year and wreaking damage. Some said, "Just let it go. There are too many bad memories. The cause is hopeless." The people of New Orleans didn't buy that, and neither did the team. This was our home. With this game we were going to show everyone the passion and emotion that New Orleans possessed. The team was rising, the people were rising, and the city was rising. On Monday night, we would show the world that New Orleans was not only coming back, we were coming back stronger.

This would be my first chance to play in front of the home crowd in the Superdome. I finally had the opportunity to be in front of our fans—my fans. These were the people who had welcomed me with open arms after the injury, rehab, and free agency signing. I felt like I had something to prove to them. I wanted to show them I'd been a worthwhile investment and I could lead them.

That game symbolized recovery for me, for the Saints, and for the region. We were coming back. No matter what anybody said—the skeptics who thought I'd never throw again, the critics who didn't believe New Orleans could recover, those who said it wasn't smart to invest money in something that would just flood again—none of that would matter after we showcased our team on Monday night.

There was a pregame concert by the Goo Goo Dolls outside the Dome, and U2 and Green Day played on the field before the game. It was fitting that they came together that night to sing their own version of "The Saints Are Coming"—almost a foreshadowing of the outcome of that game . . . and of what the next four years would hold. It all had to start somewhere, so why not now? There was such an energy that night, an atmosphere of joy. The fans were ready to cheer us on to the first-place spot in the division.

However, we didn't get to enjoy the festivities leading up to the game. We were focused with great intensity on giving it everything we had, just as Sean Payton had prepared us to do. He did something the Saturday before the game I will never forget.

WINNING ONE
FOR THE PEOPLE

ON PAPER, THE WEEK leading up to our first home game was just like any other game week. We spent the same amount of time preparing as we had for Green Bay. As usual, we showed up for practice, weight training, and team meetings. We watched film like we always did to prepare for the Falcons. But there was something different going on under the surface that week, and we felt it the moment we walked into the Dome.

On the Saturday before the Atlanta matchup, Coach Payton switched our practice venue from the Saints' facility near the airport to the Superdome. This was our last practice to go over our game plan and fine-tune our attack for Monday night. He also changed the time of the practice to the evening so we could simulate the game experience. When we walked in under the lights, a kind of reverent hush fell over us all. Even under ordinary circumstances, the Superdome at night is a pretty impressive sight. There are seventy thousand empty seats, and the stadium is eerily quiet. And that night it held more drama than usual. Those walls held the echoes of what this city had come through already and where it hoped to end up.

I had never set foot in the Superdome, let alone played a game there. For returning team members, it was their first time in the Dome post-Katrina. Sean's purpose for busing the whole team to the stadium was partly to let us try out the new turf that had been installed. But more important, he wanted us to experience the feel of the Dome before the game. He knew it would be better for any initial shock or awe to come now instead of on Monday night. It was going to be a big moment. Besides, he had something else up his sleeve for that practice under the lights.

Sean was right—we needed that trial run. It was emotional for all of us to walk onto the field and see how much work had been done to repair the Superdome. New seats had been installed for broken ones, all the video screens had been replaced, and new turf had been put in. They had used the latest type of artificial grass, which is thicker and more like real grass than what's used at most stadiums. Locker rooms, vending areas, bathrooms—everything sparkled and shined. It looked and felt like a brand-new stadium.

Standing on that field going through our drills, we couldn't help but think about what had happened here a year earlier. People had died at the Superdome, and in some ways the spot was like a refugee camp for a long time. I had seen pictures of water dripping from the ceiling and people huddled together under blankets. They were sleeping on cots scattered across the field where we now stood. Outside the Dome, thousands of people had searched for loved ones or scoured through the trash and debris for something to drink or eat. The fact that this was happening in the United States shocked everyone. With that history fresh in our minds, we felt an added sense of responsibility. Not only did we need to win Monday night, we needed to play the entire season for the people of New Orleans, who had lived through so much. The way I saw it, there was really no other choice. We had to win. And we had to keep winning because we knew what that would mean to our fans. In some small way, it was our contribution of hope.

Sean had prepared us well for what this game meant. He told us we were going to work hard that week, and just like in training camp, he was true to his word. But he emphasized that discipline was only half of the equation. There was more to this game than X's and O's. This game was about heart and desire.

We did our walk-throughs and drills and had a solid practice. We were about to head to the locker room when Sean called us up to the fifty yard line and told us to take a knee. He started off with some logistical things, like what time to arrive on Monday afternoon. He said there would be a lot of traffic and people coming for the pregame concert and that we should get there early. "Now I have something I want to show you guys," Sean said.

Suddenly the lights went out in the Superdome. It was pitch-black. Nobody made a sound. Then music began, rumbling and reverberating off the empty seats. The JumboTron fired to life. Images flickered across the massive screen. Video and still pictures from the aftermath of Katrina flashed before us.

Helicopters hovered over people struggling in the flood-waters. A man and a dog sat stranded on the roof of a house, staring calmly ahead as if it were the most natural thing in the world to be sitting on top of a house with water up to the eaves. A tall man with water to his waist carried a tiny baby in his arms. Children walked through brown water, carrying all their remaining belongings in little pink backpacks.

Telephone poles tipped over like toothpicks in sand. Waves

crashed into street signs. Cars sat upended in the streets, and some were strewn inside homes. A barge rested unceremoniously in the middle of a neighborhood in the Ninth Ward. Rubble covered every inch of the ground.

The video brought all of it back for my teammates and me. As difficult as it was to see the devastation to people's property, the most unsettling part was watching the human suffering. People stepped through the debris around dead bodies. Someone in a wheelchair had died. Another person lay facedown on the concrete with a sheet over him. Young and old waded through brackish water with their few belongings over their heads, trying to keep them dry.

The human toll represented on that screen made us want to turn our heads away. But the music and images drew us in. These were the people we were playing for now. These were the survivors, and they needed hope. They needed something good to happen.

The sheer numbers of the tragedy were devastating. But what made it most real for me was seeing those faces close-up. People hanging on to life by a thread as they were pulled out of flooded homes. A man carrying a sleeping daughter. Women hugging each other and crying. A man and his young son as they stood on an empty concrete slab, looking at what they'd lost. Children who couldn't find their parents and held up signs with the names of their siblings. A boy in a life jacket as he clung to the top of a submerged car. You could almost taste the hurt and frustration and loss and anger.

In the flickering light of the screen, I looked at the guys on our team. There wasn't a dry eye among us as we watched this explosion of pain and suffering. When we saw the images of the Superdome with cots spread across the field, we realized we were sitting in the same spot. It made football seem less important in a way, compared to all that these people had experienced. But at the same time, it made Monday's game even more significant.

The movie ended. We sat there for a few moments as the lights came back on. We were all wiping away tears, feeling as if we'd just relived the past year in half an hour.

Sean turned to us. He had seen the video before, but he was just as moved as we were. Choking back the emotion, he said, "You want to make this night special? Then you go out and win this game for these people. They deserve it. But you need to win this game."

Up to this point, we knew how much it meant to the organization to be back on our home turf. We knew how much it meant to the players to be playing home games in the Dome again instead of staying in hotels and flying all over the country. But that night was a reminder that this was about a lot more than football. We got a glimpse into the depth of the pain our city had experienced. And in that moment I thought, *If playing this game with all the fire and passion in our hearts can give something to this city—and to the folks who are still stranded in Houston and other parts of the country—we are going to lay it all on the line. We will win this game.* These people had seen enough nightmares from Katrina. They deserved our best.

The final piece of our game plan was in place now. We steeled our resolve not just to play the game better, but to live our lives better. We could not turn back the hands of time and take away any hurt our fans had experienced—that was impossible. But we knew how much our fans identified with the team. With that connection, we hoped they could latch on to some of our hope. We could lead them back to higher ground, where they could get a glimpse of a better future.

One picture that was taken inside the Superdome during those dark days of wind, rain, and oppressive heat is emblazoned in my mind as a symbol of hope. It was taken after part of the ceiling had torn off. The sun had peeked through the clouds above and sent a shaft of light onto the field. That huge square of sunlight hit at about the fifteen yard line. The photographer's frame captured a young boy, maybe ten or twelve years old, sprinting along the field between the scattered cots and people. As much as sorrow and loss were represented in that stadium, there was also an innocence to the picture. That kid was doing what kids do on a football field—he was having fun. He was pretending he was Joe Horn or Deuce McAllister. Nothing about his situation had improved. He had still lost everything. But his heart made him want to run and play, to not give up believing.

That's what we wanted to be to everyone who watched us. We wanted to run fast and play hard, as if we had nothing to lose. We couldn't erase anything that had happened, but we could help people focus on what was ahead rather than on what was behind us. We wanted to be like that little boy.

Wrong Turn

The buildup to the Atlanta game was unlike anything I'd experienced before, and the story lines were rich. Two undefeated teams. Two rivals from the same division. The devastation of a year earlier and now the restored Superdome. The last time people had gathered inside, they were looking for shelter from a storm. Now we would gather to celebrate the rebirth of a city and the hope of restoration. There was a lot riding on that Monday night game, and we felt it.

I was ready to play in front of our fans for the first time and show them I was the quarterback who was going to lead the Saints into a new era. It was a big moment for the city and a big moment for me. The road to that game was difficult—and I'm not just speaking figuratively.

The game started at 7:30. Coach Payton told us to be at the stadium two hours prior to kickoff, at 5:30. I don't like to cut things close, so I planned to get there by 4:30, three hours before the game. I like to take my time, study the game plan, get my shoulder stretched, make sure my pads are ready, and go through the whole routine the way I'm used to. I am a creature of habit.

The team stayed at a hotel next to the airport the night before every home game. I figured it would take only about twenty minutes to drive to the Dome, but I decided to leave earlier—a little before 4:00. My adrenaline was pumping already, and I was anxious to get to the stadium. Almost immediately I hit some traffic. By now I knew my way around New Orleans fairly well, so instead of staying on the interstate, I got off and jetted over to another street. I figured it had to be shorter than sitting in traffic.

The shortcut was backed up as well, so I turned off on another street. But that one was backed up even more than the ones I'd been on before. After making several more turns, I suddenly realized I had no idea where I was. I looked at my watch. Almost 5:00. I decided I needed to cut my losses and try to work my way back to the interstate.

Almost an hour and a half after leaving the hotel, I was nearing the off-ramp exit of I-10 at Poydras, which goes right down to the stadium. It was 5:25, and I still wasn't at the Dome. I should have been there an hour ago, but there I was, sitting in a sea of Saints fans with banners and gold and black makeup. Little did they know their team's quarterback was in the car beside them, trying to get to work. I was stuck, and there was no way out of it. I was sweating, all the time thinking, *How could this happen? Especially for something so important!* I'd had nightmares about showing up late to a game before, but this time it was really happening. And it couldn't have been at a more inopportune time.

I finally got down the ramp and headed toward the stadium. It was 5:29. I was supposed to be in the locker room in one minute. I was driving a 1997 Land Rover Defender—one of those boxy-looking off-roaders with a safari roof rack on top. I pulled up to the gate and gave the attendant my parking pass.

"I don't think you're going to make it in there," she said, looking at my carrier.

"No, I'm fine." I looked at the concrete overhang and saw I had a couple of inches to spare. No problem. What was really getting me flustered at that moment wasn't my car or the parking garage. It was the fact that this was such an important moment, and I was going to show up in the locker room late.

The attendant could tell I wasn't going to be deterred, so she gave me a look and waved me on. "Okay, you can try."

"Don't worry; it's going to fit."

I drove forward pretty fast and made it under the concrete overhang. But what I failed to notice was a metal pipe that ran along the bottom edge of the overhang. Sparks flew everywhere, and there was the most terrible sound of crunching metal I've ever heard. The car stopped, and immediately I looked at my watch because I couldn't bear to look at my roof. *How is this happening?*

I backed out, scraping the top of the car on the pipe again. I exited the garage, trying not to look at the woman who had given me fair warning. I pulled up on the curb next to the garage and called our director of security, Geoff Santini.

"Santini, I need help. I'm late, and my car won't fit in the parking garage. Is there anything you can do?"

"All right, there's a security guy out there. I'll call him, and he'll come get you."

Fans walked by the car, eyeing the mangled roof rack and then looking in the window. "Hey, it's Drew Brees! Aren't you supposed to be inside getting ready for the game?"

I waved and smiled, scanning for the security guard. The second he came out, I grabbed my stuff, jumped out of the car, and tossed my keys in the air to him.

"I have to get to the locker room."

He made the catch. "Don't worry. I'll take care of it." It was my first completion of the night.

I sprinted to the locker room. Everyone else was there already. I was sweating, and my heart was racing. The last thing I wanted was to have my teammates see me stroll in late and think, *This guy's not taking it seriously. He doesn't understand the gravity of this game.*

"Where have you been?" Sean Payton asked.

I was out of breath. "Coach, long story. I'll have to explain later. I need to get ready."

Before every game I have a fairly strict routine I follow to help me get ready, mentally and physically. I always stretch and go over the game plan. Then I head onto the field to throw routes to the receivers with time to spare before the pregame festivities. That day I couldn't do any of the things I normally did. About all I had time to do was change into my gear. I was flustered and frustrated with myself, and I was getting worked up into a bad frame of mind.

Mickey Loomis, our general manager, came up to me on the field and put his hand on my shoulder. "I heard you had a little trouble getting to the stadium today."

"Yeah, I kind of got stuck in traffic and tried to take a shortcut and got lost."

He smiled at me. "Just relax, Drew. Everything's fine. You're here, and you're ready to play."

A calm came over me. Mickey's words put me at ease, and I was able to get my head together again. I went back to the locker room to get ready to play. It was a good lesson for me about focusing on the challenge ahead instead of being paralyzed by my mistakes or worrying about what others were thinking about me. I had to relax and put my energy into the important game ahead. I owed that to myself, my teammates, and this city.

Sellout

That night we had a sellout crowd. More than seventy thousand people were there, and it was ESPN's most-watched broadcast to date.

The Falcons were favored to win. They had won the NFC South in 2004 and had been only one game away from making the Super Bowl after losing to Philadelphia in the NFC Championship Game. They had plenty of talent too: Jim Mora, a former coach for New Orleans, was now head coach for Atlanta, and they also had offensive weapons like quarterback Michael Vick and running back Warrick Dunn.

That night, surrounded by seventy thousand screaming fans, my teammates and I realized that what Sean Payton had said was true. This was much more than just a game.

You have to understand this about the Saints fans: they are some of the most loyal fans in the world. Don't get me wrong—when I played in San Diego, the fans were great. They were loud and supportive, and there were plenty of Chargers faithful. But a lot of people who live in San Diego are transplants from other parts of the country. What that meant was that many fans would cheer for us most of the season but root for their home team when they came to town. At times in San Diego, it felt like there were more people cheering for the other team than for us.

Not so in New Orleans. On game day, the city shuts down. Everybody who can goes to the game, and those who don't have tickets close up shop to watch on TV. And everybody is wearing either a Saints jersey or some form of black and gold. After the game, everything opens up again, and it's a citywide party. So much of the culture around here is centered on the team, and people take a Saints win as a win for themselves. It was time to go out there and make our city proud.

We kicked off to Atlanta and stopped them on their first drive. On every play the crowd got louder. On the fourth play of the game, Michael Koenen of the Falcons went back to punt, but Steve Gleason looped straight up the middle and blocked it. The ball bounced into the end zone, and Curtis Deloatch landed on it for our first touchdown of the game. The crowd went nuts. It was the loudest one-time roar I have ever heard in a stadium. That moment served as a confirmation: this night belonged to New Orleans.

At the end of the first quarter we ran a double reverse, and Devery Henderson took the ball the final eleven yards into the end zone. John Carney added three field goals to the scoreboard. We played lights out that night on defense and managed the game extremely well on offense. Our defense put a ton of pressure on Michael Vick, sacking him five times. We shut down their running game as well.

We won the game 23–3, bringing our record to 3–0. Even better, we had taken control of the NFC South. The fans were wildly appreciative. We had gone from setting our sights on winning just one game to winning three in a row. Now the question was: could the streak continue?

ONE
AT A TIME

CHAPTER ELEVEN

THERE'S ALWAYS A DANGER after the buildup and emotion of a Monday night game that a team can lose momentum and intensity by the time the next Sunday rolls around. That Monday night was no exception. Sean Payton didn't want that to happen to us, and he warned us of the danger as we got ready to face Carolina, another NFC South opponent. Sean's message to the team as we prepared for Carolina was this: "The media started out saying you wouldn't win three games all year. Now they're going to be telling you how great you are, and they're going to want you to look ahead and speculate about how far we'll go. They'll try to stuff you so full of cheese that you will lose your focus. Let's not forget what it has taken to get to this point. Remember that we need to continue to improve each day. Don't eat the cheese."

Disappointingly, we didn't heed Sean's message. We got behind early in the game but managed to start fighting our way back. We were not able to recover a late onside kick that could have given us a chance to tie or win the game, and the Panthers won 21–18. But we learned a lesson that day: your emotions and intensity have to match your preparation. We just did not have it that day.

We couldn't afford to hang our heads over the loss because Tampa Bay was right around the corner—our second game at the Superdome. There wasn't as much media blitz this time, but the fans gave us just as much support and volume as they had at the previous game. They were ready for us to return home.

We needed home field advantage that game, especially in the fourth quarter. We were down 21–17. We had just held Tampa Bay on third down, and they were punting to Reggie Bush, our rookie running back. As Reggie got ready to receive the ball, he started motioning to the fans to make more noise. The roar inside the Dome crescendoed until it sounded like a freight train. By the time the ball was snapped, I thought it couldn't get any louder, but as Reggie took the ball on our thirty-five yard line and began his return, the noise level rose even higher. Reggie passed midfield, and you could have sworn a jet was taking off from the stadium. When he passed the goal line after running sixty-five yards and scoring his first NFL touchdown, the entire place went berserk. That touchdown was the final score of the game—we won 24–21.

At 4–1 we were among the top teams in the NFC. But we couldn't relax now—with each game of the season, the stakes kept getting higher. We had to get ready for the next challenge: Philadelphia was coming to town. Philly was widely regarded as a strong Super Bowl favorite that season. The team was a perennial contender, and they had been to the Super Bowl two years earlier. Two of the NFC's best were going head-to-head.

At that point we weren't thinking or talking about the playoffs. Our mind-set was still "one game at a time." We had survived training camp that way. We had won four out of five that way. Each day we tried to concentrate on doing what we were supposed to do, doing it the right way, and not looking too far ahead. The media and the fans were talking about how important it was to clinch the first-round bye as the first or second seed, but for now we were taking things one step at a time.

Prior to being head coach in New Orleans, Sean Payton had coached in the NFC East for nine years, most of that time as an offensive coordinator for the Giants and the Cowboys. On many occasions he had battled wits with Philly's defensive coordinator Jim Johnson, one of the greatest defensive coaches of all time, and Sean had a pretty stellar record against him. We respected Philly, but we felt like we had an edge with Sean, and that gave us confidence.

We jumped out to an early lead against Philly, and at halftime we were up 17–3. The Eagles came back and scored three straight touchdowns, which gave them a 24–17 lead at the start of the fourth quarter. We knew we needed a spark. We hadn't done anything well offensively the entire second half, and we needed to score in a big way.

As important as the communication is from coaches about which plays to run, there's also interaction that takes place between players on the sidelines throughout the course of a game. The offensive line is constantly communicating with me about what they're seeing and how we will handle protections. I also gather my receivers together and say, "Hey, I like this matchup, so let's attack this particular corner or safety. Be alert for me to give you a signal that adjusts the route." The signal might be a nod or a wink—something simple to trigger a change in our offense.

As the fourth quarter began, we saw an opportunity to make a game-changing play. We called a play at the line of scrimmage, and as the defense was hurriedly getting set, we identified the matchup we had been waiting for. I met Joe Horn's eyes and gave him a nod, and he winked back to acknowledge that he had picked up on my signal. What was supposed to be a fifteen-yard stop route now turned into a stutter and go, right past strong safety Michael Lewis.

The ball was like a hot potato in my hands—I couldn't get rid of it fast enough. Joe ran down the field so fast the secondary might as well have been standing still. He caught the ball on the run and waltzed into the end zone to tie the game 24–24.

There was still some time left, about thirteen minutes. Philadelphia got the ball and sustained their drive for a few plays, but our defense stopped them. They were forced to punt.

We had about eight and a half minutes to play and were starting on our own fifteen yard line. We began a methodical march down the field that chewed up the clock. It was one third down after another—third and short, third and long, third and five. And then with three seconds left on the clock, John Carney lined up for a thirty-one-yard field goal. We had just run sixteen plays and chewed up the final eight and a half minutes of the game. The clock ran out as the ball sailed through the uprights, and we won, 27–24.

It was a huge win for us, and it also communicated a lot to the fans. It's one thing to explode and score lots of points and win going away. It's another to hit some snags and keep plugging away and eventually scrabble out a win. Our fans had been beaten down for so long and had gotten their hearts broken by so many tough losses. They'd also been knocked down by Katrina and its aftermath, and many were still struggling to rebuild their homes and restore their communities. On every side it felt like the system was against them. Then our team came along and started winning. Suddenly it felt like the tune in New Orleans was changing a little. In some ways, the struggles the city faced were akin to the hole in the top of the Dome during the storm. It let the water in, but later, when the skies cleared, it also let in the rays of sunshine.

Life can be like that. I've learned over and over that closed doors mean God will open something else. A window, maybe, or a back door. Sometimes you just have to look hard for that opening.

Walking Up the Down Escalator

At some point during each season you know you're going to face a situation where everything seems to be working against you and you have to fight through the adversity with all you've got. You don't play as well as you had wanted to or you get a bad break or have an off day. Those moments are guaranteed to come, so when they happen, you can't let them shock you or take you by surprise. Always expect the unexpected. When it feels like you're walking up the down escalator, you'd better be ready with a good solution.

After the Philadelphia game, we sat at 5–1 going into a bye week, and we were feeling pretty good about ourselves. We then proceeded to lose three out of the next four games. We were definitely in a slump. We hadn't been blown out, but we certainly hadn't played like we knew we could, and now we were sitting at 6–4. Next up was a trip to Atlanta. This was our time to show we had some solutions.

We had beaten the Falcons at home on opening night, but the vibe from Atlanta was *You only beat us because it was the first game back at the Dome, and you were riding the emotions of your fans. There's no way you're going to come into our house and beat us again.* There was a real sense of urgency for our team. We had just lost two in a row, and we knew we had to get back on track quickly.

The Georgia Dome was rocking when the game began. The first play from scrimmage we ran and got stuffed. The second play from scrimmage we ran and got stuffed. We had moved a total of three yards so far, and now we were stuck at our own twenty-four yard line. The place was going wild.

During that week of game planning, we had noticed a big play opportunity for us against their defense. The Falcons were used to seeing our two receivers run up and run double in. The safety would squat on the inside receiver, and the cornerback would assume it was a double in and try to jump underneath the outside receiver. That's the play they anticipated now on third down and seven. However, on the first third down and long of the game, our plan was to change it up.

We still sent the inside receiver on an in route, but this time the outside receiver ran a deep post over the top. With the safety and corner anticipating the double in like they had seen on film, Devery Henderson ran right past both of them, and seventy-six yards later he was standing in the end zone for a touchdown. Better yet, we had made an immediate statement about our readiness to play this game. And we had taken the crowd out of the game right from the start.

Atlanta hung tight with us all through the first half. At the end of the second quarter, we were up 14–6 and driving with just over a minute left. We were on the Falcons' forty-eight yard line when I put up a Hail Mary as the clock was running out. Usually those passes get intercepted or batted down in the end zone, and the half is over. Still, it was worth a shot. I bought time, stepped up into the clean pocket, then launched it. The ball slipped past a ring of Falcons defenders and landed in Terrance Copper's hands for a touchdown. Saints lead, 21–6.

It was an emotional high to walk into that locker room at the half. We were back. We had prepared well for the game, preaching that week about getting back to the fundamentals and understanding the philosophy of what wins and loses football games: striving for ball security on offense, making big plays, having great third-down efficiency, and playing situational football. Besides that, we knew why we were playing. Not just for a win, but for the people of New Orleans. We won 31–13.

The next week we beat the 49ers, and then it was on the road to Texas Stadium to play the Cowboys. All of America was talking about Dallas at the time. Tony Romo had taken over as quarterback. They were on a roll, and the consensus was that they were the strongest team in the NFC. After the tough stretch we'd been through, the early buzz about our team had died down. But both teams were 8–4, and both of us had offenses and defenses in the top five in the league. Also, with Chicago sitting at 10–2 and in position for the number one seed in the NFC, the winner of this game would likely claim the number two seed. This was a huge game.

Coach Payton emphasized to us the importance of a win against Dallas. We needed it to garner a first-round bye and home field advantage for the playoffs. But it was also a big game for Sean personally. He had been with Dallas before going to New Orleans, and this was his chance to go up against his former team, coached by Bill Parcells, one of his mentors. It was obvious that Bill had a big influence on Sean, especially that first year when Sean was establishing his identity as a head coach in the NFL. I continue to hear plenty of Bill Parcells stories and quotes from Sean, and I even possess a copy of the "Bill Parcells Ten Commandments of a Starting Quarterback." Sean wouldn't show it, but you could tell how much this game meant to him.

Texas Stadium held some connections for me, too. It was where I had won the 5A state championship my senior year of high school, back in 1996. That place held some good memories, and I was hoping we'd add another. As a team we tried to look at this game just like any other on the schedule and not get distracted by all the story lines, but it was tough. There was a lot of emotion and history on the line.

We were originally scheduled to play at noon. But we were into the flex schedule part of the season, and our game was important enough to move to Sunday night. John Madden and Al Michaels would call it on a national stage. The game kept getting bigger while we fought to keep it in perspective.

We got off to a slow start in the first quarter. We were stopped on our first drive by a DeMarcus Ware sack, and when Dallas got the ball, Julius Jones broke into a huge run for seventy-seven yards and a touchdown: 7–0. In the second quarter we answered with three consecutive touchdowns, the last of which came at the end of the half to put us up 21–7 going into the locker room at halftime.

What I remember most is how focused we were as a team. We knew how much this game meant to Sean and also knew that once again on a national stage, we could prove to people that we were for real. We were locked in on every play, every call, thinking about executing it to perfection. We'd talked that week about being as aggressive as we had been all season, and we were. To my surprise, there were thousands of Saints fans there—a tough thing to pull off at Texas Stadium. How our fans got tickets, I don't know, but they did a good job making it seem as much like a home game as possible for us.

Near the end of the game, the fans did something I'll remember forever. As we scored more points and it became clear Dallas couldn't come back, the Cowboys fans started leaving the stadium and the Saints fans filtered down to field level. By this time we had already scored forty-two points and were simply trying to run out the clock. I looked up into the stands once to see the blue and white shirts heading for the exits and a sea of black and gold coming down toward the field. Our fans took up the first ten rows around the entire stadium. And then we heard their voices.

"Who dat! Who dat say dey gonna beat dem Saints?" The Saints fans, decked out with beads and New Orleans jerseys, couldn't hold in their excitement. It was like Mardi Gras had taken over in Texas Stadium. Their chants communicated to us, *We love you guys. You're making this season special. You're making this trying time a little easier. You are giving us a home. You are lifting our spirits. And we love you for that!*

The final score was 42–17. To be honest, it felt really good to win after hearing all week how good the Cowboys were. We knew our team. We knew we could do this. And it felt good that our fans had our backs, even when we were on the road.

Inching toward the Playoffs

The win at Dallas put us at 9–4, and we were flying pretty high as we looked back on the pivotal goals we'd accomplished during the season. If we won the next week against the Washington Redskins, chances were good we would have the number two seed locked. What we forgot was that we weren't there yet. We still had three games to play, and it was too early to let up.

We lost sight of that against the Redskins, and we paid for it. We lost 16–10 . . . and in front of our fans too. We had a chance to win at the end, but with the clock winding down, we failed to convert a fourth-down play. Game over. Our record fell to 9–5, and we were all disappointed. I remember walking into the locker room after the game and seeing shirts that read *NFC South Champions* in everyone's lockers. I started fuming at the thought that the shirts had been put in our lockers after half-time with the assumption we would win. Now it was just adding insult to injury. It turned out that Carolina and Atlanta also lost, so we clinched the division title anyway. I was relieved, but I hated feeling like we'd backed our way into a championship. It was a wake-up call for us though, and we needed it. In order to be considered a great team, you have to be able to handle the success just like you do the defeats. Learn from them and get better because of them.

Some great memories from that year came even after the defeats. Each week after the game I would go into Sean's office in the locker room and talk. We would discuss our verdict on the day's game and what we would have done differently. This really helped build the bond, trust factor, and confidence level between us. I respected him very much and wanted to know how he felt, especially in the early stages of developing the team. Plus, coming off my injury, I needed some affirmation from him at times. And maybe that went both ways. I always tried to be positive, and I made sure Sean knew that no matter what the circumstances with our team, we would be okay. We had one of those moments after the Washington loss. We discussed the critical mistakes and missed opportunities in the game, and then he stated that we would find out what type of team we had by the way we handled a defeat like this.

The next week we headed to New York to play the Giants. It was a Christmas Eve game, and we were looking for momentum going into the playoffs. The pressure was on because the Giants were in a dogfight with four other teams for the last playoff spot. We needed that game to give us a first-round bye in the playoffs. In my eyes it was simple: we had to win.

On the Giants' first drive, Eli Manning threw a fifty-five-yard touchdown pass to Plaxico Burress. At that moment we had a choice to make: either we could let that deflate us, or we could use it to motivate us.

As the final score showed, it was the latter. All cylinders were firing on offense, despite a 20 to 40 mph wind that blew throughout the game. We came back after Manning's completion and scored thirty unanswered points. We rushed for more than two hundred yards and controlled the ball well. Our defense didn't let New York cross the fifty yard line the rest of the night. We were at the top of our game, which is exactly how you want to close the season.

The next night the Eagles beat the Cowboys, and that sealed the number two seed for us. In our final game against the Panthers, Sean decided to pull the starters after we scored a quick touchdown on our first drive. Although we lost that game, bringing our record to 10–6, our fans couldn't have been happier.

It's amazing the difference a year makes in the NFL. In 2005 with the Chargers, we could have been 10–6 and not made the playoffs at all. In 2006 a 10–6 record gave us the number two seed and a first-round bye.

Play Number 26

Philadelphia beat the Giants in the wild card game, which brought them to the Superdome for a huge matchup in the divisional round of the playoffs. It was only the second time in the history of the New Orleans Saints franchise that we had been in the divisional round, and it was our first time hosting. We were giving something special to our city—something they'd never experienced before.

The game against the Eagles earlier in the season had been a close one—we'd won an emotional thriller in the final moments of the game by only three points. It's difficult to beat a team twice in the same year, particularly one as talented as Philadelphia, so we knew we would need to bring our best. Philly was rolling, and quarterback Jeff Garcia, who had taken over for Donovan McNabb due to a midseason injury, was playing lights out. Everybody expected an offensive showdown since ours were the two highest scoring offenses in the NFL.

We scored first, but by halftime the Eagles had taken the lead 14–13 and had some momentum. In the third quarter Brian Westbrook broke through our defense for a sixty-two-yard touchdown run. That put Philadelphia up 21–13. You could feel the tension in the Superdome. But just as they had done all season, the fans knew they needed to lift us up. They started cheering louder and louder, and we fed off their enthusiasm.

The linchpin in that game turned out to be our veteran running back, Deuce McAllister. He was really the heart and soul of our team. Joe Horn was one of the emotional leaders—very vocal and a fan favorite—but Deuce was the stalwart figure who kept us glued together.

Deuce had so much invested in our team. He had worked hard through a lot of tough seasons. He had watched Katrina slam into New Orleans. He had suffered an ACL injury and endured a grueling rehab to get back up to speed for 2006. A lot of people questioned whether he could return as the Saints' number one running back. "He probably won't be as strong," they warned.

But not only did Deuce come back 100 percent that year, he arguably was giving one of the best performances of his career in this playoff game. And it's a good thing, because this is when it counted. He was in front of the fans who loved him, in a city that could identify with his heart and drive and pure will.

Deuce had a five-yard touchdown run, dragging a pile of Eagles with him, to pull us to 21–20. To this day, that run is one of the best individual efforts I have ever seen. His will and desire to stay on his feet and get in the end zone were unparalleled. When we got the ball again, it was time to feed the horse one more time. I hit Deuce with a short pass that he took eleven yards to the end zone, showing great athleticism as he juked defenders in the open field. We had a 27–21 lead heading into the fourth quarter, thanks to two big touchdowns from number 26. Our defense held Philadelphia to a field goal on the next drive, and we kept our lead, 27–24, the same score from our earlier meeting that year.

When we took possession of the ball with a little more than eight minutes remaining, we had a golden opportunity to wind down the clock and score some points to put the game away for good, and Deuce was the man for the job. I fed him the ball six times, and we marched down the field methodically while the seconds continued to burn off the clock, getting us closer and closer to the NFC Championship Game. But with three minutes to go, we fumbled the ball on a botched pitchout to Reggie Bush, giving Philly another opportunity. They had the ball near midfield, but on fourth down they decided to punt rather than take a chance and go for it. They had enough time-outs that if they could force us to go three and out on offense and get the ball back quickly, they would have a better opportunity to tie the game.

Since we were inside the two-minute warning, all we needed was a first down and we'd be going to the NFC Championship Game—for the first time in Saints history. Once again Sean dialed it up for Number 26. I handed off to Deuce, and he gained four yards. On second down I handed it off to Deuce again. He got five more yards and forced Philly to use their final time-out. That brought us to third down, and we needed just one yard for a first down. Then we could take a knee to run out the clock and win the game. Deuce had carried us the whole way, and we weren't about to abandon the plan now. Sean called Deuce's number again. He crashed through the line and punched our ticket to the NFC Championship Game as the referee signaled a first down. The Superdome erupted.

When the game was over, our team went over to the stands, circling and high-fiving anyone reaching out to us. This victory belonged to them as much as it did to us.

We were one game from the Super Bowl.

Bless You, Boys

We knew the road to the Super Bowl went through Chicago. The Bears had finished the regular season with a 13–3 record. If Seattle had beaten them in Chicago, they would have played us in the Superdome, but it wasn't meant to be. As we mentally prepared for the next game, watching from the comfort of our couches, the Bears beat the Seahawks 27–24 in overtime. We'd be seeing them in the championship game.

All we heard that week was how dome teams can't win on the road in the playoffs in hostile environments. We didn't buy into that, but we did understand the importance of a fast start in those difficult weather conditions. Unfortunately, we started slowly in Chicago by doing all the things we said going into the game we wouldn't do. We turned it over two times and made a few mental errors in the first half. By late in the second quarter we found ourselves down 16–0. We finally put together a drive during the last two minutes of the half and scored on a thirteen-yard pass to Marques Colston. That brought the score to 16–7, and it gave us a little momentum as we headed into the locker room.

On our first drive of the second half, I threw a pass to Reggie Bush that went for eighty-eight yards and another touchdown. Now we were only trailing by two. When we got the ball back, we really felt like this was going to be it. We finally had the opportunity to take the lead after being behind the whole game. This had been our modus operandi all season. Face the storm, and bounce back.

It was cold in Chicago. The wind was howling at Soldier Field, making the twenty-degree weather feel even more frigid. We drove into Bears territory and set up to kick a forty-seven-yard field goal. We missed. After that I was called for intentional grounding in the end zone, which gave the Bears two more points. In the fourth quarter the snow started coming down, and the harder it fell, the further the game slipped away from us. The Bears scored twenty-one unanswered points in the fourth quarter and ended up winning 39–14. They were on their way to the Super Bowl. We were on our way home.

It was tough to lose—especially after how far we'd come that season, after how much adversity we'd fought. As we headed back to the locker room, we all shared the same resolve: *Next time we play this game, it's going to be at our place.* We had no problem going on the road and beating a team; we'd done it plenty of times. But we also knew what an energy and motivation our fans gave us and the confidence we could play with at home. We knew no one could win a game like that in *our* dome with *our* fans.

If you had told us before the season started, "You're going to the NFC championship," I think we all would have been a little shocked—and just happy to have made it that far. By all counts, it was such an unlikely scenario. A new coach. A 3–13 season. A hurricane. A busted shoulder. And now . . . we were only one game away from the big dance.

As we were walking off the field after the game, a photographer took a shot of a few of us from behind. All you could see was our jerseys and our heads hanging down a little. That photo made it onto the front page of the New Orleans

Times-Picayune the next day. In big letters above the article, the headline read, "Thank You, Boys."

To this day I still get people saying that to me. The guys and I will be walking down the street, and we'll hear it from the vendors at the shops and from the people passing. They usually have that distinctive New Orleans accent. You can tell they've seen a lot and been through a lot, but they'd never trade this city for any other place in the world. It's a regular chorus from folks like these: "Thank you, baby. We love you. Bless you, boys."

When we returned, the city was still celebrating our season and expressing their appreciation. Because of a snow delay at the Chicago airport, we didn't arrive in New Orleans until around 2 a.m. I didn't know then that thousands of fans would be waiting for us when we arrived, clapping and cheering as we drove down the half-mile-long road to get back to the highway. It was an amazing sight. You could sense how much this season had meant to them.

It had been quite a year—the reopening of the Dome on that first Monday night, the nail-biter against Philadelphia, the Who Dat crowd in Dallas, the playoff win against Philly, and then the first NFC Championship Game appearance. I had desperately needed it. Our team had desperately needed it. And so had the fans.

A great stadium can do only so much. It takes great fans to create a home field advantage. They need passion, emotion, and faith . . . and our fans have plenty of that. We would need all three in large measure as our journey continued.

WHO DAT?

CHAPTER TWELVE

THERE'S SOMETHING YOU have to understand if you want to appreciate the unique culture of the Saints, and that's the Who Dat phenomenon.

It's difficult to explain Who Dat to people who aren't from New Orleans. It's so wrapped up in the city and the team and the people of this area. I've actually researched the phrase and found out it has its roots in jazz and was used in minstrel and vaudeville shows in the late 1800s and early 1900s. In comedy routines a character would become frightened and then say, "Who dat?" Literally, of course, it's short for "Who is that?" But there's more to it than just a contraction of words.

The phrase was used in songs, routines, and movies during the 1930s. Different sports teams in the South have used it over the years, and there was even a legal battle over who owned the rights to the phrase. According to Louisiana lore, the "Who dat?" cheer originated at Patterson High School football games and then made its way to LSU. Eventually fans brought it to the

Saints, where it has stuck ever since. Sportscaster Ron Swoboda was the first to popularize the chant when he set it to music and put it on the radio in 1983. The phenomenon really took off in 2006, when Bobby Hebert, a quarterback with the Saints in the 1980s and early 1990s, talked about "Who Dat Nation" on his WWL radio program. He was referring to the Saints faithful all across the country who believed in our team no matter our record and had created a community-wide sense of ownership and pride in us.

The climate of New Orleans is infused just as strongly with Cajun culture as it is with its connection to the Saints. The French Acadians were driven out of Canada and wound up here in the mid-1700s. Their traditions and customs inter-mingled with those of Native Americans in the area and even-tually those of freed slaves as well. There were a lot of different influences mixing together to make up the Cajun culture and dialect. You can always tell people of Cajun descent because of the unique way they speak. It's part slang, part art, and part shortening words. So instead of saying, "Would you please hand me the water?" you would say, "Han' me dat der wata."

I bought my son, Baylen, a book called *Petite Rouge*. It's the Cajun version of Little Red Riding Hood, written as a native from New Orleans would tell it. When I read it out loud to Baylen, it forces me to talk in that style. It's a hilarious bedtime story because it offers a distinct Cajun interpretation of the familiar tale. A duck is sent by her mother to bring some gumbo to her grandmother, but she's warned not to go through the swamp. And it's not a wolf that's after her—it's a gator!

As far as our team goes, it's hard to say exactly how the "Who dat?" chant came to be such a motto and defining mark. All I know is that it fits and it's here to stay. If you're walking down a street in New Orleans and you say "Who dat?" with the right intonation, anyone from Louisiana will give you a nod of approval to let you know you're one of us.

"Who dat say dey gonna beat dem Saints?"

Points of Purpose

In a way, our team is a microcosm of New Orleans as a whole. As is the case for the city, we all hail from a variety of backgrounds, but we have melded together into a unified and distinct culture. And like New Orleans, most of our players have had their share of adversity along the way.

When you look only on the surface, you have no idea what challenges a guy has faced in his life. When you see the talent on our team, you probably wouldn't guess that some of our best players were late-round draft picks or weren't drafted at all. They had to battle every inch of the way to even get a chance at playing. Many of them were, at one point in their careers, the last roster spot or relegated to the practice squad. Others were released and "out on the street," with no team to call home. They were essentially kicked in the gut and told, *You're really not good enough to be in the NFL.* Some Saints players had to fight their way back from a really tough injury, like I did, and defy those who said they would never recover. Forget the draft rankings—these are the guys you want on your side. You know what they've been through—and how much stronger they are because of it. And when you go through tough times together, there's nothing that unites you more.

One of our outstanding running backs is Pierre Thomas. He was an undrafted free agent who came to New Orleans in 2007. At the time we had just drafted a running back in the fourth round, and Pierre was really fighting for the fifth spot. There are only three spots guaranteed on the roster for a running back. With four other guys ahead of him, he had to be thinking, *There's no way I'm going to make this team.* His chances looked pretty bleak. But Pierre had an optimistic attitude that defied his circumstances. He believed that if he did things the right way and kept his chin up and gave it everything he had, good things were bound to happen. Sure enough, we found a spot for him. You make room for guys like that. He gave us no other choice—he had too big of a heart and he fought too hard for us to let him walk away.

Pierre's attitude toward his work was refreshing because he consistently communicated, *I don't care where I play—just put me anywhere. I want to help.* He started off playing on every special teams unit and finally got the opportunity to start at running back the last game of the 2007 season when other players were out due to injury. He had over one hundred yards in both rushing and receiving against Chicago, which was something no Saint had ever done. Nothing has ever been given to Pierre—he's had to earn it all. He wasn't born on third base, as our linebackers coach Joe Vitt would say. He's had to fight tooth and nail just to get into the batter's box. Those are the kinds of people you want on your team. Those are the kinds of people you root for.

Marques Colston was a seventh-round pick out of Hofstra in 2006. When he first came to us, I didn't even know his name until midway through training camp, when he was about the only receiver who was healthy. He was playing every position he was asked to play and catching every ball I threw to him. *Who is this guy?* I thought. *Where did he come from?* I love stories of guys who played at small schools, weren't highly touted, and were drafted low. Marques was almost drafted as Mr. Irrelevant, which is the nickname given to the last pick in the draft every year. They give an award for it and everything. Not really something you strive for, but if you look at it in the right way, that chip on your shoulder can serve as positive motivation.

We had no expectations about a guy who came in as the

252nd pick, but he approached every task assigned to him with such class. It was really because of his emergence that we traded Donté Stallworth to Philly at the end of training camp in 2006. We knew Marques could be a special player, and he proved himself by catching a record number of balls in his first two seasons. And in an era of flamboyant receivers who tend to revel in on-field antics and off-field drama, you'd be lucky to hear Marques say more than a few words. He is humble, but at the same time he remains hungry. If you saw him practice today, you'd be amazed to note that he still works like the rookie who came in fighting for a spot on the team in 2006. There is always something to prove.

One of my best friends from the team is Billy Miller, a tight end from USC who was drafted by the Broncos in 1999. At six foot three and 220 pounds then, Billy started off as a receiver but soon realized that his best chance to make it in the NFL would be to bulk up and play tight end. He played in Denver, Houston, and Cleveland before coming to New Orleans, and with each move he had to fight to claim a place on the team. There were plenty of times throughout his career when he could have easily given up because the pressure was too much or the coach was too hard or the injury he was fighting was too painful. But each time he went through such an ordeal, he looked back at all he'd been through in the past. Experience told him he had what it took to pull through again. Plus, Billy made sure there were a few specific things he had mastered that he could do better than anyone else. Don't get me wrong—he worked to be good at everything, but he made sure that those were his plays and his opportunity to contribute to the team in a big way. Those pass plays of his became our bread and butter, and I have never had more confidence throwing to a guy.

As I look at the players who make it into the NFL and last more than a couple of years, I notice a consistent thread. It's not always the first-round picks and the most naturally gifted players who rise to the top. It's often the journeymen—the ones who persevere through trials and are able to handle the unexpected challenges that come their way.

When I was a kid, I tended to be the best athlete at school or on the team. I was picked first for dodgeball or kickball or whatever we were playing in the schoolyard. Even in high school, things came fairly easily for me . . . until the ACL injury my junior year, that is. But in a strange way, I am actually thankful for that injury, in that it allowed me to learn how to face adversity at a young age. Would I quit, or would I fight through it? From my perspective, it's when the rug gets pulled out from under you that you really find your calling in life. Those defining moments don't have to be tragedies. When they're viewed through the lens of God's plans, they can be "points of purpose" in your life.

I really believe adversity is a path to opportunity. But sometimes it's difficult in the moment to see that God has a bigger vision for the future than you can grasp. It may be years before you can look back and truly appreciate the journey God has taken you on. And usually, it's one you wouldn't have chosen. I wouldn't have chosen an ACL injury or a dislocated throwing shoulder, but those were the cards that were dealt. The only choice I did have was what I would do with that adversity when it came my direction. I also learned that despite the circumstances you find yourself in, it's wise to worry only about the things you can control. You can't control if you get injured or if the team decides to draft someone else to take your job, but you can control your attitude and your preparation. Every day you can dedicate yourself to becoming the best you can be. Thinking about it now, I'm grateful for the way those difficult experiences transformed my personal life—and how the same thing can be true for other people.

Sometimes I wonder what might have happened if I hadn't had that injury at the end of the 2005 season. If I hadn't had to walk that road of recovery, I certainly wouldn't have wound up in New Orleans and experienced the real life that sprang from that comeback. I wouldn't have met the folks who are now my friends and teammates in New Orleans or had so many incredible opportunities that have come my way. And if I hadn't had the injury in high school, I probably wouldn't have attended Purdue and I wouldn't have met Brittany. God used all those things to work together for good in my life, and I'm grateful not just for the victories but also for the tough times that guided me and helped me become who I am.

This principle that any situation, no matter how bad, can ultimately make you stronger isn't only true on the football field. It applies to every facet of life, whether you're battling an illness or dealing with a layoff or facing a financial setback. But just like in a game, it's not enough to simply know it in your head; you have to take action. Knowledge alone doesn't change anyone. You have to get to the point where you not only accept it but own it and put it into practice. That's the only way you'll see a change.

I can't help but think of the people from New Orleans who were displaced by Katrina. It would have been easier for them to move to Atlanta or Houston long-term. But most people refused to do that. They came back, and they were determined to bring their city back. No matter how hard it was, they committed to making New Orleans better than it was before. I believe each one of us has a calling for our lives, and it's up to us to pursue that with everything we have. In the end, there's a reward for having done the right thing, the thing you were called to. When you do, your children and grandchildren and the generations to follow will be blessed by your actions.

Just about every important stage in my life has begun with

a huge negative. Those were truly "why me" moments. *Why do I have to go through this?* Now I know that I am who I am because of those things. They gave me strength I didn't have before. They helped me establish my identity and purpose in life, and they gave me perspective about the struggles that people face every day.

The next time you're up against one of those difficult times, you might not be able to see it as an opportunity to gain power and confidence, but it is—you can bank on it. You have to prepare now to trust and have faith that it's happening for a reason. And when it comes, you can lean into the adversity, put your shoulder down, push through it, and learn from it. Through those experiences, God will mold you into the person he wants you to be. The person you're meant to be.

Setting an Example

To my surprise, some of those challenges in my life have been the very things God has used to make me a better leader. The low points have given me the chance to regroup and refocus on what's most important. And those experiences have also given me empathy for others when they are going through a tough situation.

Every team I've been on has taught me a lot about leadership—some examples I want to emulate and others I make a note to avoid. One principle I've learned is that a leader can't ask anybody to do what he is not willing to do himself. As a quarterback, I know the guys on my team are looking to me to set the tone. For one thing, they want me to produce on the field. I touch the ball on every down and have to make the decision about who else is going to be involved in advancing the ball. My teammates are relying on me, and I have to be ready to play. But it's not just about football. I also have a moral responsibility to model personal integrity, discipline, and the right attitude to the rest of my team. I have to manage my offense and breed confidence in those guys. If they see me getting flustered or pressed, that's going to affect them negatively. They need to see me act cool and poised so they can do the same.

From my vantage point, I can see things throughout a game that others might not, so I can be a teacher to the guys. But it's not a one-way deal. They see things from their perspective that I miss, and I need to be humble enough to listen and learn. Part of a quarterback's job is to both coach and be coached.

Another thing I've learned about leadership is the importance of work ethic. Throughout the week of preparations before a game, I make it my goal to be one of the first ones to the practice facility in the morning and the last to leave. I stay late every day to practice my footwork, throw more routes, and talk through concepts with the receivers and coaches. That's not heroic; it's just part of the job. And it's not for show. I know I always need to keep practicing and getting better and gaining more confidence. You are either getting better or getting worse, but you are never staying the same. When the guys observe that their quarterback is doing everything possible to help the team win and succeed, and when they realize he's going to fight for them, they'll play their hearts out for him. Leading by example is the only way I know how to lead.

In my role as a quarterback I've found it helps to understand each of the guys on my team. Every player is different—and not just physically. Through practice and trial and error, you discover how they're most comfortable catching the ball. You also learn their mental and emotional makeup—how they respond to pressure, what pushes their buttons. You find out how they react when they miss an assignment or drop a pass. I also discovered early on that everyone is motivated in different ways. Some guys are spurred on when you get hyped up and loud and vocal, but others do better with a simple look or a nod. Other guys would rather have you pull them aside and talk with them in private.

One aspect of leadership a lot of people overlook is the importance of showing how much you care. When other people see that you are genuinely concerned about them and truly invested in them, they'll trust you. There's no faking it, and there's no amount of talent that can make up for the lack of it. When your teammates know that you have their best interest at heart, the by-product is that they'll go out there and fight for you. They'll *win* for you.

Some people look at their home team and think, *If only we had that free agent. If only our team could pay for that receiver or running back.* I don't waste time thinking about those kinds of acquisitions. If those players come to us, great. But here's the way I look at it: I'll take the less talented guy with the big heart every time. I love the old saying "It's not the size of the dog in the fight, but the size of the fight in the dog." Give me someone I can depend on so I know what I am getting every time, and I'll show you a winner.

As history has proven time and time again, the most gifted athletes are not necessarily the ones who win championships. There's a hidden factor that burns deep inside a player that you can't see on a stat sheet or a highlight reel. When a bigger, prototypical quarterback looks at me from the other side of the field or when the crowd looks down as I'm walking into the stadium, I sometimes try to visualize what they're think-ing. Maybe they assume I'm too short for my position or that there's no way I can get the job done. In my heart I know I'm going to show them something. I've got to prove myself every time I step onto the field. I know how hard I've worked, and I know how many people believe in me. I want the guys on my team to know I believe in them too. Whenever we walk out onto the field, we can hold our heads high, silently saying, *You all haven't seen anything yet.*

A Call to Christian Athletes

I am very proud of my faith. Being a Christian is who I am. I read the Word of God in the Bible every day, and I do my best to live out the teachings found inside. On a daily basis I ask God to show me his will and allow me to see the purposes he has for my life. Then I try to carry out those purposes in all I do. I also strive to live with a healthy fear of God. But don't take this the wrong way. In my view, fearing God means you have so much love and respect for him that you don't want to let him down and you would do anything to serve him. I believe that when you fear God, you don't need to fear anything else—no man, no task, no obstacle or challenge. Because when God is with you, you can accomplish anything and overcome any obstacles.

God has made every person unique, and although we are all different, he created each of us with the ability to achieve greatness. Of course, there are bumps along the way, and we will all face our share of adversity. This is what shapes us as people and as Christians and allows us to move forward stronger than we were before, ready to reach heights we never thought possible. Our faith is a constant work in progress, and the journey of a Christian is never finished on this earth. We always need to be working toward strengthening our bond with the Lord and improving our relationships with others.

The challenge of a Christian athlete is to live the life that we preach and understand that we have been given a platform to make a positive impact in the lives of many people, especially kids. What bugs me more than anything else is seeing guys profess their faith on game day with a point to the sky while the cameras are rolling and then walk out of the locker room into a life of sin. I'm not saying we never make mistakes. We are all human, and therefore we are all sinners.

Nobody is perfect. The Lord knows I have committed my fair share of sins and made some stupid decisions. But the key is to learn from those mistakes and commit to ourselves and to God that we will clean up our lives where necessary. As athletes, we live in an age of media where our every move is documented and scrutinized, and sometimes we feel like certain things we say or do are misconstrued or taken out of context. The national media usually focuses on athletes who make poor decisions, and therefore that becomes the general perception about athletes. Unfortunately the status quo does not sell papers, but drama and controversy do. As athletes, we must continue to fight that perception and show fans that the reality is different—that most of us take great responsibility in representing our communities and organizations the best we can. Football is one of those sports that has the ability to transcend just being a game or a form of entertainment to become a source of hope and pride for so many fans. We recognize this and constantly find ways to connect with those who make this game great—the fans.

I believe that everybody deserves to have his or her own relationship with God. Yes, there are fundamental beliefs and values that are consistent for all Christians. But when it comes to our own individual walks with God, they are specific to each person. While I am not afraid to talk about my faith, I tend to be less outspoken than others might be. I think it's great for other people to be more vocal—I love to see enthusiastic Christians who have the power of the Lord running through them. But that's just not my personality.

I want people to take Christ seriously, so I try not to treat him flippantly by throwing around some catchphrase or code words that only Christians will understand. I want people to see that my faith is authentic—not only in my words but also in the way I live my life. There are a lot of skeptics out there who get disillusioned when they see people who talk about God but don't have the actions to back it up. My desire is that people will see me as a man of God who is genuinely trying to live out my faith with my wife, my son, my team, and the community I live and serve in. I also hope those who don't know Christ will be able to look at the way Christian athletes carry themselves and see that they are making their lives define the game, rather than letting the game define their lives.

TO WHOM MUCH IS GIVEN...

CHAPTER THIRTEEN

ONE OF THE GUIDING PRINCIPLES in my life is from a parable of Jesus: "To whom much is given . . . much will be required." In other words, if you have been blessed, it's your responsibility to bless others with what you've been given. God hasn't given those gifts just for your own good but for the good of others as well. Early in my football career I recognized the need to give back to the community. I see it as my responsibility, but also my privilege, to be generous with what God has entrusted to me.

Over the years I've seen players become as passionate about their charity work as they are about football, and the common denominator seems to be that they have suffered through something difficult or experienced some loss in their own lives. One of my mentors and friends, Doug Flutie, is that type of guy. His son, Doug Jr., has autism, and Doug has made it his mission to raise awareness about the disorder and fund research to help those affected by it.

For a long time Brittany and I had a desire to channel our giving and fund-raising to specific projects that would make a difference in people's lives. So in 2003, after a lot of thought and prayer, we established the Brees Dream Foundation, a 501(c)(3) tax-exempt charity.

We came up with the concept and name for the Brees Dream Foundation on our honeymoon. It was our joint vision, but really it was Brittany's passion that ensured it came to fruition. In a way, we think of it as our first baby. Our foundation is personal to us not only because of the people who inspired it but because it was our dream, our way to give back after all the blessings we have been given.

Our original mission for the foundation was to advance cancer research projects and improve the quality of life for patients with cancer, especially children. Part of the inspiration for this idea came from Brittany's aunt Judith Zopp. She and Brittany were very close, and when Brittany was in college, Aunt Judie, as Brit called her, went through several stages of treatment for both lung cancer and brain cancer. We watched her struggle valiantly as the treatments, including partial lung removal, radiation, Gamma Knife rays, chemotherapy, and full-brain radiation, sapped her strength. Though her body continued to decline, her attitude and spirit never did. She managed to go to work every day after the chemo in the earlier stages. And all the way to the end, she somehow remained upbeat and positive, and her warm, loving spirit always shone through. She was and still is an inspiration to Brittany and me.

After that experience, cancer was no longer a theoretical concept for us; it was personal. Aunt Judie died on September 3, 2000, the beginning of my senior year of college. It was her life that was the catalyst for our vision. We wanted to help other Aunt Judies in the world.

As we became more familiar with the cancer treatment

centers, our hearts especially went out to children with illnesses. We now work closely with children's hospitals in New Orleans and San Diego and other organizations that treat kids with debilitating diseases. The Hope Lodge, which is affiliated with the American Cancer Society, provides housing for families with sick children who are coming from out of town for treatment. It offers a comforting place to stay, a "home away from home" for families who are going through so much upheaval in their lives. Whatever the length of their stay, they know the Hope Lodge will be available for them. The Brees Dream Foundation helps make that stay as comfortable and peaceful as possible.

There's something about watching an innocent child suffer that cuts to your core. Not only are these kids in unimaginable pain, but they haven't had an opportunity to lead a "normal" life yet, to just be a kid. At times, I think one of the most important parts of treatment can be simply putting smiles on kids' faces or letting them know you're there for them, encouraging them that they can pull through.

We're very involved with some projects in Southern California from my time with the Chargers, and we still have a great relationship with the San Diego community. One of the most exciting opportunities has been a project at the hematology/oncology ward at Rady Children's Hospital. In May 2010 we hosted a golf tournament that raised more than $100,000, which helped complete funding for Carley's Magical Gardens, a pavilion in the hospital with a tree house, bronze animals, and a garden play area, where kids can relax and dream.

Since we established the foundation in 2003, Brittany had another aunt, Ann Jones, who passed away—this time from pancreatic cancer. It took her quickly and came as a shock to the whole family. Much like Aunt Judie, Aunt Ann was one of those people who held the family together. This experience was another reminder of why we feel compelled to do everything we can to help with cancer research and provide support for patients. We hope to put up two plaques beside Carley's Magical Gardens with Aunt Judie's and Aunt Ann's names on them to commemorate their lives and the type of people they were.

We've also worked with an organization in San Diego called Friends of Scott. There was a young man named Scott Delgadillo, who died of cancer in 2001. His family started a foundation to fund different programs for children with life-threatening diseases. One of the programs we are especially excited about is for kids who miss their prom or formal dance due to illness. By hosting the Annual Unforgettable Prom night, this organization gives sick children a chance to get dressed up, ride in a limo, and celebrate a special evening. It's a simple way for them to enjoy something cancer took from their lives. And since everything from the formalwear to the catered food is donated, this free event is a blessing to the parents as well as the kids.

The Brees Dream Foundation might sound pretty official, but in reality, the whole organization is just Brittany, me, and my marketing agent and good friend, Chris Stuart. And since the three of us take no pay for our work, we operate at nearly zero overhead cost. Our philosophy is simple—a dollar in is a dollar out. All the money raised in a specific community stays in that community. Our passion is clear—to help people. We don't want anything to get in the way of that.

A New Vision

Although New Orleans and San Diego get most of the media attention, we are still thrilled to be making an impact back at Purdue University. In West Lafayette, Indiana, we support the

Purdue Athletes Life Success program (PALS), a free camp offered during the summer for about four hundred kids. It was once run by the National Youth Sports program, but it looked like it would have to shut down when their federal funding was pulled. We'd seen research about how positively this camp was impacting the kids long-term, and we didn't want to let the program die, so our foundation took it over. We fund it through a charity golf tournament and a special corporate relationship with Purdue Employees Federal Credit Union.

The camp uses sports to teach kids life skills—teamwork, discipline, leadership, and a good attitude. There's also an art program, a computer program, and a financial literacy program that partners with the credit union. I'm the spokesperson for Visa's practical money skills program, which teaches kids how to manage their money and live within their means. I strongly believe that the earlier you can start teaching kids how to manage and save their money, the better equipped they'll be when they get to college and into their careers.

When I signed with New Orleans in 2006, we broadened the scope of our foundation to encompass the rebuilding efforts in the city, but our vision remained centered on kids. Less than a year removed from Katrina, we saw that there were still so many needs in New Orleans. We wanted to help rebuild schools, parks, playgrounds, and athletic fields, as well as fund child care programs, after-school programs, internships, and even teachers' salaries at schools that needed it. I am a firm believer that when you provide kids with a healthy learning environment and constructive after-school activities like sports or clubs or the arts, you are keeping them out of trouble and putting them in the best position to succeed. After all the children of New Orleans had gone through—being displaced from their schools, having their parks destroyed, and losing some of their familiar, safe places—we felt this was the least we could do. We didn't want them to lose out on any more of their childhood. The kids here have captured our hearts, and we know how vital the next generation is to the growth of the community.

In a lot of ways, this city and I have had parallel journeys. New Orleans was trying to come back at the same time I was rehabbing my shoulder and trying to resurrect my career. I had to learn how to throw again and then rebuild my arm strength, and it was the same with the city. There were areas where the floodwaters completely knocked homes and buildings off their foundations, and people had a chance to start over, to bring things back even better than they were before.

Somebody once said to me, "If you love New Orleans, it will love you back. But if you hate it, it will hate you back." Brittany and I have found that as we've grown to love this city, it has given us more love than we ever could have expected. And as we've become involved in charitable work, the payback for us—emotionally and spiritually—has been far beyond what we will ever be able to provide for it.

Still, the needs were overwhelming at first. Where do you start when everything is devastated? Brittany and I had to ask ourselves some hard questions to figure out what the priorities should be. We felt like one of the best ways for the city to get back on its feet was to bring people home again. We kept coming back to a few central questions: What was going to attract people who had been displaced to return to New Orleans? What would draw people who had never lived here but could discover this as a land of opportunity and a great place to raise kids, like we had?

Across the board, parents want to give their children opportunities for success in life, and we figured some of their top priorities would be schools and sports programs. That's why we targeted education, parks, athletics, and other youth activities.

Those improvements were tangible rays of hope for the residents too—reminders that they could have confidence in their city and that the rebuilding would continue.

It took about a year to identify twelve projects in town we wanted to tackle, and in June 2007, with the help of our partner, Operation Kids, we launched the Rebuilding Dreams in New Orleans campaign. These twelve projects totaled $1.8 million and were targeted at the needs of children in the area. Some of the organizations we were helping had been let down before—federal money had been misappropriated, or those who had promised money hadn't followed through. We told those groups, "We are committing to raise this money, or it will come out of our pockets. And the money is going to go where we've promised. You *will* see results." We wanted to send the message that no matter how things had been done in the past, we were going to be dependable and reliable. They could count on us.

In May 2009, we completed the $1.8 million funding that went to those twelve organizations. One that really captured my heart was Lusher Charter School. Prior to Katrina, the building had housed another school that had been closed due to poor academic performance and other issues. When the hurricane hit, the empty facility was used as a shelter for the homeless and those escaping the storm. By the time the dust settled, the school was in terrible disrepair. But due to some extraordinary leadership, as well as the commitment of parents and children to return to their neighborhood, a new school was established in its place: Lusher Charter School.

They already had a strong music, theater, and dance program—the one thing they were missing was an athletic program. We were able to put about $750,000 toward a new athletic field and a weight room for training. Brittany and I go there to visit from time to time, and when we do, we feel like alumni. As we walk around, kids will casually say, "Hey, Drew," and keep walking. They don't rush up for an autograph or a picture—I'm just part of the Lusher family now. That's a great feeling.

Another big project was a school right down the street from our house called Samuel J. Green Charter School. It's a school for kindergarten through eighth grade that emphasizes culinary arts—hence its nickname, the Edible Schoolyard. They have a greenhouse and a garden where they grow fruits, vegetables, and spices right on the school grounds. They learn about the science of growing and what flourishes in different climates and at different times of the year. Then they use that food each day in the classroom and the lunchroom.

New Orleans has a long tradition in cuisine, so this school really fits the unique persona of our city. Plus, the opportunities it provides cultivate a sense of pride, self-esteem, and confidence in kids. Many students and their families come to school on the weekends to tend to their row of vegetables or fruit. We provided Samuel J. Green Charter School with $250,000 for the development of their Edible Schoolyard as well as the installation of a professional kitchen.

Over the years it has been fun to partner with other groups that have a similar vision for the city. Organizations we support like the Idea Village attract young, entrepreneurial talent to New Orleans to establish small businesses and bring jobs and stability to the city. The Brees Dream Foundation has been able to identify organizations that have great plans and solid leadership in place but need a little extra to get over the top and complete funding. We pride ourselves in finding these causes and helping to close out funding for some great projects in a way that will have a significant impact. The thought that this city could come back stronger was once only a dream. Now we can see the light at the end of the tunnel, but we must keep our heads down and press forward because there is still a lot of work left to do. We must stay focused and embrace the opportunity.

Giving back to the community isn't only about money, either. As a professional athlete, whether you like it or not, you're a role model. A lot of people—especially kids—look up to you. I know that when I was a kid, I watched the pros' every move, hung on their every word, and tried to model my life after theirs. As important as it is to share the blessings I've been given, my heart needs to be in the right place too. I need to do the right things for the right reasons—out of a heart that cares about others and genuinely wants to make a difference.

I want kids to look at me and say, "When I grow up, I want to make that kind of impact on the world." It's not just about being a good athlete on the field; it's also about being a giving person off the field.

As a quarterback, I can't think of many thrills quite like seeing your team come together and accomplish an objective you've been working toward all season. That's kind of how I feel about getting to see these different pieces of the foundation come together too. I love watching each person on the team working toward a common goal and making a difference.

Our Biggest Fans

As professional athletes, we can sometimes get wrapped up in things like goals and records and championships and trophies. We're concerned about contracts and bonuses and the business side of the game. We can pay a lot of attention to the media and all the publicity. But what really helps keep us grounded is when we hear from some of our most special fans.

Devan Muller was a little five-year-old with a big smile who came to a Saints practice in the 2007 off-season. He had gone through a major heart surgery, and things weren't going well for him. Through the Make-A-Wish Foundation, he was given the chance to have one of his dreams come true. He was a huge Saints fan, and his wish was to attend a Saints practice. He wanted to meet some of the players and throw the ball with me. So we brought Devan into the team meeting room during an off-season practice, took him out to the field, and gave him a chance to step into the huddle. He even got to follow alongside us while we ran drills. Afterward Devan stayed out on the field, and the two of us played catch and talked. I've never seen a kid grin so big for so long.

We've had the opportunity to meet other kids through Make-A-Wish, and one boy even did an honorary coin toss in the middle of the field on game day. We'll do whatever we can to let those kids live out a dream. Without fail, they're more of an inspiration to me than I could ever be to them.

We've gotten letters from parents saying, "Our son passed away this last week, but what he was constantly talking about until the end was the opportunity to come and be with you and meet the team. It was a dream come true for us. Thank you for giving that joy and happiness to our child." Letters like that from a hurting parent put everything in perspective. You have a brush with one of those special little guys, and you realize how fortunate you really are. You also realize that others around you are going through tough times—challenges that most people can't even imagine.

There are also success stories, where parents write and say, "My son is doing great. He was given a couple of months to live, but now he's doing well and the doctors think he might pull through it. We think when he came to practice and threw the ball with you, it was a huge turning point. It gave him something to look forward to, and he wants to come back again when he's cancer-free."

These kids may be our fans, but *they* are our heroes. Some of them might not have much time left on earth, but they're fighting every day to live life to the fullest. They motivate us as a team to be all we can be—a team worthy of the special kids who want to be close to us.

I think a lot about the term *calling.* Brittany and I felt that when we came to New Orleans. I sensed that God was bringing us here for a reason. Most people think they're called somewhere because of what they can do for a community or a cause. But to me, it's also because that community can help *you* along where you need it. The truth is, as much as Brittany and I have invested in New Orleans in terms of football and the foundation, this city has given it all back to us tenfold. I will always be thankful—to the people of this city and to the God who called me here.

BUILDING A CHAMPIONSHIP TEAM

CHAPTER FOURTEEN

ALTHOUGH MY SHOULDER had made it through the 2006 season just fine and had gotten stronger every week, I still felt there was a lot of progress to be made before the 2007 season rolled around. Dr. Andrews had said it would be at least an eight-month rehab process just to get back on the field, but that it would take about two years before I would feel "normal" again. I wasn't sure what he meant at the time, but I was beginning to understand. I kept working on strengthening and conditioning exercises during the off-season. I had moments when I was throwing the ball as well as I'd ever thrown it, but it was taking time to become as consistent as I wanted to be. It sounds weird to say that after coming off the best season of my career, but even after all the time and maintenance I'd put into my shoulder that year, I knew there was still room for improvement. The retooling of my throwing motion during rehab had made a big difference in my efficiency and the way my arm felt. I knew that with more time and repetition, my shoulder would only get stronger.

My goal for each year is simple: to be better than I was the year before. You can't always look at the stats to make that conclusion, either. Sometimes you are only able to determine your progress by digging deep and evaluating yourself. As I looked ahead to 2007, I was building from the baseline of where I'd finished the season in 2006. That year I felt like I became stronger each game. Now I felt it was time to focus on raising the bar, setting my sights a little higher.

As difficult as it is to rebuild a shoulder, building a great team is a tougher task. Creating a championship team is even more challenging. To explain how we rose to the top, I have to go back to 2006 and revisit some decisions that were made about me and the other players on the team.

New Orleans certainly had other options for quarterback in 2006. There were other healthy free agents they could have chosen, or they could have stayed the course with Aaron Brooks, their quarterback at the time. They could have drafted Heisman Trophy winner Matt Leinart from USC, or if Leinart wasn't available, they could have picked Vince Young or Jay Cutler. They knew there were no guarantees that I would be able to rehab and make a complete comeback. But despite the odds stacked against me, New Orleans believed in me. I responded to their belief, and it propelled me to exceed all expectations.

Some people still ask me what would have happened if I had gone to Miami instead, but I don't like to spend time looking back. Because of the way things worked out after the injury, I had the chance to come to New Orleans and make a difference. I believe that was part of God's plan, and I embraced it with all my heart.

There were other hard decisions the Saints had to make. When Sean Payton got to New Orleans, he knew they had to start over and build the organization up the right way. He convinced the owner, Tom Benson, and the general manager, Mickey Loomis, that the team really needed to bring in guys who would help them build a new foundation and a new core. Together they worked at changing the attitude and culture of the team by bringing in hardworking players who were committed and willing to fight through whatever challenges came their way.

Building a championship team is not an overnight process. It's not all that different from the reconstruction after Katrina. You have to go through some pain and tearing down before you can get to work on the rebuilding process. Coach Payton knew he had to make some tough decisions about the type of players we didn't want for the year ahead. The guys from the 2005 season had lived on the road, away from their families for long stretches. They practiced at high schools, stayed in different hotels and apartments, and had no place to call home. It's easy to lose direction and stray from the course when you don't have a solid foundation of home and family. These tense conditions caused a great deal of division among the team, and I have heard players refer to this frustration as "Katrina anger." Unfortunately, that anger brought out the worst in some guys. It became obvious that there were certain attitudes and personalities from the previous season that didn't fit with the vision they were trying to build. Those players would not be there next year.

For the most part, the guys who were brought in weren't well-paid free agents. At the time, this was not an easy place to attract high-level players. Instead, a lot of the new recruits were castaways. They'd been told by other organizations that they didn't have what it took to remain on the team. When they got to New Orleans, they were given a home.

Even though 2006 started out as a rebuilding year for us on all levels, it ended up as a storybook year—the best in franchise history up to that point. We made incredible strides toward building a culture and an atmosphere that was conducive to winning. After we made it to the NFC Championship Game in 2006, that put the pressure on in 2007. We really felt like we could make it to the Super Bowl. We had the talent, we had the confidence, and we believed all the pieces were in place to win everything.

However, team building and personnel are only part of the process. Ironically, handling success can be just as tough as handling adversity—maybe tougher. When you get knocked down, you learn to get back up. Everybody knows that intuitively. When you lose, you learn and grow from the mistakes and figure out how to overcome them. But when you succeed, you have to realize that just because you did it once doesn't make it any easier the second time. It's human nature to relax and feel entitled. If you want to win consistently, you have to fight that tendency with everything in you. When you reach the top of the mountain, don't forget how hard it was to get there in the first place.

In the NFL, each year means starting over. Every season there's a new team, a new set of challenges, new dynamics, and a new opportunity to grow together. Did we have what it took to handle the success of the previous season?

A Season of Setbacks

We began the 2007 season with a game against Indianapolis. According to a new tradition, the Super Bowl–winning team from the previous year hosts the Thursday night NFL Kickoff game to mark the start of the season. We had missed playing the Colts by a game the previous year and felt like we were ready to take on the champs. It was a good game for the first half, and at halftime the score was tied 10–10.

We lost 41–10. To put it mildly, we had a rough second half. It was beyond disappointing. We were embarrassed. Humiliated. That was not the New Orleans Saints on the field. We didn't remember the last time we had been beaten like that.

Convinced that the Indianapolis game had been a fluke, we headed to Tampa Bay with fresh confidence. Still, we knew this wouldn't be a cakewalk. Anytime you're playing a divisional opponent, you have to be ready for a fight. We had beaten the Buccaneers twice in 2006, so they had that extra motivation from the previous season. Going into that game, all of us were in the same frame of mind: we were going to turn things around. No losing two in a row. We were going to show everyone the *real* Saints team.

We ended up losing 31–14. At one point in the game we were down 28–0. Another embarrassment.

Our expectation was to make it to the Super Bowl that year, and here we had lost the first two games of the season. But that was our problem. We were thinking about the Super Bowl. We weren't thinking about winning one game at a time and then putting our energy into winning the next one.

After getting a whupping those first two games, we came back to the Superdome for *Monday Night Football* against Tennessee. Our attitude was *Okay, we're really going to turn things around. Now is the time to step up. Stop the bleeding.*

The Titans were a good team that year—in fact, they ended up making it to the playoffs. The final score showed what they were made of. We lost 31–14 for the second week in a row, and we were sitting at 0–3 going into our bye week.

During the bye week each player self-scouts and evaluates. It's when we consider what we've done well and where we've come up short. When we looked at our play from the season so far, we had to be honest and say, "We haven't done anything well." We decided to wipe the slate clean and start again. The rest during that week was good for us—physically and mentally—and we thought we had some things figured out about how to move ahead.

Some fans would probably turn on their team at 0–3. The boobirds would come out, and you'd hear them as you went into the tunnel. But our fans were the opposite. They kept encouraging us, and their attitude was *Look, we know you're playing hard; we know you're trying. We're still here for you; we're still pulling for you.* They reciprocated the support we gave them in the hard times after Katrina. There's a unique back-and-forth between our team and New Orleans that's hard to explain. We gave them strength when they needed it, and they gave it right back to us. We help each other fight through whatever we're facing.

They were behind us when we faced Carolina the next week. But that game turned out to be a heartbreaker for all of us. We were leading in the fourth quarter, deep in Carolina territory, and we couldn't get the ball in the end zone. We lined up for an easy field goal, but it was blocked. Carolina came back to tie us, and as time expired, they kicked a fifty-two-yard field goal. They eked out a win, 16–13.

Now we were 0–4 for the first time since 1996. Numbers aren't everything to me, but in those first four games, I had thrown only one touchdown . . . and nine interceptions. Those are stats you don't like to remember. As we headed off the field after the Carolina game, the air went out of the Dome. We'd been to the championship game the year before, and here we were bringing up the rear in our division. We were facing a huge amount of adversity again—but this time it was because we had dug our own hole. We were pretty shell-shocked by the whole thing and wondered what had happened. We were losing confidence in our own abilities.

I had thrown only eleven interceptions during the whole 2006 season, and I threw nine in just the first four games of 2007. Everybody trusted me to take care of the ball. I had let them down. I knew that was not me. That was not the type of player I strove to be. I wanted my team to be able to count on me.

Before the Carolina game, one of our receivers, David Patten, had pulled me aside. DP, or the Big Chief, as we all called him, had been signed by the Saints that year from Washington and had been a key part of New England's offense for all three of their Super Bowl wins. He was a veteran player who had seen a lot, and he became a great friend and mentor for me over the next two years. In that moment he showed me some tough love. He told me that people were saying I had lost confidence, and he felt like I needed to step up a bit more as a leader and as the quarterback of our team. This lit a fire under me that still burns today. The fact is, he was right—I *had* lost a little confidence and was beginning to put undue pressure on myself. Had 2006 been a fluke? I was so desperate for us to succeed that I was trying to make it happen as opposed to letting it happen. I was trying to force every play instead of just feeling and reacting to the game. When you hit a stretch like that in your career, it's vital to focus on the little things and fall back on the fundamentals of the game. If you can't do that, you can't play. Trust the process, trust your routine, and trust your preparation—that's what gives you the confidence to relax and play at a high level on game day. I needed the Big Chief to remind me of that.

The next Sunday we played at Seattle, and they were heavily favored. We scored three touchdowns in the second quarter and won 28–17 in front of a national audience. Just what we needed to get back on track.

The next week we came out on top against Atlanta and

continued the streak by beating San Francisco. In the next game we faced Jacksonville, another eventual playoff team and heavy favorite. We put up forty-one points and won. That meant we'd won four in a row. We'd evened out our record, 4–4. I remember guys from the media asking, "Who wants to play the New Orleans Saints now?" We fed on that kind of talk, and our confidence rose a little. We were down but not out. We'd been hit, but we were fighting back. The Superdome was rocking, and people were fired up. In the last twelve games I played some of the best football of my career, throwing twenty-seven touchdowns to nine interceptions. Quite a change from the one to nine ratio from the first four weeks. I was also approaching the two-year mark since the surgery, and my arm was feeling stronger than ever, even before the injury.

Unfortunately, though, the hole we'd carved for ourselves was pretty deep. In order to stay in contention for the playoffs, we had to win almost every game left in the season. It was not meant to be. Despite our best efforts to recover from a bad start, we finished the year at 7–9, missing the postseason entirely.

Like it or not, you can learn a lot more from losing than you typically do from winning. Our record may not have been pretty that year, but we came away with some valuable lessons about not taking anything for granted and about finishing well. In that sense, 2007 and 2008 were very similar—both seasons had high expectations, and both seasons were disappointments. But there were foundations being laid that we couldn't see . . . yet.

Ha-ooh!

Each year I've tried to do something new during the off-season to inspire my teammates and help bring us together. The chants we do during the pregame are not for anyone but us, so we don't talk about it to the media or explain it until after the season is over. The chant may come to me while Brittany and I are traveling or while I'm in the car or at some other random moment. Or I'll read something that really resonates with me or hear a story that sparks an idea. From there, I figure out a way to communicate it so the whole team can take part and then get feedback from other leaders on the team about how to tweak it to fit our profile.

As we were getting ready for the 2008 season, I felt like we needed something fresh; we needed to shake things up a bit. I've heard that the definition of insanity is to continue to do the same things the same way and expect a different outcome. We'd been doing the same thing the last two years, and it was time to let the guys know that this was a new team, aiming for new results. We'd had a disappointing year in 2007, and we didn't want to fall short of our ultimate goal again. We were switching gears, and 2008 was a new year and another chance for a fresh start.

I thought about it a long time. How could I bring something different, unexpected, and a little surprising to help the team? It clicked with me that the pregame chant was the perfect avenue. Usually a quarterback isn't doing that type of thing—it tends to be the defensive players who take the emotional lead. They're traditionally the ones who get in people's faces and butt heads to get everyone fired up before the game. I'm on the opposite end of the spectrum—in terms of both position and personality. I tend to slow things down and stay calm, cool, and poised. A quarterback can't let the emotion of the moment affect his methodical, precise movements. But that year I felt like, as a leader for our team, I needed to get outside my comfort zone. I needed to be the one to get in there with the guys and get them hyped up for the game.

A movie called *300* was released about that time. It was

loosely based on the Battle of Thermopylae, which was fought in 480 BC. I was inspired by that film, particularly by the scene where the Spartans are marching to the sea to meet the Persians. They come across the Arcadians, another tribe of Greeks willing to join the fight. These men make a fierce presence—there's a huge crowd of them, and they are decked out with weapons and helmets. But the leader of the Arcadians seems disappointed that there are only three hundred Spartans. He says he thought Sparta would at least match their commitment in terms of the number of soldiers.

In response, the Spartan king Leonidas points at one of the Arcadian warriors and asks his profession. "I'm a potter." He asks another, who responds that he is a sculptor. The third is a blacksmith.

Leonidas turns to his warriors and says, "Spartans! What is your profession?"

As one they hold up their spears and say, "Ha-ooh! Ha-ooh! Ha-ooh!"

"You see, old friend," Leonidas says to the Arcadian commander, "I brought more soldiers than you did."

I loved the mentality of the Spartans: *We are soldiers. That's our identity. That's what we were trained to do. And we won't waste our time looking at who or what we don't have; we choose to look at what we do have.*

I will never relate football to war, nor will I refer to football players as soldiers. The men and women of our military risk their lives every day in the line of duty, and we play a game. But at the same time, our game is violent. So you'd better have something to get your mind right before stepping onto that field.

Here's the chant I came up with based on that scene:

I would say, "Who are we?"

And the response from my team was "Saints!"

I would repeat, "Who are we?"

"Saints!"

Then I'd say, "Are we ready?"

The team would respond, "Ha-ooh!"

"Are we ready?"

"Ha-ooh!"

Then I would repeat the whole thing again: "Who are we?"

"Saints!"

"Who are we?"

"Saints!"

"Are we ready?"

"Ha-ooh!"

"Are we ready?"

"Ha-ooh!"

Another pivotal scene in the film shows a Persian messenger wearing the skulls of dead enemies. He basically tells the Spartans they have to surrender or they'll all be killed. King Leonidas has a problem with that, and he pulls out his sword and points it at the messenger, who backs up toward a gaping well. The messenger says, "This is blasphemy!"

King Leonidas screams, "This is Sparta!" and kicks the messenger into the hole.

So to our pregame chant I added, "This is New Orleans!"

And the team responded, "Ha-ooh! Ha-ooh! Ha-ooh!"

That routine got us ready to play each week. It started the adrenaline pumping, and it gave us the mind-set that we were a band of brothers who wouldn't back down from anyone or anything.

To be honest, it felt strange at first, motivating my team that way—it's much more loud and emotional than I tend to be. But then again, in order to accomplish something you've never accomplished before, you have to do something you've never done before. You have to take it to the next level. You have to let go of your security blanket and take a chance.

This was a small thing, but when it comes down to it, it's all the little things added together that lead to victory. The road to a Super Bowl win is a process of bringing a team together and accomplishing your goals, step-by-step. We were teammates, bound by the blood, sweat, and tears of many years of struggle, and we were ready to fight. We'd go onto the field, stick together no matter what, and do all we could to defeat a worthy opponent. Ha-ooh!

Seesaw Season

In 2008 we were back and forth, up and down, all season long. The first game was in New Orleans, and Hurricane Gustav was coming through. It brought back some terrible memories for the people of New Orleans as they anticipated another storm and wondered if all their rebuilding work would be washed away. After what we'd learned from Katrina, nobody wanted to mess around with hurricanes, so all of New Orleans was evacuated. The Saints went to Indianapolis and practiced at Lucas Oil Stadium while our city weathered the storm. The levees had been rebuilt by then, but at the time they were only strong enough to withstand the onslaught of a Category 3 hurricane. Thankfully Gustav wasn't beyond a Category 3 when it hit, and the levees held. New Orleans was safe. We returned to our city at the end of the week once we were in the clear.

On Sunday the Dome was rocking as Tampa Bay came to town. You might think the storm would have kept the fans at home, checking for damage and getting things back in order. It didn't. Their mentality was *Our Saints need us. We want to be there to support them.* That's just how they are.

We were behind 20–17 in the fourth quarter. We got the ball and scored a touchdown, which launched us into the lead with about eight minutes left. Tampa Bay drove into our territory, but we picked off a fourth-down pass with less than a minute left in the game. It was a dramatic win, 24–20. It meant a lot to us, especially with everything that had happened that week: the evacuation, practicing elsewhere, and being away from our families. Coming back and seeing that the fans had found a way to get to the stadium really fired us up.

The season whipped the opposite direction the next game. We were up 24–15 in Washington in the fourth quarter, and somehow we managed to lose 29–24. Then we headed to Denver, which is always a difficult place to play. We were down 21–3 in the second quarter. We fought back and had a chance to take the lead with a field goal at the two-minute mark, but the kick sailed right and the Broncos held on to win, 34–32.

We beat San Francisco when they came to the Superdome, putting our record at 2–2. The Vikings were on the horizon for Monday night. We felt like we'd put the negatives behind us, and we were ready to make a run. It was an exciting game to watch—Reggie Bush ran two punts back for touchdowns, Minnesota's Antoine Winfield blocked a field goal and returned it for a touchdown, and there were two field goals of more than fifty yards. Unfortunately, we missed a field goal at the end again, and the Vikings made theirs to win, 30–27.

That was a tough loss at home, but we bounced back to beat the Raiders the next week. That put us at 3–3. Then we went to Carolina and lost. It seemed like every game was back and forth—win, loss, win, loss. We knew if we kept it up, we'd wind up 8–8, and we were not an 8–8 team. We had no consistency, no winning streak, no momentum. It felt like the minute we got the bus accelerating, somebody would throw on the parking brake.

There was one key moment late in the season against Tampa Bay. We were playing at Raymond James Stadium in one of those late-November Florida monsoons. It was a divisional must-win game for us. With less than four minutes to go, we had the ball with the score tied 20–20. This was one of those perfect scenarios where you can calmly lead your team down the field, converting a few critical third-down throws, and then line up to kick the game-winning field goal. Instead, on the third play of the drive, I got impatient and tried to force a completion. It was intercepted, and the Buccaneers kicked a field goal to go ahead 23–20. We had one more chance to either tie or win the game, but I threw another interception. They ran out the clock, and we lost.

I walked to the locker room utterly dejected. It was the worst I have ever felt after a game while wearing a Saints uniform. Within a three-minute time frame, I had blown two chances for us to win. I made a commitment right then and there that I never wanted to let down so many people who were counting on me. This was a huge divisional game—a must-win—and I didn't get the job done. I knew the opportunity would come again, and when it did, I would be ready.

Those 2007 and 2008 seasons were tough ones to go through. But they were struggles we had to face and over-come as a team in order to reach new heights and accomplish bigger things. Sometimes you have to take a few steps back-ward in order to advance to your ultimate goal. Without the lessons we learned during the low points of those seasons—things like perseverance and fight and coming together as a team—I don't know that we would have accomplished what we did in 2009.

An Old Foe

Despite the disappointments of that season, there were some high points that stood out, like the trip to England to play against my former team, the Chargers. They'd had a rough start to the season just like we had, and both teams were 3–4 when we arrived in London. This was the first time I'd played against my old team since my injury, since signing on with the Saints. We were staying outside London, practicing on torn-up soccer fields, far from the familiar routines of home. But it didn't matter where we were playing. My teammates knew how much that game meant to me. As much as you try to make it just another game, it was hard to ignore the weight of the matchup.

The game was held at Wembley Stadium. Marty Schottenheimer had been replaced by Norv Turner by then, but Philip Rivers was their quarterback; and I knew a lot of the players and coaches who were still with the team. I wasn't looking for revenge, and although there was a part of me that wanted to make them sorry they hadn't kept me, that wasn't my real motivation. It was more like I wanted to show them their investment in me for those years was paying off. Or maybe I needed that final game to completely sever my emotional ties to the team. Whatever it was, the game was a big deal to me.

Sure enough, the game gave me the closure with San Diego I needed. It was strange to stand on the sideline, looking at my old team from fifty yards away. Those guys used to be my teammates. They were wearing the jersey I used to wear. But as familiar as some of those things were, playing opposite the Chargers gave me the confirmation that I was now where I belonged. There was no doubt in my mind. I'd known it at a gut level ever since I felt the call to New Orleans in 2006. But this matchup sealed it and gave me a sense of peace.

It was a great game, and we won 37–32. In the locker room afterward, Sean Payton gave me a game ball, and the guys came up to me to say how happy they were for me. My boy Billy Miller probably had one of the best games of his Saints career that day, and he let me know after the game how important it was to him to win that one for me. In the midst of a rocky season, that was another experience that drew our team a little closer together.

The Record

In 2008 there were records set—and one that was *almost* broken. We might not have made an appearance at the playoffs, but the year had some highlights. We walked away with the single-season franchise records for both scoring (461) and yards (6,571). And there was another record that hit me pretty close to home.

Dan Marino holds the single-season passing yardage record at 5,084 yards. It's one of those hallowed achievements in football history. In the final play of the season, at the Superdome, I was probably the only person in the stadium and among TV viewers in America who didn't know we were one pass away from breaking it.

Going into the last two games of the season, we were 7–7 and out of playoff contention. We figured it out on paper and knew we would have to throw for nearly 760 yards in those final games in order to break Marino's record. That's a pretty far-fetched aspiration for just two games. I put it out of my head and focused on the game at hand. The most important thing was for our team to finish strong—in my eyes the team's record should always be a higher priority than an individual player's stats.

We went to Detroit and put on quite an offensive show. We threw for 350 yards. I say *we* not to be humble but to show that our offense is a team effort. Your offensive line has to do a great job communicating and blocking to allow you to get the ball off, and your receivers and backs have to make some plays to bail you out from time to time. Dan Marino would say the same thing.

Going into the final game, we needed 402 passing yards to break the record. You just don't go into a game saying, "Hey, I think we're going to throw for four hundred yards tonight." It's not that easy. You have to take each play as it comes and fight for each completion. Plus, we were playing the Carolina Panthers, who were trying to win the division and get the number two seed. That would give them a week to rest and then home field advantage in the divisional round of the play-offs. They weren't resting their starters—they came ready to play and weren't about to hand us four hundred passing yards.

Sean Payton pulled me into his office before the game against the Panthers. "We're going to get this record," he said. There was a hint of a smile on his face, but I could tell he meant business. There was no question everybody on the team wanted it. But for me as a quarterback, I couldn't go into a game playing only for a record. That would be making the same mistake we'd made at the beginning of 2007, when we'd prematurely set our sights on the Super Bowl. You have to take it one play at a time. You can't lose sight of that step-by-step process. As we started the game, I was thinking, *One play at a time. Don't let the record influence your decision making. Play the game to win. If we get the record, that's the way it was meant to happen. Otherwise, don't sweat it.*

The first quarter was ugly, and we went scoreless. Most of the second quarter wasn't much better, though we did hit a field goal. We weren't clicking offensively. We probably only had about eighty yards passing, so at that point I was thinking, *There's no way we can break the record now. No way.*

But during a two-minute drive before the half, we got a chunk of passing yards and scored to start closing the gap on the lead. That made it 23–10. For the first time all game, it felt like something was stirring in the team.

Even so, nobody told me about our progress toward the

record during the game. That was how I preferred it. It's like a pitcher who has a no-hitter going—nobody wants to say anything to him and break his concentration.

On the Panthers' first possession of the second half, they went down the field and scored. They were up 30–10 going into the fourth quarter.

On the second play of the final quarter, we scored, making it 30–17. We stopped Carolina and got the ball back. At this point we had no other choice but to be in our two-minute offense the entire fourth quarter. I threw the ball on almost every play, just trying to get down the field. We scored again, throwing eleven passes on a twelve-play touchdown drive to make it 30–24. To win the game, we knew our defense had to hold the Panthers and our offense had to score one more touchdown. We got the ball back again and made a quick touchdown to pull ahead 31–30. The crowd was going wild. We had been losing by twenty points going into the fourth quarter and now we were winning. It was unbelievable!

We kicked off with 3:11 on the clock. Our defense had held all quarter, but Jake Delhomme marched the Panthers downfield, using almost all of the clock. With the final seconds ticking away, they kicked a forty-two-yard field goal to take the lead, 33–31.

I looked up at the clock after the ball sailed through the uprights. It read 0:01.

Carolina still had to kick off to us, and everyone in the stadium knew what they were going to do. They would squib kick it down the middle of the field, and as soon as one of our guys touched it, the clock would run. We could try to pitch it around and head for the end zone, but without a penalty, that would be our last play. The offense really had no chance to get on the field unless the Panthers made a mistake.

The Panthers squibbed the kick as we expected, but it

wasn't right down the middle of the field, and the ball went out-of-bounds. Our guys didn't touch it, so no time expired, and we would be getting the ball at our forty yard line. There was still one second left. One more chance for the offense to get back on the field.

I went onto the field knowing there was only one way for us to win the game. We had the ball at our thirty-five yard line because of a penalty. We didn't have time to set up for a field goal, so my only option was to throw a Hail Mary into the end zone. What I hadn't noticed was a fan in the stands counting down the number of yards we needed to break the Marino record. We needed fifteen yards to tie it and sixteen yards to break it. Everybody else knew it but me.

"Hail Mary, right, Coach?" I said to Sean. I didn't even think there was a question about it.

I got about halfway out to the huddle when he called me back to the sideline. The coaches had all been talking and strategizing, but it seemed like a no-brainer to me.

"Drew, tell you what," Sean said. "It's probably a little far out for a Hail Mary. Just tell the receivers as they're lining up to get in the Hail Mary formation, but then run down only about twenty yards and turn around. You throw it to whoever's open, and they can start pitching it and head for the end zone."

I got into the huddle and told the guys about the forma-tion, but I didn't communicate the play clearly. They heard "Hail Mary" but didn't understand the rest of what we were doing. I dropped back to throw, and immediately I could tell there was a sense of confusion. You're never sure how a team will defend that Hail Mary pass. Sometimes they play way downfield, and sometimes they bring up defenders to press or bump the receivers. We weren't technically running a Hail Mary play, so the rules on where the receivers would go were a little fuzzy.

I wound up throwing to a receiver who wasn't even looking for the ball, and it fell incomplete. If we had completed that pass, which was twenty-five yards downfield, maybe we could have flipped it back enough times to score. Worst-case scenario, we would have set a new passing record. Instead, we came up sixteen yards short.

Everybody was devastated, but at that point I still had no idea why. I figured they were sharing in my own frustration of coming back from being twenty points down in the fourth quarter, taking the lead, only to give it right back. That was why I was upset. It wasn't until later that I realized how close we'd come. At the end of that season I was named the 2008 offensive player of the year, but I would have traded that title for a chance at the playoffs.

I mentioned it before, but I love this phrase I heard a long time ago: "Experience is what you gain when you don't get what you want." I get a kick out of this because it's absolutely true in my life. It seems like that's the only way I learn. Sometimes you get thrown into the fire, and sometimes you get burned. But you gain experience from those losses and the times you get kicked while you're down. When you keep working toward your goal but don't get what you want, remembering this allows you to really appreciate, at the end of the journey, what you've been through to get there. There is nothing like the satisfaction that comes when you finally achieve what you set your hopes on, when the experience you've gained from the ups and downs pays off.

The highs and lows weren't over for me personally. The next year would hold one of the best things that ever happened to me—and one of the most crushing losses of my life.

GAINS
AND LOSSES

CHAPTER FIFTEEN

ONE OF THE STRANGE THINGS about life is the way our deepest sorrows can coexist with our greatest joys. Sometimes the good is woven in so tightly with the difficult times that it's almost impossible to separate the two. That's how the year 2009 was for my family and me: full of highs and lows, beginnings and endings, new life and death.

God's Gift to Our Family

My son, Baylen, has been one of God's most incredible gifts to Brittany and me. There's no question he has changed my entire life, my whole way of looking at things. Before he was even able to talk, he was such an inspiration to me and helped me put life in perspective. Being a father has made my preparations each week and everything I do as a football player that much better, because I know that, no matter what happens, when I come home at night, he's going to be there.

Brittany and I had wanted to begin our family in the off-season of 2006, but my injury threw a wrench into those plans. Then the minute we signed with New Orleans, there was so much to do. I was focused on rehab, and I also had to reestablish myself and my career. We had to find a home, and once we did, we needed to fix it up so we could live there. All of that made us rethink the timing and push back having children. After the 2008 season was over, we prayed about it and talked more about the roots we were putting down. We felt good about being in New Orleans, and we were looking forward to raising our children here. We both thought this was the time to start our family.

Brittany was the most unbelievable pregnant woman. Beforehand she warned me that pregnancy can really change a woman's behavior. "Listen, when I get pregnant, I'm going to have these cravings and mood swings," she would say. "You'd just better be ready for all of this."

She was trying to prepare me for the physical, mental, and emotional fluctuations that were bound to come. I knew about the hormonal changes that get stirred up in a woman's body when she becomes pregnant and how much turmoil that can cause. On top of that, we'd heard horror stories of the first trimester and how hard it is because of morning sickness and fatigue and changes in the body. But in Brittany's case, we weren't even positive she was pregnant at first. She had no morning sickness or mood swings or any signs to tell us otherwise. When we went in for what we thought was the eight-week ultrasound, the doctor said the baby was already almost three months along.

One of the tough things about moving to a new city was finding a doctor. We wanted to make sure the person who brought our child into the world was the best. After asking several people for recommendations and going in for a visit, we decided on Dr. Liz Lapeyre. As a first-time parent, you really have no idea how many things you just don't know. I think I asked more questions than Brittany did at the visit. Liz has five children of her own, and she was great. No matter what time we texted her with crazy questions, she always responded. She was the first person to ever see and hold our son, and now she is a big part of our family.

But at that moment I just stared at Dr. Lapeyre. "Are you sure?" I said.

She gave me a look. "Your baby is twelve weeks along."

I didn't need her to break down the math for me. This had obviously happened on the first try.

Before the pregnancy, Brittany had set a goal to be in the best shape of her life going into it and then to do her best to maintain that strength and stamina right up to the due date. She stuck to that and really saw it through. After all we'd learned about the importance of diet and sleep habits from Dr. Heitsch, she believed that being in shape and eating well would help her deal with the changes to come. She cut out most caffeine and continued to exercise hard throughout the *entire* pregnancy. She was nine months pregnant and still working out. People couldn't believe what great shape she was in. Brittany talks a lot about my discipline in terms of training and getting ready to play each game, but I was in awe of her work ethic and daily regimen.

Throughout the pregnancy it was amazing to watch not just Baylen's growth inside of Brittany but also the way her body naturally responded to the new life. She was meant to be a mom. She did whatever she could to care for the baby growing inside her. And if I can say so myself, she was a sexy pregnant woman! People talk about the "pregnancy glow," but Brittany really did have a glow about her that was remarkable. Plus, I also couldn't get over the amazing fact that what she was carrying inside her was a product of our love. She was the happiest I had ever seen her, and we would sit up for hours at night and watch her belly shift from side to side. Baylen was nonstop from the get-go.

A lot of people tried to prepare me for the birthing process. I kept hearing, "You haven't seen anything till you see your child born." And they were right. If you don't believe in God or if you have any kind of reservations about your faith, watch a baby being born. It's hard to witness an event like that as anything other than a miracle from God, evidence of his handiwork.

Leading up to the delivery, I was really nervous for Brittany. I wanted everything to go well, but there was only so much I could control. I tried to prepare myself mentally in case something went wrong or they needed to do a C-section. You hear stories about thirty-hour labors and the intensity of the pain. I'd experienced my share of pain on the field, but nothing like this.

My role in the delivery was to be her coach. "Brittany, what do you want me to do? I'll hold your hand. You can squeeze my hand off if you want. You can punch me in the arm. You can do whatever you want. I'm here to support you and help you any way I can."

As it turned out, my biggest job during the delivery was to hold one of her legs. I wound up providing the leverage for the final push. Brittany was a champ. She only had to push for an hour, but that was some hard-core pushing. To my surprise, the first words out of her mouth after Baylen popped out were "That wasn't so bad. Let's do it again." He was born seven pounds, seven ounces, at 2:22 p.m. on January 15, 2009—which also happened to be my thirtieth birthday. I don't think you can write a better script or story for the birth of your first child.

Some people have asked how I would compare the Super Bowl win to the birth of my son, and I'd say the emotions were similar. I was crying as I watched Baylen come into the world, and it was such a special moment to see Brittany hold her firstborn child. Then there was the incredible feeling of holding this tiny baby in my arms for the first time, looking at Brittany and laughing and crying at the same time, saying, "We created this little guy." It was an amazing experience. The way I saw it, that day in the hospital and that moment on the field in Miami were both dreams come true—all the waiting, all the preparation, and the feeling that God had done all this and worked it out in his own time.

In some ways I think Baylen was the missing link in our lives. I can't wait to get home at night because I get a chance to read him a story before he goes to sleep and maybe change a diaper or two. It doesn't matter what we're doing; I'm just glad I get to be with him. That prospect helps me focus throughout the day and get everything accomplished so I can make it home as soon as possible. In the past, I might have called Brittany and said, "Hey, babe, I'm going to be thirty or forty-five minutes late." I can't make that excuse anymore because if I don't make it home in time, Baylen is already asleep in his bed. This little guy has been part of the process of my becoming more responsible in areas of my life I hadn't really thought much about before.

I can't wait to be all-time quarterback for my kids. I'm visualizing the backyard matchups already. And the girl, when she comes along, will be right there in the middle of the game. I'm fairly sure we'll have a girl at some point because I don't think Brittany will stop until that happens. She loves having a little boy, but her eyes light up whenever we talk about the possibility of a Brees girl.

The Name

If you want to know the truth about the name *Baylen*, we made it up.

Brittany and I kept the baby name book industry in business

for the last five months of her pregnancy. We settled on a list of names for boys and a list for girls and then whittled them each down from there, almost like the baby name playoffs. But from the minute we discovered we were having a boy, we nixed all five of those boys' names and started over. They just didn't feel quite right.

Brittany would suggest a name, and I never once said, "Oh, that's nice. I like that." Instead, I would say, "No, there was a kid back home named Buford who used to pick on me in second grade. We can't name him that." Of course we never seriously considered Buford Brees, but you get the picture. Suddenly, instead of having lots of names in the running, there were no names at all in the baby name playoffs.

We turned to the books again. We bought every baby name book we could find, poring through them and going online to look up every name that's ever been given to a child on the planet. But no matter how hard we tried, we couldn't find anything we liked. We were settled on the middle name Robert, after my grandfather Robert Ray Akins, the legendary Texas football coach, but we weren't making any progress on the first name.

It was the fourth quarter in the baby name playoffs, and time was running out. As I recall, two days before Baylen was born, Brittany looked at me, inspired. "What about Baylen?" She didn't find it in any of the books we'd bought or on any of the Web sites. It just came out of her mouth.

My first reaction was "It sounds like it's missing a letter. Maybe an *r* somewhere in there."

I'd heard of Braylen before and even Daylen, but I'd never met a Baylen. At first all I could think about was a farmer balin' hay.

"I don't know."

"I like it; it's the one," she said.

I should have known right then that the playoffs were over. She called everybody she knew, asking, "What do you think about the name *Baylen*?"

Everybody loved it. And I have to admit, it grew on me. Now when I look at my son, I can't imagine him as anything but Baylen. As usual, it was a good call on Brittany's part.

The Hair

In the 2008 off-season, I started growing out my hair during training camp and continued throughout the season. Because of the way 2007 had gone, I decided to be like Samson—to let my hair get long as we built up our strength to win. It grew. And grew.

I have a picture of my dad holding me when I was a baby, and he had that classic long hair that was in style in the 1970s. The shaggy rock band look. When we discovered Baylen was on his way, I thought, *I want my son to be able to look back at old pictures and say the same thing about me that I said about my own dad. Who knows what the trend will be when he's a teenager.*

I said to Brittany, "I'm going to have long hair when he's born."

I'm a pretty clean-cut, short hair kind of guy, but by then my hair was almost down to my shoulders. Baylen will always have those pictures to look back on . . . and laugh at.

Commitment

After experiencing the pain of my parents' divorce, I was determined to break that cycle for my children. It's so easy for people to be hurt by their parents and then wind up doing the same to their own kids. My parents didn't mean to hurt my brother and me, but there's no way around it: divorce is painful.

I wanted to make sure I didn't repeat the same dynamic for the next generation.

Some people ask, "How can you be so sure? You can never say never, right?"

Here's what I believe. When I said "I do" to Brittany, I meant it. Nobody is going to tear us apart. As an added motivation, I know what it was like to deal with the impact of divorce, and I never want my child to have to experience growing up in two separate households. So when I put the ring on Brittany's finger, I said, "For better or for worse, till death do us part." Period. No matter how bad it could possibly get, I am committed. It's not about my happiness. It's not about a feeling. I committed myself to her for the rest of my life, and I promise *never* to walk away.

Because of that promise, there are certain things my wife and I have promised to each other about the way we interact. For example, when we argue—and we do have disagreements—she knows I will never tell her to shut up. Ever. I will say, "Sweetie, please, could you be quiet for a second? Can I make my point?" That has happened a few times. But I will never tell her to shut up or disrespect her, because we see that as one of the ways people close the lines of communication. Also, I will never call her ugly names or use profanity when we're arguing. I want her to feel safe to come to me and tell me what's on her heart so we can grow closer in our relationship. If I shut her down, nothing gets settled, and whatever we were fighting about will just fester and get bigger.

I feel like God has given us each other for a purpose, and if God gives you someone to work with that closely, you need to listen and learn. There's no excuse for acting in ways that lead to broken hearts or a fracturing of the relationship. I don't want to push my wife down; I want to see her reach her full potential. I want to enrich her. I want to love her and give myself up for her, just like the Bible commands husbands to do.

Brittany and I have had some difficult times in our mar-
riage—I think everyone does. The adversity can either pull
you together or pull you apart. Some of the most trying circumstances we've been through together have created a lasting
bond that's growing tighter every day. But it takes work, and
it takes commitment. It's not about being the perfect husband
or the perfect wife, because you're going to fail. I fail all the
time. It's about forgiving each other, listening to each other,
learning from each other, and allowing God to cement your
relationship through the hard times.

The thing God requires from us in that equation is commitment. If you give yourself an out, eventually you will take that
out. If you say, "I promise to stay as long as we both shall love,"
then there will come a point where you don't feel love. I guarantee it. What has to happen, instead, is that when you're in,
you're all the way in. There's no backing out. Quitting can't
be an option. If you allow yourself to say, "Well, if it gets bad
enough, I'll leave," how are you going to know when you've
reached that point? Brittany and I have vowed to stick it out,
no matter what, and will never even consider leaving. My hope
is that this kind of commitment will provide Baylen with a
strong family and also give him a good role model for his own
relationships down the road.

Whose Son Is He?

Our extended families try to see which of us Baylen takes after
most. My family will say, "I can't believe how much he looks
like you!" Brittany's side of the family says, "I can't believe
how much he looks like Brittany."

There's no question he has my blue eyes and my ears. But
he has her nose and mouth. As he grows, there are times when
I'll look at him at just the right angle or in a photo and it's

scary how much he looks like me. Then the other day we saw a picture of Brittany as a kid, and if you took away her long, blonde hair, they would be identical.

Brittany thinks he has my personality because he is all over the place. He's a ball of nonstop energy who can't sit still, and that's very much the way I am. He loves being outside and being around people. He likes constant stimulation and wants to be part of whatever's going on. It's no wonder he loved it when I held him up after the Super Bowl with all the confetti coming down, the lights glaring, the fireworks flashing, and the people celebrating. He didn't know what was going on, but he loved being in the middle of the action. When he's older, I'll be able to explain to him exactly what he was part of that night.

I do worry sometimes about the expectations he might feel being the son of an NFL quarterback. I saw that pressure in my little brother as we were growing up. Since we're so close in age, he had to follow in my footsteps as we went to high school. People asked why he wasn't a quarterback like I was. I don't want that to happen with my son. I would love to give him every opportunity to do whatever he wants in life. If he wants to play sports, we'll give him that chance. If he wants to be an artist or fly airplanes or build houses—I don't care. Whatever talents he's given by God, that's what I want him to do because I know that's what will make him most fulfilled and happy—following the path that was set out for him.

Baylen was the best thing that happened to me in 2009. But there was also a tremendous loss that year, a few weeks before the 2009 season began. It's one of those things that's difficult to talk about, but there's no way to truly understand my story without that piece. As I looked into the stands after the Super Bowl win and picked out many of my family, friends, and mentors who have been instrumental over the years, there was one face missing.

My Darkest Valley

There are some trials in life that you wonder how you'll ever get through. My mother's death was one of those. The news came on August 7, 2009, and I left training camp immediately to be with my family. I can honestly say that was one of the toughest experiences of my life.

My mom was an outstanding athlete from a sports-minded family, as well as a successful attorney in Austin, Texas, and at one time the president of the Austin Bar Association. But I didn't know her as an attorney or a political figure in town. I just knew her as my mom, the one who took care of my bumps and bruises. She gave me opportunities to play the sports I loved and get the best education I could. She was the one who sat beside me and helped me decide to continue with football when I was ready to quit in high school. She helped foster a vision of who I could be and encouraged me to go after my dreams. I owe a lot to my mother for these things.

My mother was there for me during a lot of crucial points in my childhood, yet there were also many times I needed her and she wasn't there. She had a pattern of unhealthy relationships, and as I progressed through high school, I gradually gained the maturity to see that ours was headed in the same direction. She was consumed with getting her own way, even if it wasn't in the best interest of her children. This caused some tense moments between us. But starting in my junior year of college through my first year in the NFL, the relationship with my mom really started to deteriorate. There were a variety of factors that created even more turmoil, and soon the divide between us became so wide that we spent the next eight years barely speaking to one another. It seemed like we could never get on the same page, and whenever we did get together, it resulted in emotionally charged confrontations. These issues took a toll on both of us, and it wasn't until after her death that I found out the reasons for many of these problems.

Brittany and I turned to the church and our faith more than ever during that time. For our premarital counseling, we met with a psychologist who volunteered at the church, and we were able to talk about the issues with my mom. The psychologist recognized immediately that the problems that existed between us were not normal in a parent-child relationship, and there could be something else going on. It was the first time someone had opened my eyes to the fact that my mom could be suffering from mental illness. As a kid, I never thought that my parent would have a problem like that. I was so accustomed to the extreme highs and the depressed lows that her behavior seemed normal to me. Had I only known then what I know now, I could have handled the situation differently. I ask myself the question often: *Could I have saved her?*

By the time I moved to New Orleans in the spring of 2006, Mom and I weren't communicating for long stretches. I felt like I was losing out on time with the family I used to be so close with. I tried to compartmentalize the situation with my mom so I could focus on all the positive things going on in my life. We were having a great season as a Saints team that year, and it was an unbelievable experience to be part of the resurgence of this city. But I couldn't shut out the effects of the separation from my mom. There was a piece of me that was always hurting for her because of the strain we had experienced. I had no idea what the future of our relationship would be—or even if there was a future for us. The only way I knew how to cope with it was to pray every night for her and for our relationship and to throw myself into every other aspect of my life, hoping that would make up for her absence.

When we found out Brittany was pregnant in 2008, a big thought looming in the back of our minds was my mom. When and how were we going to tell her? What kind of relationship would she have with our child? Would she do the same kinds of hurtful things to my child that she had done to me? How would Brittany and I handle it when she hit one of her dark periods like she so often did? As a parent, I knew I would give my life for my child, but I never thought I'd have to protect my child from my own parent. I had long since forgiven my mother and hoped she had forgiven me. But what you can forgive, you sometimes shouldn't forget. You have to remember if you're going to learn from those mistakes.

During her pregnancy, Brittany e-mailed back and forth often with my mom. She kept her up-to-date on her doctor visits, her due date, and the baby's progress. For quite some time my mom had been looking forward to a teaching trip to Ukraine. She would be gone for six months on a Fulbright teaching scholarship, working as an instructor at the University of Kiev. Things seemed to be looking up. She left in January, a few days after Baylen's birth. During that time, Brittany e-mailed pictures of Baylen and corresponded with my mom while she was in Ukraine. Mom and Brittany seemed to be getting closer through the communication. They also found common ground in talking about Ukraine, since Brittany is 50 percent Ukrainian. Mom even sent some small gifts to us from the country, and that meant a lot to Brittany. "I think things are getting better," she said to me once. There was an encouraging sign that spring when Mom e-mailed me from Ukraine: "Oh, I can't wait to meet my little grandson." I read those words and felt a flicker of hope for the future. We weren't there yet, but we were at least moving forward.

Mom was due back in the United States in the summer, and we were trying to figure out a time for her to visit that would work around her schedule and the start of the 2009 season. As I looked forward to the possibility of her visit, I had really mixed feelings. On one hand, after our communications while she was in Ukraine, I felt very eager to reconnect. On the other hand, the last face-to-face meeting between us had not gone well. Plus, Brittany and I were still unsure as to the role my mom would play in Baylen's life. I was hoping to begin a new chapter in the relationship with my mom, but there is no way to candy-coat history. The full truth is that my mom and I had a toxic relationship. When we were together, I felt like I was a different person. The negativity turned me into someone I did not want to be. I prayed about it constantly. I asked God to help us communicate and have a relationship. I searched for Bible verses that would help. I asked family members and friends for advice. But no matter how much I prayed and searched, I couldn't get past Mom's destructive attitude and how low I felt whenever we talked. After eight years of trying to salvage things, I was discouraged by how little progress had been made.

I loved my mother very much, and I always will. I never intended to hurt her, although I know I did. And now I don't want to hurt anyone who knew her and respected her by telling my side of our story. After all, she was my mother. But our relationship was a consistently difficult one. It was always on my mind, no matter what was happening around me. A lot has been written over the years speculating about what really happened between us. I'm hoping that others with strained relationships will find a little comfort and direction from my experiences, and maybe even learn from our mistakes. I truly believe people are brought into our lives for many reasons. Whatever those relationships are like, they teach us lessons. It's what you learn from those situations that makes you who you are. I made many mistakes with my mother and our relationship. There are so many things that now I wish I could change or would do differently. I learned that there are many things she did that I will never do as a parent. I have also learned that a lot of the best of my mom lives in me. At this point I have to forgive myself and learn my lessons.

When the News Came

On the first Friday in August, in the middle of training camp, Brittany came to the Saints practice facility unexpectedly. We had just finished practice, and Sean Payton came up to me. "Drew, Brittany is here. You need to go talk to her." I looked over at her holding Baylen, and immediately I could feel that something was very wrong. Although Brittany had brought Baylen to practices plenty of times, this was a closed practice, and under normal circumstances, no one would be allowed in.

I ran to her. She said, "Hold your son, Drew. I am going to tell you something, but I need you to hold your son. I need you to know we are going to get through this."

I took Baylen in my arms and sat down. She started to sob but was able to muster the strength to say, "Baby, your mom just passed away." All I could do was hold my son and my wife and cry. My heart sank to the ground, and I couldn't speak. *What happened?* We'd been planning her visit, and now we were planning her funeral instead.

Brittany said that she had gotten the call from my brother, Reid, and it appeared to be a suicide. I could not believe what I was hearing. This had to be a bad dream. I took some time with Brittany and Baylen and then tried to gather myself before going in to talk with Sean. I thought I was fine when I walked into his office, but the minute he stood up, I could see the sympathy in his eyes. I lost it. It took me a while to rein in my emotions before sitting down and talking about what had happened. Sean and I talked for a long while, and his words were very comforting at a difficult time. He was there to listen, and he also had some words of wisdom and encouragement as I dealt with this loss, both short-term and long-term. He told me to take as much time as I needed. "Allow yourself to grieve," he said. "You don't ever want to look back and realize you didn't let yourself feel what you needed to feel. We all handle the death of a loved one in different ways, but make sure you take enough time to do it properly. Don't worry about getting back here. We will be here for you when you return."

I walked very slowly back to my locker, still in a daze about the news I had heard. I gathered my things and tried to leave as quickly as possible, so as to not draw attention from any of my teammates. I called my brother as soon as I could to make sure he was okay and to find out exactly what had happened. I was waiting for him to tell me this was all a horrible joke or a big misunderstanding. He didn't. I asked him if it was possible that it wasn't a suicide or if there was some kind of confusion. It had to have been an accident. My brother confirmed my worst fear, as he had been the one who talked to the police that day. My mother had been visiting a friend in Colorado. She had packed prescription sleeping pills, pain pills, and antidepressants, some of which dated back to the 1990s.

I flew out to Denver the next day to be with my brother and to see my mother one last time. Being with Reid that day, when we were both in such a vulnerable state, felt right. We had been the two most important people in Mom's life, and it seemed appropriate for us to be able to say good-bye to her together. Having this time with Reid made it all a little easier.

My mom had left handwritten notes for certain people when she passed away. One of those notes was for me and Brittany and another was for Baylen. It was very hard to read them, but I hoped there would be some answers in them. As we started getting more information, the reality began to sink in that she had indeed taken her own life. The question that haunted all of us was "Why?"

We were hoping the cause of death would stay private, but unfortunately it became public once the toxicology report and autopsy were final. It took three months to get the official results, and we thought maybe by then the media would just leave it alone. They didn't. It's devastating enough to deal with the death of a parent, but facing her suicide seemed almost unbearable.

In the three weeks after her passing, as we all talked and worked through things as a family, I probably learned more about my mom than I had known my whole life. I had no idea about her early days and the secret mental and emotional problems she'd had. Even from childhood, she'd dealt with those demons by disguising them or hiding them. Family members tried to confront her and get her help, but she would become defensive and deny she had a problem. Her struggles only worsened as she got older. She certainly didn't talk about these issues with Reid and me, and she did her best to be there for us and be the best mother she could be in spite of her illness.

Mom's death was a crushing blow to our entire family. We made it through the memorial services, but they were extremely tough and emotional. I really appreciated all the people who came to the services to support our family. Our team owner, Tom Benson, flew Coach Payton and my closest teammates to the service. I hope they all know how much that meant to me.

Sometimes the best way to heal is by knowing how many people care. There's no way to describe the pain and all the questions that haunt you after something like that happens. I still couldn't accept the fact that my mom would never see her grandson. It was all she had talked about for the last six months—how excited she was to hold that little boy. I was overcome with feelings of regret, sadness, and shame that bubbled up from deep inside.

For the first time I was starting to realize how much her constant, internal pain drove her to do some of the things she did. It didn't excuse her behavior, but things made more sense to me. And when I thought about how she took her own life, I knew she must have been in such a lonely, dark place for her to feel like that was the only option. Instead of being angry at her for the ultimate selfish act, I felt sad for her. I knew she had acted out of her pain.

Unanswered Questions

Even with my new perspective about Mom's history, the first few weeks after her death were filled with confusion and unanswered questions. I felt anger at her for leaving us, guilt for not reaching out more effectively, and remorse over our strained relationship.

I also struggled with the spiritual implications of her choice. I sought counsel from people who know a lot more about the Bible than I do. Some Christians believe suicide is an unpardonable sin. They think God can't forgive such a heinous act. But friends and spiritual leaders in my life were able to show me how the Scriptures reveal the depth of God's love. The way to a relationship with God isn't by doing good things or keeping rules. My mom made mistakes in her life, but so have I. All of us have. The way to an eternal relationship is by accepting the grace God offers us. Had my mom asked for God's forgiveness as she had taken her own life? Did she have God's grace in her heart when she passed? If you have God's grace in your life, you can't be separated from him by a bad decision. Understanding more of the love of God gives me the comfort that my mother really is in heaven. And I feel confident she will be smiling down on us forever, because that is what she promised in her letter to me.

I had agonized over the broken relationship with my mother for many years. When she died, the truth about her emotional problems and mental issues spilled onto the deck of my life. That was the most intense time of mourning I've ever experienced. But gradually God started bringing healing in my life. I came to the realization that Mom was no longer in pain. I didn't have to hurt for her any longer. That relieved me, and in a way it gave me strength and enabled me to use all the concern and worry I once had for her in more constructive ways. I felt that for once in her life, my mother was finally at peace. Mom's death also brought the rest of the family much closer. We needed each other to mourn, and after going through that difficult crucible, we're stronger now than we've ever been. I never would have chosen to go down that path. But somehow God has brought good out of it anyway.

As the 2009 season got underway, the grief lessened and I began to see all the great times I'd had with my mom and all the good things she had given me. In a way, everything I'd been through gave me an incredible internal strength I never would have had otherwise. Who would have guessed that a season that started out in the midst of such a dark valley would end up on a mountaintop.

THE YEAR OF FINISHING STRONG

CHAPTER SIXTEEN

WITH ALL THAT had happened with Mom, my 2009 pre-season was off to a really rocky start. In the past I'd always been able to compartmentalize certain things and focus on the task at hand, but I'd never experienced anything like this before. The players and coaches were very supportive and told me to take all the time I needed, but I was honestly glad to be back with the team and get to work. Anything to take my mind off the tragedy of my mother's death.

As a team, we knew we needed to make this our year to change things. We'd been floundering the past two seasons, and it was time for a shake-up. If you want to do something you've never done, you have to prepare by doing something you've never done. We evaluated everything from 2007 and 2008 and found that the common denominator in the games we lost was "finishing." As we watched game clips and discussed what had gone wrong, that word kept bouncing off the walls. *Finish*. What would have happened in those seasons if we had finished half the games we'd lost in the closing moments? We would have been playoff bound, if not divisional champs.

As I looked around at my teammates that year, I saw we had a lot of people with God-given talent. But we needed something more than that—talent will get you only so far. Champions are forged from commitment, preparation, and discipline. I believed we could go a long way if we were willing to buy into everything that was being taught. I'm always looking for ways to motivate myself and others in the off-season. I told the guys that if we finished every game, we could not only win the division—we could get a first-round bye and be the number one seed. Even better, we could win it all. Instead of focusing on a bunch of different things we needed to do, we pinpointed just one. We kept it simple, and that phrase *finish strong* stuck. We all believed that was exactly what we needed to do.

On a Monday morning in April, we had our first off-season meeting to kick off our program. We went over the basic stuff—welcome; here is a recap of last season; this is what we expect from players; here are some things we need to improve upon as we look ahead. I had gotten the okay from Coach to have ten minutes with the team, both players and coaches, at the end of the meeting.

I had found a book with vignettes about average people who had done extraordinary things simply because they'd focused on finishing well. The book was *Finish Strong* by Dan Green, and I bought a copy for every member of the team. I also gave everyone a wristband that said, "Finish Strong." I read some favorite quotes that struck me about the power of seeing something through to completion. I was passionate about this, and I wanted the other guys to catch the same vision for the season ahead.

Finish strong became one of our themes for the year. In the weight room we promised to make the last repetition the best of the day. As we watched film, we focused even harder during those last fifteen minutes. And we took it out onto the field too. At the end of games when we might have faltered in the past, we hung tough. The offense made big plays, the defense created turnovers, and the special teams came up with game-winning field goals or returns. It was not just a mantra but a way of life. We took that phrase seriously, and it paid off.

That year was the most intense off-season and preseason I've ever seen. Our defense's mentality was *We've got something to prove to everybody.* Our offense saw their attitude and countered, *You're not pushing us around.* It got competitive fast. And it was truly a case of iron sharpening iron. We made each other better. We were confident we had one of the best offenses in the league. Our defense had heard enough about them being the weak link on the team. Our new defensive coordinator, Gregg Williams, created a new culture among the players: they were going to dial up the pressure, play aggressively, and not apologize. That attitude and talent came together, and I was seeing things I'd never seen before from our defense.

When the season began, we were prepared. No other team could bring more pressure than we'd already seen in practice. We had a fast and brutal defense and a high-powered, light-'em-up offense. And to top it all off, we had a healthy dose of confidence and were gaining that swagger with each workday. We believed there was no team we couldn't stop on defense and no team we couldn't outscore on offense.

Nine, Ten, Win Again

Before the season, in late June 2009, I took a USO trip to Guantanamo Bay, Cuba. Ever since I watched *A Few Good Men*, I've dreamed about visiting Guantanamo Bay. Gitmo's reputation as a tough and rugged environment for the Marines always made it appealing to me. I thought this might be my last opportunity to visit the troops there since President Obama had announced they were shutting down the operation. I have the utmost respect for our military, and I believe they're protecting us from enemies we can't even imagine. Because they do what they do, you and I can safely do what we do every day. To be there with those guys I look up to so much was the ultimate experience.

One morning the Marines invited me to get up and do physical training with them. I was jacked—I felt like I was going to a playoff game. I got up at 5 a.m. and hustled out. It was still dark when we arrived at the meeting point, a place they called the "mosquito tree." And for good reason. Not only were you fighting the thick, humid air, but you had to keep moving or else the mosquitoes would get you.

We got into formation and started running. I was following along in step, listening to the cadence, and there was a leader off to the side who would yell to help us stay in stride. We were running in three rows, with ten to twelve per row. He called off, "Left, right, left"—nothing complex—but the inflection in his voice and the rhythm of the footsteps washed over us. Somehow the chant kept us locked in and focused on what we were doing. He wasn't just telling us what to do; he was leading us.

This was new to me. I was trying to listen to the words and repeat them back like the Marines did, but I was a little hesitant at first, not wanting to shout out the wrong thing. They were yelling fast, and I was having trouble understanding some of what I was hearing, especially as the run progressed and everyone started breathing a little harder. The others seemed to know every word by heart, and they weren't shy about belting it out. But by the end of the training session, I had both the rhythm and the words, and I began shouting everything back to the leader like I was one of them.

As soon as I got the hang of the running and chanting, something clicked inside. I thought, *This is awesome.* I knew a part of that experience would stick with me, and there would be something for me to take back to my team. Sure enough, at one point in the run, they started a chant. Here's what the leader called out:

"When I say, 'One,' you say, 'Two.' When I say, 'Kill,' you say, 'For you.'

"One."

"Two!"

"Kill."

"For you!"

"When I say, 'Three,' you say, 'Four.' When I say, 'Kill,' you say, 'Some more.'

"One."

"Two!"

"Kill."

"For you!"

"Three."

"Four!"

"Kill."

"Some more!"

And then it was "Five, six. Kill, for kicks! Seven, eight. Kill, it's great! Nine, ten! Kill, again!" Each time he would go back to one and start over, so it took forever to get all the way through this chant. And you really had to pay attention closely if you wanted to keep up.

I'll admit, the words of the chant are harsh, but they're appropriate for these proud few. A Marine is not trained to keep the peace or direct traffic. A Marine is trained to kill and break things and mess up the plans of the enemy. The military doesn't kill for kicks, of course—it's just a chant. Of anybody on the planet, they know the seriousness and gravity of the mission. They live with the reality and the consequences of that responsibility every day.

As soon as I heard the chant, I knew it was something that would resonate with my teammates. But I figured the NFL wouldn't approve of me urging players to go out and kill. So I changed *kill* to *win*. Here's how our chant went during 2009:

"One, two! Win, for you. Three, four! Win, some more! Five, six! Win, for kicks! Seven, eight! Win, it's great! Nine, ten! Win, again!"

The chant is a reminder that as we play, we're striving to win not just for ourselves but for each other. And we're not just winning for the team; we're winning for the city and for our fans too. Every time we step onto the field, we're playing to win. And the next week when we come back, we're going to do it all over again. That was our philosophy for the season. Everybody would get hyped up before each game, and then we'd bring it in, and with every hand in the middle, I'd say, "*Win* on three. One, two, three. Win!"

There was a feeling of ownership and unity with the chant. We wanted to make other teams say, "What are they doing? Those Saints have something special, a unique bond." The cadence became popular, even though most people didn't understand what we were saying. It gave us an us–against–the–world mentality: if you're part of our team, you're part of a brotherhood that plays together and trusts each other and will fight to the end.

Starting Out Strong

For our first game, we played at home against a new Detroit Lions team. They had lost all sixteen games the year before, but there were many new faces on the sideline now—and they were hungry for a fresh start. We were prepared to get their best performance and their best game.

We blazed out onto the field with reckless abandon, not caring who we were playing. We scored on the first two possessions and kept adding to the lead, finally winning 45–27. That day was a career high in touchdown passes for me. It was just one of those games. Everybody was given opportunities and everyone made plays. It also made me the first player in history to throw six touchdown passes on opening day.

It felt good for our team to light it up for forty-five points, especially since the first game is always a question mark in regard to the other team's defense. No team shows much in the preseason, so it didn't help to watch film. Plus, the Lions had a new coaching staff, so we couldn't base much on past precedent. It was a good start to come out strong in the face of those unknowns.

But most significantly, we were starting to see what kind of a team we could be. You don't get that in preseason; it comes when you unite and face a common opponent. It comes when you collectively take on the challenges that are thrown your way. In the first game we saw all the weapons we possessed. We felt like we could step onto the field and score anytime we wanted.

The second game of the season was big because Philadelphia had just smoked Carolina, the winner of our division in 2008. Philadelphia had manhandled the Panthers on the road, and now we were headed to their territory. After the way they beat the daylights out of our rival, the Eagles were arguably the favorites in the NFC at that point. Lincoln Financial Field is traditionally a tough venue, and we knew the crowd would be a big factor in the game. It was going to be loud. We had to be ready for a sixteen-round championship bout.

We had built up a little history with Philly recently, this being the fourth time we had faced them in as many years. There had been some tough battles between the two teams, and every game had been decided in the fourth quarter. We knew we'd have to be at the top of our game offensively, and our key mind-set was to simply take care of the football. That's always the case, but it was especially important in that game since their defense thrives on turnovers. We needed to take it one drive at a time, one series at a time. We had to handle their pass rush. And most of all, we had to play with confidence and be explosive and take advantage of big plays whenever we could.

We methodically worked the ball on the first drive, and I hit Marques Colston for a fifteen-yard score. Their quarterback Kevin Kolb answered with a seventy-one-yard touchdown pass to DeSean Jackson to tie it up. (Kolb was starting that game because Donovan McNabb was out with a rib injury.) The first half we kept going back and forth like that. Both teams scored points in the last two minutes of the second quarter, and we went into halftime up 17–13. We'd played pretty well, but not great. We knew we could do better.

In the third quarter we opened up on them and scored quickly. We had to kick off to begin the second half, but our special teams forced a fumble and gave us a short field for a quick touchdown. Two plays later, we intercepted a pass and our offense came in and scored again. Later, Reggie Bush had a nineteen-yard touchdown run. Darren Sharper ran an interception ninety-seven yards for a touchdown. We were putting points on the scoreboard at will.

Toward the end of the game we were deep in our territory on our half yard line. It was fourth down, and we were up 41–20. There was really no way Philadelphia could come back unless we did something stupid. But statistically a team that punts out of their own end zone usually gets scored on quickly.

I went over to the sideline and said to Sean, "Coach, let's take a safety. We don't want to kick out of our own end zone."

Joe Vitt, our assistant head coach, has been around the league for thirty-one years, and he's Sean's trusted adviser. Joe headed over, and the three of us talked. We agreed that taking a safety was the smart thing to do, so I took the snap, ran along the back of the end zone, and tossed the ball out-of-bounds. We gave up two points but gained thirty yards of field position, and now there was no way they could block our kick and score quickly. I appreciated Sean's willingness to accept my input on plays and situations like this one. I just know that if I do recommend something, I had better make it work. Sean and I communicate very well together, and I would love it if I never had to play for any other coach.

We felt really good about the way we'd played on both sides of the ball. Only two games into the season, we had already scored ninety-three points. If we kept that up, chances were we were going to win a few games. But that wasn't our focus now. We weren't thinking about the Super Bowl. We just kept marching ahead to the next Sunday.

The third game we beat Buffalo by twenty points. In the fourth week we won 24–10 against the Jets, who had come onto the field unbeaten. Even so, I didn't feel like we'd even scratched the surface of our potential. I also knew we hadn't really faced adversity yet. We'd won every game up to that point by a double-digit spread, and we hadn't been forced to come up with a big defensive stop at the end of a game or run a two-minute drive and kick a last-minute field goal. We had finished the games we'd been in, but we hadn't come close to losing. What would happen when we did?

Battle of the Unbeatens

We were four games into the season, and so far we were undefeated. Every time we stepped onto the field, we had a vision that we could win. We *would* win.

In our fifth game, the week after our bye, we faced the

New York Giants. Five games in, they were also undefeated. They'd won the Super Bowl in 2007 and had been the number one seed in 2008, and this year they were at or near the top of the NFC in every category. They had the number one–ranked defense going into that game as well.

In each of the previous three seasons we had lost after the bye week. We decided that in order to get a result we'd never had before, we had to do something we'd never done before. Sean shook up the schedule and actually allowed the players more time off to refresh our bodies and minds. He was treating us like professionals, and it was our job to act accordingly.

The extra days off fueled the focus and intensity we put into preparation when we returned from the bye week. Plus, we had the added motivation of the Giants' vaunted defense, their impressive history, and their undefeated record. Additionally, Eli Manning was coming back to play in his hometown for the first time since he had entered the league. And there was also the drama of one of our players meeting up with his old team. Jeremy Shockey had been drafted by the Giants and had been on the team that won the Super Bowl in 2007. However, an injury to his left leg and ankle prevented him from playing in the postseason, and things turned sour with the team after that. He was traded to the Saints in 2008, and this was his first matchup against his old team.

Until Jeremy came to the Saints, we didn't have any players who really wore their emotions on their sleeves quite like he did. His personality was just what our team needed—someone with confidence and a little swagger. Jeremy was vocal. He was bold. He could get pretty fired up at times. And he had the attitude that if a ball was thrown anywhere close to him, it was his. He didn't care about getting hit; he was going to get that ball. There's a zone that Jeremy gets into—a certain frame of mind—and when he's in his element, he can't be stopped.

There's no linebacker or safety in the league who can cover him consistently. Someone might stop him here or there, but Jeremy is going to come back the next series and make a play. Guaranteed. I know that it can be tough changing teams, especially the day before training camp, which is when we acquired him, but he quickly bought into our philosophy of spreading the ball around and sacrificing for the good of the offense. His overall statistics have suffered because of it, but our success has risen to an all-time high.

Getting off to a quick start in this game was important to set the tone. Our philosophy was that the Giants may have had the number one defense in the league on paper, but they hadn't played anyone like us yet. We wanted to get the crowd involved from the start and then take over the game. That's exactly what we did. We scored thirty-four points in the first half on our way to a 48–27 win. We had stunned them. And with a touchdown catch and victory in the bag, Shockey had his revenge.

We were 5–0, and already people were looking ahead and talking about the Vikings and Saints. I knew it was too early to be counting any of our chickens, but in the back of my mind I was thinking, *Get ready to play those guys in the NFC championship.*

On the other side, in the AFC, we were watching the Colts go undefeated. They had some close games, but they were finishing them and winning. *Get ready to face the Colts in the Super Bowl,* I thought. Every time something came on TV about the Colts, I looked at it like a boxer at a weigh-in, where you stand nose to nose. That's how I envisioned the season playing out. We were going to win home field advantage, and the Vikings were coming to New Orleans. Then we would beat Indianapolis in Miami.

Rarely do things play out as projected because there are so

many variables in this game. A wild card team might make a run, or the favored team goes into a late-season swoon. But I could envision that scenario playing out, and if it did, I was going to be prepared.

Remember This Place

Next up was a road trip to Miami, and it was there we faced adversity for the first time all season. I knew we'd eventually have to be tested, and I was looking forward to it. You know it is going to come, so you might as well embrace it. I was anxious to see how we would respond. To that point, we had overwhelmed our opponents with scoring and defense. Miami proved to be a big challenge.

There's only one way to find out what's deep inside, only one way to forge your team's identity. That's through the tough times. When things don't go your way, how will you react? Will you give up? roll over? Or will you fight? All week long the buzz from outside the organization was that the Saints were good when we scored, but we couldn't win the close game. What would happen in a nail-biter? or when a dome team played in the heat of Miami?

One of Sean Payton's greatest strengths as a head coach is finding a way to give his players a simple yet concise motivational message when they're preparing for a game. That week he told our team that we would need every bullet in our gun—every weapon in our arsenal—to win this game at this moment in the season. "Expect to play the toughest game of the year on Sunday," he said.

We played as terribly as we possibly could at the beginning of the game. Early in the first quarter I made a bad decision and threw an interception when we were backed up in our own territory. Another one came a little later as a ball was tipped at the line of scrimmage. Those two interceptions turned into fourteen points for them. Penalties stopped drives, and missed assignments resulted in a barrage of negative plays. With every stop they made, the Dolphins defense got tougher to handle. At one point midway through the second quarter, I looked up at the scoreboard to see us trailing 24–3. We had violated all the rules about protecting the ball. Plus, we were playing on the road against a wildcat offense, meaning they can run and pound you all day and chew up the clock.

Late in the second quarter the Dolphins were driving, and our defense came up with a big turnover. We got the ball at our own forty-nine. We ran a couple of plays and made it to the twenty-one yard line with seventeen seconds left before the half. We had no time-outs. I couldn't take a sack, and any throw I made needed to be in the end zone or out-of-bounds to stop the clock. We could not get caught in-bounds, or else the clock would run out and we would miss our chance at a field goal.

We needed something good to happen. We needed some momentum. And soon. I took the snap from the shotgun and surveyed the defense. I saw Marques Colston up the seam just inside the five yard line. I had a quick decision to make. He wasn't technically in the end zone, but I felt like there was a place I could throw the ball where he could adjust his position to catch it and then reach across the goal line for a touchdown. It was worth a chance. Plus, I trusted the big man to make a play. I turned the ball loose, and he caught it at the two yard line, spun around, and thrust the ball toward the goal line. The referee signaled a touchdown, with five seconds left on the clock.

It wasn't time to celebrate yet, though. The review booth took over, and as we watched the replay on the JumboTron, it was clear that Marques came up inches short of the touchdown.

Without any time-outs left, we used the review time to strategize. We were in a predicament because as soon as they determined it wasn't a touchdown, they'd set the ball, the clock would start, and we'd have to be ready to snap the ball. A conservative coach would have attempted a field goal. Take the three points and head into the locker room. But the way I saw it, there was a huge difference between going into the second half down 24–6 as opposed to 24–10. On the other hand, if the Dolphins stopped us, that would be a huge momentum factor in their favor.

I was standing next to Sean as he went through the scenario, and he decided to send the field goal unit on.

"Coach, I'll get it," I said. "We need a touchdown here. I'll get it."

That's all I said, and that was all I needed to say. He knew exactly what I meant: I would sneak the ball over the line for the touchdown.

"Are you sure?"

"I'll get it."

Joe Vitt came over and joined the discussion. Sean trusts him like nobody else. Joe nodded at Sean, then looked me in the eye. "Do it."

"All right," Sean said. "Explain to the guys what you're doing."

He got the field goal team off the field and sent the offense back on. We huddled quickly, and I said, "Okay, we only have a few seconds left. We have to score. No false starts. I'm going over the top with the ball."

Miami had called a time-out previously to make sure they knew the situation, and now they were bowed up, ready for a goal line stand. We snapped the ball, and immediately I went airborne. Normally I could dive into a gap between one of the guys, but they'd filled all those gaps. There was no place for me to go but up and over. I broke the plane of the goal line, reaching out with the ball before the Miami defense engulfed me.

As crazy as it sounds, I knew as soon as we scored on that play we were going to win the game. I don't score many touchdowns, and when I do, I'm typically not emotional. I like what Bear Bryant said about "acting like you've been there before." But that day the emotion swept over me. I ran into the end zone and spiked the ball, and the crowd booed. They knew what I was saying to them: *This is the first of many. We are not done here. We'll be back soon.*

That touchdown was just what we needed. As we headed off the field, it almost felt as if we had the lead. The momentum shift was that big. Even though we'd played poorly much of the first half, we were into the game now. We knew we could use the adversity to propel us.

On the first series in the third quarter, Darren Sharper intercepted a pass and ran it all the way back for a touchdown. We traded a couple of scores and then rattled off a series of touchdowns. We scored twenty-two points in the fourth quarter and won 46–34.

I'll never forget the feeling of walking off the field after that game. We probably had about ten thousand Saints fans there, all of them decked out in black and gold and Mardi Gras beads. Once again they proved to be the difference in shifting the momentum to our favor. We greeted them after the game along the inner bowl of the stadium with high fives and appreciation. It was an awesome sensation.

All season we'd been hearing about our lack of a test and how we couldn't withstand a pressure-packed game. We had proved the critics wrong. And just as important, we'd come back from a twenty-one-point deficit. Winning like that on the road reaffirmed we had something special. As we headed into the locker room afterward, Coach Payton turned to us and said, "You'd better remember this place and the way you feel right now. We're coming back here in February, and we are going to have this same feeling then."

You can never rest on your previous performance and let down your guard for the next game, but there's nothing that can compare to that feeling on game day after a win. Those are the moments every retired player says he misses the most. After all the preparations, the training, the butterflies and jitters, there's nothing quite like sitting in the locker room with the guys you've been in the trenches with. We made it our goal to get back to the Miami locker room in February and have that same feeling after the Super Bowl.

Fighting Back

The game against Atlanta was *Monday Night Football* at its finest. We were 6–0 and on the heels of an emotional, come-from-behind victory. I always worry about how we'll bounce back from games like that. As much as adversity tests you, success will as well.

Atlanta was 4–2. They were a divisional opponent who had been to the playoffs in 2008. It was a big game because if we won, we'd take control of the division. If we lost, Atlanta would be just one game behind us. We knew what was at stake.

Atlanta struck first and kept the pressure on. I was sacked and fumbled the ball deep in our territory. They returned it a few yards for a touchdown. Another bad start.

However, in the second quarter we came back with three touchdowns. We were ahead 28–14 at the half. It turned into a wild finish with an onside kick recovery by the Falcons at the end of the fourth quarter. We didn't finish the game as strong as we wanted to, but it was a solid performance and we did what we needed to win.

Coming up against Carolina, the coaches wanted to keep us focused on the future and not our past accomplishments. Carolina had won our division the previous year and had been the number two seed in the NFC. Since I had signed on with the Saints, we had not beaten them in the Superdome. Two of those losses were on last-second field goals. The Panthers had no respect for our home field. We needed to instill a little fear and get back some respect.

But once again we didn't get things off to a very good start. Right off the bat they scored two unanswered touchdowns. I threw an interception and had a fumble that they recovered. All we could muster before halftime was two field goals. We were down 17–6 at the half, and the mentality very easily could have been *Here we go again, losing to Carolina at home.*

The Saints had never been 8–0 in their entire history, so winning that game would mean a franchise record. Things weren't looking promising at halftime. At the start of the third quarter, though, we scored a quick touchdown on a four-play drive that included a sixty-three-yard pass to Devery Henderson. That's when the tide turned. Our defense stopped Carolina deep in our territory on a crucial third down, allowing only a field goal. We got the ball back and scored another touchdown in the last seconds of the third quarter, tying the game 20–20.

We were down to the wire with another game that could go either way. But on our wrists were these rubber bracelets that said, "Finish Strong."

We got the ball in the middle of the fourth quarter and drove into their territory. We kicked a field goal for our first lead of the game. A few plays later, Anthony Hargrove forced a fumble and jogged in for a touchdown, making the final score 30–20. For the first time ever, the New Orleans Saints were 8–0. We had set the franchise record.

Once again we'd fought back from a fourteen-point deficit, and we were proving to our opponents and ourselves that we weren't going to accept defeat. Every time we stepped on the field, we expected to win, no matter what the situation. That three-game stretch—Miami, Atlanta, and Carolina—was a turning point in our season. It solidified our winning mentality, and I believe it set us up for everything we would accomplish later. We had found a lot of ways to win, but the common thread was that we had to overcome significant adversity in each game. In Miami it was the twenty-one-point comeback in the fourth quarter. Against Atlanta it was equaling our emotion from the week before on a national stage against a divisional opponent and grinding out a win. And with Carolina we came off a short week to face an opponent that historically had our number at home and then fought back from a fourteen-point deficit to set a franchise record for consecutive wins. Now we were battle-tested and ready for any challenge that lay ahead.

Any Given Sunday

The next week was one of those notorious games where you know on any given Sunday any team can beat any other team in the league. On paper it should have been a blowout. We were 8–0; the Rams were 1–7. But no team is entitled to a victory simply because they show up. Sure enough, as the game began, we weren't clicking. Their offense did a great job retaining possession of the ball and keeping us off the field. It was an ugly first half, and after only four offensive possessions, we were tied 14–14 going in at the half.

In each game so far that season, it seemed like someone different would step up and create momentum for us. One week it would be a defensive stop; another time it would be a special teams play or a touchdown reception; and in another game a big run seemed to open the floodgates. But against St. Louis, things were just blah. The offense wasn't flowing, and we needed a spark.

That spark finally came in the form of Courtney Roby and his ninety-seven-yard kickoff return. It was exactly what we needed to start the second half, and that run electrified our sideline. We led for the rest of the game, and at the end, when they had a chance to win, our defense held tough. We won 28–23.

It was certainly not a perfect game for us. Sometimes you have to grind your way through and find a way to win. They aren't always pretty, but a win is a win is a win, as we like to say.

In the week leading up to the Tampa Bay game, the coaches put it on the line. Sure, we were 9–0, but our last few games were nowhere near the performances we'd had earlier in the season. It had been weeks since we'd put together offense, defense, and special teams in one game. Offense had been turning the ball over and getting off to a slow start. Defense had been giving up too much yardage. Special teams had a big play in St. Louis, but we needed more consistency. Tampa Bay was a big rival, and they didn't fear us. If we wanted to win, we'd have to go in and play our most complete game of the season.

The Bucs went down on their first drive and scored seven points, but that was their last score for the rest of the game. Our defense forced four turnovers. Offensively it was a slower start again, but we finally got rolling and won the game 38–7. We'd finally put everything together again. Just in time too. We needed the momentum because New England was up next.

Brady and Belichick

People around the country had been asking, "Can the Saints stand up to a really good team like the Patriots? Can they beat Brady and Belichick?" This team knew how to win. They'd proved that with four trips to the Super Bowl—and three World Championships—in the past decade. They had an excellent quarterback, a defensive guru as head coach, and great personnel all around. It was clear we'd need our best game to beat them.

They were 7–3, but they had experienced some tough breaks along the way. They'd been ahead seventeen points in the fourth quarter against the Colts, and then came the infamous fourth-down play in their own territory late in the game. Our record may have been better, but there was no question this was a tough team.

We didn't need a motivational talk for this matchup. When the big games come around, we eliminate distractions and ignore the peripheral stuff, like the question of an undefeated season or the comparisons of Brees vs. Brady. More than anyone else, I knew this wasn't about me or a quarterback rivalry. It was our team against their team, our offense against their defense. It also wasn't responding to the media as they descended and tried to get us to give bulletin board quotes for the other team. "How are you going to stop Moss? Can they stand up to your receivers?" I understand they're just doing their jobs, but my job is to try to focus and prepare and not say anything that could be used to motivate the other team.

Our first priority was turnovers. Period. We had to better take care of the ball on offense and do whatever we could to take away the ball on defense. We hammered away at those fundamentals. Even at 10–0, we felt like we still had something to prove. We wanted to show everyone that we belonged in the upper echelon of teams. We wanted respect, and the only way to get that was to earn it. And the only way to earn it that week was by beating the Patriots.

The night before a game, our team always gets a recap

of the keys to victory and a motivational story or speech from Joe Vitt, our fiery and passionate assistant head coach. These moments with Coach Vitt have become legendary, from his talks about teams he has coached in his thirty-plus-year career to highlight clips from *Rocky, Gladiator, Goodfellas,* or our own season. On this occasion, Coach Vitt charged us to think about all the people in our lives who had brought us to where we were right then. He encouraged us to think about how much they'd taught us, believed in us, and loved us. There was a moment of silence as we all reflected on those individuals. Coach Vitt then said, "Guess what? They will all be watching you Monday night." That set the tone, and we never looked back.

The first play of the game made a statement: I sent a deep ball down the sideline to Devery Henderson for a huge play. This was our night. We scored on all but one possession in the first half and continued the onslaught into the second half on our way to a 38–17 victory. We also set a club record for average yards per play, which may not seem like a big deal, but averaging ten yards per play is a ton. Our aggressive mind-set served us well as we put together a complete team perfor-mance, and it was also the game that finally caused people to believe in us. In their minds, we weren't for real until we beat a team like the Patriots.

At that point in the season, there were two teams at 11–0: the Saints and the Colts. We were flying in the locker room. We knew we had achieved our goal for that week. But an emo-tional win on Monday sometimes means disaster on Sunday.

Steep Hills Yet to Climb

The Washington Redskins played an amazing game against us the next week. When you're 11–0, you know every time you step on the field, you're getting the opponent's best because they would love to knock off the undefeated team. The scariest teams to go up against under those circumstances are those you think have nothing to lose. Teams that are out of playoff contention are often the most dangerous because this game is their Super Bowl.

Once we were past New England, it felt like we were in the homestretch. An undefeated season was within our grasp. But our coaches warned us in advance that the game in Washington would be hostile, cold, and physical. The Redskins would try to take away our perfect record. Sean emphasized that in some cases, like the New England game, the hill to climb wasn't as steep as you'd originally thought. But he warned that this hill in Washington was going to be treacherous. He was right.

Almost immediately they went up 10–0. Another bad start. We came back and tied the score. Their offense stayed on the field and kept pushing, driving, and before we knew it, we were down by ten in the fourth quarter. We kicked a field goal to close the gap to seven. With the clock winding down, they had a chance at an easy twenty-three-yard field goal. The ball missed to the right. That would have sealed the game for them, but we now had an open window.

This was our moment to finish strong. It took us thirty-three seconds to drive eighty yards in five plays and score the tying touchdown. In overtime we recovered a fumble and hit an eighteen-yard field goal to end the game. We could finally let out a sigh of relief. We were undefeated in twelve games. We had finished strong.

A week earlier, people had been wondering if we could beat a team like the Patriots. Now they were saying the only team on our schedule that had a chance to beat us was the Cowboys. But Sean Payton was clear about Atlanta. Divisional games on the road are always tough. There are no gimmies, no matter what the team's record or standing. The most important game of the season is always the next game.

All year we had been playing with confidence. When we walked onto the field, we felt like we were going to win. We believed somebody on our team was going to make a big play, and no one was sitting around waiting for it. We all wanted to be that person.

The game against the Falcons was pretty low-scoring by our standards. Our defense did a great job of holding them to field goals in the first half, but we didn't get many opportunities offensively. At the beginning of the fourth quarter, we were tied 23–23. We drove down and kicked a field goal to take the lead, chewing up over eight minutes on the clock along the way. With a little over a minute to go, our defense came up with a big fourth-down stop. We took a knee and won the game 26–23. It was one of those wins we really had to sweat for. The kind that made us feel like we were being prepared for something. And maybe we were. Dallas was coming the next week.

Letdown

Heading into the Dallas game, we had a lot going for us. We were 13–0, and they were 8–5. We had the home field advantage. And all week we'd been hearing about how poorly the Cowboys play in December.

But even with those factors in our favor, we knew how talented the Cowboys were. They also had something to prove from the game in 2006 when we went to Dallas on a Sunday night and beat them badly. Whatever the outcome of this game, it was possible that we could face them in the playoffs in the near future.

They took a 14–0 lead quickly, and it was 17–3 at halftime.

In the third quarter they scored again, making it 24–3. We nailed two touchdowns in the fourth quarter to pull to 24–17. When their field goal attempt bounced off the upright with a little more than two minutes left, I thought we were on our way, just like in the Washington game. I was going to throw a Hail Mary, and then we would score and win in overtime. Instead, I got sacked and fumbled the ball. Time ran out.

The undefeated season dream was over, and we were all extremely disappointed. It was a tough day in the locker room because you don't get many chances at perfection in the NFL. Only two teams have accomplished that feat in the regular season: the Patriots and the Dolphins. To go so far—three games shy of a perfect regular season—and come up short was a big blow. Now that dream was gone . . . *and* we'd lost to a rival team.

It was too early to throw in the towel, though. While we played and strove for a perfect season, that loss to Dallas might have been the best thing that could have happened to us in the long run. In many cases, disappointment is what prepares you to achieve greatness in the future. This loss also identified some glaring problems that had been swept under the rug for some time. You see, as long as you're winning, you are much more apt to let the little things slide. Winning cures everything in our business. We were due for a wake-up call. There were too many little things that were beginning to catch up with us. Fundamentals and details were lacking on both sides of the ball and needed to be corrected. Whether it was a blocking scheme or a route concept on offense or a coverage scheme or a blitz adjustment on defense, we weren't as sharp as we'd been earlier in the season. It was true that we had quite a few injuries and young players who were thrust into the lineup, but no excuses. Sometimes a loss allows you to recognize your weaknesses and make corrections, and in the end you'll be better off for it.

Home field advantage was on our minds the next week against Tampa Bay. But we faltered again—this time in overtime. Going into that game we talked about our slow starts with Atlanta, Washington, and Dallas, so the coaching point was a fast start. We must have listened well because after three possessions, we were leading 17–0.

However, our offense would not score any more points that day. The Bucs, on the other hand, converted a field goal and two touchdowns to tie us with under three minutes to play in the fourth quarter. We drove down the field, and with time running out, we set up for a thirty-seven-yard field goal from the right hash mark. Garrett Hartley lined up for the game-winning kick, but his attempt sailed wide left. He was crushed. But the game came down to a lot more than that one play— we simply didn't finish well. We went into overtime, and they won the coin toss, drove into our territory, and kicked a forty-seven-yard field goal. Game over. We lost, 20–17.

If you ever wanted to see a textbook case of "losing by inches," this was it. There were three drives where we missed getting a first down by six inches or less. When you're winning, certain things might go wrong, but you brush over them. Suddenly, those little things—those inches—were costing us games. This was the end of our season, when we were supposed to be peaking. We weren't even close.

We played Carolina in the final game of the regular season. That game was supposed to determine home field advantage throughout the playoffs, but Minnesota had also lost their last two games and already had four losses, so we had the number one seed no matter what. Before the game Coach Payton called me into his office. I knew he would probably be asking me to sit out the last game to avoid any potential injuries, so Flutie's mantra was running around in my head: "Never let your backup see the field." But after we talked, it was clear to both of us that the best thing to do was to rest certain guys and for our team to get healthy and ready to go. We wanted all the weapons in the arsenal going into the first playoff game. I was excited to see Mark Brunell get to start under the circumstances. He deserved it.

We ended up losing to Carolina, 23–10. That brought us to three losses in a row to finish out the season—not exactly how you want to go into the playoffs. The questions started flying. "How are you guys going to be ready to play? Which Saints team is going to show up? Is it the 13–0 Saints? Or is it the team that finished 0–3?" It was true—we really hadn't played a complete game in about five tries, going all the way back to New England. We also knew that the teams who tend to do the best in the playoffs are the ones on the rise. They're hitting the playoffs on a five- or six-game winning streak as opposed to a three-game losing streak. But none of that was about to stop us. One of the strengths of our team is our ability to ignore the critics, disregard the media, and block out any distractions. We try to focus on the process and trust the plan.

One of my mentors, Tom House, calls me every Monday after a game—something he has done since 2006. It's helpful to have someone who's an outsider looking in, and almost without fail, he offers me one observation that hits the bull's-eye. He called me after the Dallas loss and said something that stuck.

"Drew, sometimes you focus so much on the result that you lose track of the process. You're thinking so much about winning, winning, winning that you forget the process it takes to win." Tom said something else that took me a while to understand at first. "There are certainly times when you can care too little. But there are also times when you can care too much."

Tom was right: we were putting too much pressure on

ourselves. We had forgotten that the game of football is simple. Obviously you have to work hard and do whatever it takes to achieve your goals. But there's a point where you have to relax. You have to trust what you've learned and put your confidence in the people who have put you in your position. Once you've prepared as well as you can, it's time to relax and play. That releases the pressure to perform and allows you to be who you were meant to be.

There's a saying I love that goes like this: "The will to win means nothing without the will to prepare." In other words, you need to put as much emphasis on the process as you do on the result. It was time to get back to the basics and remember the process: one game at a time.

The message Coach Payton had for everybody was "Listen up, guys. Forget what everybody's saying. The media is going to try to tell you that no team has ever lost the last three games of the season and then come back and won the first playoff game. They'll give you every reason why resting players is the wrong decision. What you have to do is believe in what we're doing and trust the plan and the process. We're going to get our guys healthy and put ourselves in the best position to win the next game."

It's human nature at 13–0 to get carried away and somehow think we were entitled to make it to the Super Bowl. But that's not how things work. We still had to take care of business, one game at a time. If we didn't win the first playoff game, the whole season would have been for nothing. We had a sense of responsibility to prepare and get ready. It was time to block everything else out and focus on the here and now.

This time the here and now came in the form of the Arizona Cardinals.

THE ROAD TO THE SUPER BOWL

IN THE WEEKS before the playoffs, all we heard from outside the organization was that no team had gone to the Super Bowl on the heels of three regular-season losses. People speculated about which team would show up—the lackluster team from the past few weeks or the dedicated guys who had been finishing strong the majority of the season. We did our best to zero in on what our coaches were saying and ignore the questions and media hype.

We watched the first round of the playoffs with interest because the winner of the Packers–Cardinals game would face us in the Superdome. It was a wild game with a lot of back-and-forth, and Arizona eventually pulled out a win in overtime. We knew they had expended a lot of energy on that game, emotionally and physically. But if anyone was up to the challenge, it was the Cardinals. They had gone to the Super Bowl the previous year, and their offense looked outstanding against Green Bay. We had a huge opportunity ahead of us, and it was time to get prepared.

In football and in life, it's amazing how many big results depend on the little things. When you're experiencing success, it's easy to gloss over those details. As the playoffs loomed ahead, we knew we couldn't afford to get sloppy. So we encouraged each other to look at the goal sheets we'd filled out at the start of the season. What were our team goals as an offense and a defense? What personal goals did we set? Each player looked in the mirror and asked, *What can I do better? What do I need to do to fulfill my role on this team the best way possible?* In any area we were coming up short, we needed to take specific steps to adjust and modify. When we took care of the process, the end result would take care of itself.

One of the little things we wanted to focus on in the matchup against Arizona was letting our presence be felt. Our goal was to make this the most physical game we'd played all season. At that point, it wasn't about the Super Bowl. We saw only Arizona.

Making Our First Statement

As was the case in almost every big game that season, we got off on the wrong foot. On Arizona's first play from scrimmage, Tim Hightower took a handoff and ran through a big hole for a seventy-yard touchdown. That was a huge boost for Arizona, and we knew we couldn't let them capitalize on it or use it to set the tone for the rest of the game. It was time for our offense to answer the call.

We drove down the field, and with each play our intensity picked up. We tied the score on a short run by Lynell Hamilton. Then, on the very next play from scrimmage, our defense forced a fumble. Darren Sharper picked up the ball and returned it to the Cardinals' thirty-seven yard line. On that drive I found Jeremy Shockey in the end zone, propelling us into the lead. Reggie Bush kept the momentum going with a forty-six-yard touchdown run, and later he had an eighty-three-yard punt return for another touchdown. The Superdome went electric, and it was hard to hear anything in the stadium above the roar of the crowd.

We scored on five of our six possessions in the first half—finally, the fast start we'd been looking for. After seeing Arizona score fifty-one points the week before against Green Bay, we knew how important it was to score early and often.

We put the Cardinals away with a final score of 45–14. We had made a statement to any team coming into our house that we were ready. They could forget those last three games of the regular season. We had trusted our process, even though it had been questioned by the talking heads on television and other people who were throwing in their two cents. We had proved something, and now we would be hosting the NFC Championship Game for the first time in team history.

Destiny Beckons

Based on records alone, the consensus was that the Vikings and the Saints were the best teams in the NFC. The Vikings had taken some heat for losing to Chicago, Arizona, and Carolina toward the end of their season, and everyone wondered how they would do against the surging Cowboys in the NFC divisional playoff. As it turned out, there was no need to worry: the Vikings beat the Cowboys 34–3. That win gave Minnesota a date with us in the Superdome.

There's no doubt Brett Favre is a great quarterback. He plays with passion and heart every time he steps out on the field. He returned to the game and signed with Minnesota in 2009, and that season turned out to be one of his best ever. He had an all-star cast behind him too—the Vikings had a lot of weapons offensively, and their defense boasted one of the best pass rushes in the NFL.

Throughout the entire season, no team had scored a touchdown against Minnesota in the first drive of the game. We were determined to change that. After they scored on a run by Adrian Peterson, we answered with a screen pass to Pierre Thomas that he turned into a thirty-eight-yard touchdown. Was this a bit of foreshadowing about how the game would play out?

The championship game was close all the way. After we tied it up 7–7, Favre threw to Sidney Rice for another touchdown. Then I hit Devery Henderson in the back of the end zone to tie things up again, 14–14. That's how we went into the half.

In a game as tight as that one, every play, every decision, is critical. One turnover or one key completion can change the entire outcome of the game. In the second half, we got a big boost when Courtney Roby ran the opening kick back into Vikings territory for sixty-one yards. Pierre Thomas had a nine-yard run that put us up 21–14. But the Vikings came right back with another touchdown by Adrian Peterson. The score was tied again, 21–21.

Our defense came up big with a fumble recovery at the beginning of the fourth quarter. I hit Reggie Bush with a pass that was originally ruled just shy of the end zone. But after a review it was determined that as he spun around, the ball broke the plane of the goal before he went out-of-bounds. That put us up 28–21. We took the ball away again, this time deep in our territory, but we were forced to punt and Favre brought the Vikings back downfield. With about five minutes to go, Adrian Peterson rushed for his third touchdown of the day.

We couldn't manage to score, and we gave the ball to the Vikings again. They began to drive and were gaining quality yards on every play. They were in our territory at third down and fifteen, with about twenty seconds left. They were just outside field goal range, and they needed one more completion to advance the ball and attempt a long field goal that would give them the lead with mere seconds left in the game.

Things weren't looking good for us, but somehow we knew we were going to win that game. The whole team felt like we were going to stop Minnesota. We didn't know how, but we were going to find a way. Then a "destiny moment" happened.

Favre scrambled to his right and threw back across his body to the middle of the field. He has probably thrown that pass a thousand times, but this time Tracy Porter jumped in front of the receiver and intercepted the ball. That was our moment; that was our opportunity.

We went into overtime and won the toss. Pierre Thomas had a good return that set us up at our thirty-nine yard line. We drove into Viking territory but were stopped on fourth and inches just outside their forty-two. Sean had a tough decision to make: Should we go for the first down? Or should we be conservative and punt? Going for it was risky because if we didn't make it, the Vikings would have a short field. But Sean had been making those gutsy calls all year. We went for it. Pierre Thomas leaped over the line, giving us the first down.

We kept moving the ball and got to the Viking twenty-two, well within field goal range. It was up to Garrett Hartley to make the kick, and no doubt he was having flashbacks to a game earlier that season. We were playing Tampa Bay, and he'd missed a critical fourth-quarter field goal. We'd assured him that we win as a team and lose as a team, but he'd taken it hard. And now here he was getting ready to kick again—oddly enough, from almost the exact location as he'd been against Tampa Bay.

Now the kick was magnified a thousand times. With this forty-yard field goal, we go to the Super Bowl. Without it . . . well, we didn't even want to think about that possibility.

Garrett stuck it right down the middle.

He told me after the game that the night before he had woken up at 2 a.m. and called his father to describe the dream he'd had. In his dream, he'd made a game-winning kick from the right hash thirty yard line. Now that is a vision! There's no doubt in my mind that the adversity he'd faced against Tampa a month earlier had given him the strength and focus to nail this one—in his dream and in reality.

The fans went wild. Confetti flew. People screamed and hugged each other with joy. Brett Favre came up to me to shake hands. He had put his heart and soul out on the field that day. He'd been knocked around pretty hard, and he looked spent. It's a bit artificial to try to have a meaningful conversation with an opponent in the midst of so many cameras and so much noise, and when the gravity of the game hasn't even set in yet. But I was able to tell him how much I admire him and what an honor it was to share the field with him. Just knowing I was able to experience that moment with one of the greatest of all time, in a setting like that, was a memory I'll treasure for a long time.

Mission Miami

This dream was forty years in the making for the city of New Orleans. The fans had ridden the ups and downs of every season since 1967 but had never made it this far. And in the years since Katrina, the journey to the top of this mountain seemed loaded with even more meaning.

It had been four years of firsts. We snagged our first NFC South division crown. We hosted our first playoff game. We made it to an NFC championship for the first time. In 2009 we were the number one seed for the first time ever. On top of that, it was our first time hosting and winning the NFC championship. And of course, it was our first Super Bowl.

With each one of those firsts, people felt like they were part of something special. After all the losing seasons and the heartbreak of Katrina, their loyalty to their team and their city was paying off. I received a note from a man who had been a season ticket holder for forty-three years. He said he'd lived through the days of people wearing paper bags over their heads at games and calling the team the Aints. "Well, we ain't the Aints no more," he wrote.

The support from our fans wasn't confined just to the Superdome. They went with us as far as they could on our journey—and I mean that literally.

For our away games, we fly out of a private air terminal on charter flights. Traveling to and from the terminal, we have to drive down a half-mile-long frontage road off the highway. Starting in 2006 and continuing through 2009, fans would park along that road after an away game and wait for us. Win or lose, it didn't matter—we could count on them being there. It became a block party of sorts, and they brought food, played music, talked, wore their Saints jerseys, and had a good time. As we drove by, we'd roll down our windows, honk, and wave at them.

In 2009 the block party became supersized. As our winning streak continued, there were ten thousand fans waiting for us, then twenty thousand, and eventually as many as thirty thousand. It took us about ninety minutes just to make it down that half mile. It was like a parade—people surrounded our cars and leaned in to get autographs and touch us. They handed us songs they'd written about the team that incorporated players' names into the lyrics. They even threw baked goods like pralines and cookies into our windows. They showed their appreciation in every way imaginable. After a while, though, the crowd got too big, and there were safety concerns. The police put up barricades to keep people off the road, but that didn't stop us from honking and waving.

Now those fans were willing us on to "Mission Miami." No fans deserved it more.

Buildup to the Big Day

Coach Payton warned us about the two weeks leading up to the Super Bowl. He had been there before, when he was an offensive coordinator with the Giants and they made it to Super Bowl XXXV. Still, there was no way to truly prepare us for the whirlwind we were about to step into.

Most people don't realize that you have responsibilities to the league leading up to the game—the NFL requires an hour's worth of media every day. And usually that media time is in the middle of the day, so you have to structure your schedule around it. On the Tuesday before the game (which is typically a day off during the regular season), pretty much the whole day is taken up by media. We do the team picture in uniform and then get interviewed by reporters.

That probably doesn't sound like a big deal to most people, but when you're routine oriented like I am and you're getting ready for the pinnacle game in your sport, it's enough to make you sweat. I don't just have a routine I follow on game day; I have a routine I follow the entire week before a game. That preparation includes things like lifting weights, watching film, going to practice, throwing the ball, and going to sleep at a certain time. I don't let anything get in the way. With the new Super Bowl week schedule, I had to adjust and figure out alternate times to fit everything in.

Plus, there was the family aspect to consider. Brittany and Baylen were in the hotel with me, so I modified my routine to spend time with them. That discipline of being with my family is good for me—it keeps things in perspective and prevents me from overworking. My job is important to me, but I never want it to compromise the time I spend with my family.

I called a couple of friends before the game and asked their advice on how to handle the Super Bowl hoopla. Kurt Warner wears a Super Bowl ring, and I appreciate his outlook on life. His advice to me was to embrace the whole experience. A lot of guys see the media and the attention as intrusions, but he told me I had a great story to tell. As a team, we'd had an unbelievable season, and there was a lot to be excited about.

"Don't see it as a chore," he encouraged me. "Just embrace it." Kurt gave me some practical tips, like having the offensive line dinner early in the week before the crowds descended. Normally we had dinner with the big fellas on Thursday night, but that week we scheduled it for Monday instead. Finally, he encouraged me to enjoy the experience with my teammates and with Brittany and Baylen.

Kurt's words helped me go in with the mentality that all the requests and questions were an opportunity to highlight other players who don't get enough credit and to talk about our great fans and the city of New Orleans. To my surprise, I had a number of opportunities to talk about my faith as well.

Then I spoke with Trent Dilfer, another Super Bowl winner. He counseled me to come up with a routine around the new schedule and stick to it. He also advised me to pace myself, especially early in the game, and to savor the moment whenever I could.

When game day arrived, I tried to make things as normal as possible. We ate breakfast together as a team and then met at 10:00. The meeting typically lasts about an hour, and then from 11:00 until 3:00, we're on our own. The coaches don't want us out on the town, so that means we're in the hotel. This is a glimpse of what my pregame routine is like: I come to the room, study the game plan, walk through or visualize plays, and then order a sandwich and watch a movie. That's what I've found works best to get me mentally prepared for the game. On Super Bowl Sunday, instead of watching a movie, I spent time with Baylen and Brittany. I was as prepared for that game as I'd ever been, and it was a treat to just be with my family.

I never watch any of the pregame hype. I don't want anything the announcers say to influence what I'm thinking. It doesn't matter if the critics think we're going to win or lose—the important thing is for me to get my head in the right place. I would need my focus in this game more than ever.

Game Time

Sean's description of the Super Bowl—that it's "made for TV"—turned out to be on the money. The pregame lasted forever. We returned to the locker room and then sat for an eternity. Normally you prepare for the game, head onto the field, flip the coin, and play ball. But in the Super Bowl we came out of the locker room and waited. Then we watched the other team come out and waited some more. Queen Latifah sang a couple of songs, and the Walter Payton Man of the Year Award was presented. Carrie Underwood sang the national anthem, we watched the flyover, and they broke down the stage at the fifty yard line. It was nonstop distraction. We had to work to stay focused.

I was grateful for Trent's advice to pace myself. Sean reiterated that sentiment, warning that it would be easy to get pumped and then come crashing down thirty minutes later, before the game even started. You haven't taken a snap yet, and you're already exhausted. You just can't maintain that emotional high.

Finally we went onto the field for the coin toss. It was time to play Super Bowl XLIV.

As much as you prepare, you can't escape the butterflies. The Colts had a little edge in that department since most of their players had been in this spot in 2006. For most of the Saints, it was our first time in the game, and it took until late in the first quarter to finally breathe and say, "Man, it really is just a football game, like any other game." I love the scene from *Hoosiers* where the team from Hickory is playing in a huge arena. The coach has them measure the foul lane and the rim height, and they see that the floor has the exact dimensions as their own gym. Sure, there was a lot of hype surrounding this game in Miami, and there were 106 million people watching. But the field was still a hundred yards long just like in other games, and we were throwing around the same eleven-inch pigskin.

We'd prepared our whole lives for this moment. We knew how good our team was. We trusted that there was a bigger plan than what we could see. All we had to do was trust one another and play our game with great effort and full confidence.

On our first possession we went three and out. Our philosophy was to take a shot with the first third-down call of the day if we had the right matchup. We did, but my blood was pumping and I overthrew Robert Meachem by a hair. We just needed to calm down, find our rhythm, and get our legs underneath us. Peyton Manning drove the Colts down the field and hit a few passes, and they scored a field goal. We did a little better on our second possession, picking up a first down and moving to midfield, but the drive stalled and we had to punt again. At the end of the first quarter, Peyton found Pierre Garcon in the end zone. That put them up 10–0.

This was not the quick start we'd been hoping for. Being

two scores behind the Colts is not where you want to be, especially since their defense thrives off of opponents feeling like they need to be too aggressive and then overreacting. We needed to stay the course, trust the game plan, and execute to perfection. We belonged here.

Before the game, Coach Payton had given us some key words of advice: "Don't look at the scoreboard until the end of the game." We could come back. We simply needed to focus on each play, each series, one at a time. It didn't matter if we were up or down. Just trust the play and react.

We kicked a field goal on our next drive to make it 10–3, but we knew we needed more momentum going into half-time. We got the ball back and methodically drove down to their three yard line. We had first-and-goal from there after a big catch from Marques Colston, and I figured we would punch it into the end zone. Three plays later we were still a yard and a half short. Sean made a critical decision. On fourth down, instead of attempting the field goal, he took the risk to try for a touchdown. The Colts defense stopped us short. We all agreed with the call—we just didn't get the job done.

Now the momentum shifted to the Colts. We'd had the chance to tie it up, and instead we came away with no points. There were less than two minutes left in the half, and Peyton Manning is one of the best in the league at the two-minute drill. Surprisingly, Indianapolis wasn't able to convert; our defense held strong. We still had three time-outs, and we called one after both their second and third downs. They went three and out, and we had the ball with thirty-five seconds left. We drove downfield and hit a field goal as time expired, swinging the momentum back in our direction. We needed that shift to give us the guts to pull off what we were planning for the second half.

All week Sean had been talking about the onside kick play.

"It's not a matter of *if* we're going to call an onside kick; it's *when*." So when he called it in the locker room at halftime, we knew it was coming. We were ready. Sean wasn't scared to call an aggressive play like that himself, and he also instilled in us the confidence that we could pull it off. He not only tells you, "We're gonna do it," but he also says, "It's gonna work." When the second half started, it gave us an edge. *They don't even know what's coming.*

Our special teams executed the kick well, and there was a mad scramble for the ball at the bottom of the pile. There was never a thought in our minds of *What happens if we don't get the ball?* We were getting that ball. It was a scrum all right. But we got it.

When we get an opportunity like that, our offense knows we have to turn that recovery into points. And that's exactly what we did. I hit several passes right in the middle of their zone, and Pierre Thomas took a screen pass and did what he does best—bobbing and weaving through defenders and breaking tackles before finally leaping into the end zone. We pulled ahead, 13–10.

The energy had shifted in our direction. And best of all, we had kept the Colts offense on the sidelines.

There was still a lot of football left to be played, though. With a combination of passing and running, Indianapolis put together a ten-play drive and went ahead 17–13 with a little more than six minutes left in the third quarter.

Now it was our job to respond, and we drove down for a field goal to bring us within one point, 17–16. The Colts mounted a drive that took them into the fourth quarter. They made a crucial fourth down and two from our forty-six, but then their drive stalled. They set up for a fifty-one-yard field goal, but the ball sailed wide left. We would be getting the ball back with pretty good field position.

With the Colts' powerful offense, we needed to take advantage of every opportunity to score touchdowns. They had the ability to grind down the clock, and we couldn't risk coming up short at the final gun.

We methodically moved the ball downfield with a solid mix of runs and high percentage passes. We were at the two yard line when Jeremy Shockey ran a quick slant and I stuck him right in the chest with the ball, away from the defender. He leaned across the goal line, putting us up 22–17. While you usually just go ahead and kick an extra point after scoring a touchdown, in this situation there was no question: we were going for a two-point conversion.

Sean called a sprint-out pass to the right to Lance Moore. I stepped up to the line and immediately recognized that their defense was bringing all-out pressure. Just what we wanted. After getting the snap, I took five hard steps to my right. I looked up to see Lance sprinting toward the front pylon of the end zone. My throw wasn't perfect, but Lance made an incredible catch. Then he had the presence of mind to turn and get the ball across the goal line. As soon as he did, Colts defensive back Jacob Lacey kicked it out of his hands. The official on top of the play signaled that Lance didn't have full control and called it incomplete.

Lance has some of the best hands on the team. I looked at him and said, "You caught it, didn't you?"

"Yeah, I caught it!"

I went to the sideline. "Coach, he caught it."

After talking with Lance and some of the other coaches, Sean threw down the challenge flag. The replay showed that Lance had full possession of the ball and it crossed the goal line before it was dislodged. The officials reversed the ruling on the field; we were up 24–17.

That was huge. If we hadn't scored those two points, the

Colts could have taken the lead with a touchdown. Plus, the overturn of the call got us pumped up. With each play, we were feeling more and more like this was our game, like this was meant to be.

The Colts were on the march. The clock read 5:35—still enough time to come from behind. They were driving well, completing passes, getting first downs. They'd proven they could do this in the past—we'd seen Peyton Manning lead his team downfield at pivotal points and score to tie or win many times. From the sideline, I wasn't watching the game like a spectator. I was mentally preparing what we'd do if the Colts scored a touchdown. If that happened, we would need to get the ball downfield quickly and kick a field goal to win. I rehearsed possible plays for a two-minute situation in my head as I sensed the clock winding down. Three and a half minutes to go.

Suddenly I heard an ovation, and I looked up to see Tracy Porter running toward the end zone. He had stepped in front of a pass thrown on third down and five. *Boom*, he caught the ball and ran it back for a touchdown. The crowd went wild. I couldn't believe it. Our defense had done it again, and now we had a 31–17 lead.

There was still enough time on the clock for the Colts to make things interesting. At this point they could possibly score and attempt an onside kick. I would not allow myself to lose focus—I was going to be ready for whatever might happen. They mounted an incredible drive to our five yard line. On fourth and goal we stopped them with forty-four seconds to go, and the offense rushed onto the field to take one final knee and run out the clock.

As I ran out to the huddle, I looked around at the field and the stands. One thing I've learned over the years is that you have to take time to enjoy the moment and the fruit of your labor. Those moments don't come very often, so when they do, you have to soak them in so you can remember them the rest of your life. We had worked too hard and the journey had been too long to let this pass. The fans were cheering louder than I'd ever heard them before. On the sideline, the guys were embracing each other and jumping up and down with joy. The Colts knew it was over. Time ran out. Our time had come. The Saints were the Super Bowl champions!

I gave all my linemen a hug—every one of them. They had given such a dominant performance. I had been sacked only one time during the whole game. You can talk about the MVP trophy all night, but without those guys doing their job, I wouldn't have had a chance to make those plays. "I love you guys," I said. "We did it."

It's those moments, those relationships, that remind you, *Man, this is what it's all about.*

Back in 2006, when we'd made our failed run for the NFC championship, Joe Vitt had said, "When we win a championship together, we will walk together forever. Nobody can ever take that away from you. There will always be a special bond between the men in our locker room because we'll know we did this together."

He was right. No matter what happens from here on out—ten years from now, twenty, thirty, or even fifty years—we can look back to that moment and those guys who made it happen. That season will be a part of us forever.

The Baylen Moment

As soon as the game was over, there was mass chaos on the field. I was surrounded by media people ten deep. Interviewers were yelling out questions, and cameras and flashbulbs were going off everywhere. My first thought, though, was the guys on the other side of the ball. I respect them a lot—on and off the field—and

I wanted to reach out and say, "Good game." I found as many as I could, but the media barrage had me surrounded.

Then a camera came out of nowhere, and a voice said, "Hey, Drew, you just won the Super Bowl. What are you going to do now?"

"I'm going to Disney World!" I shouted.

At that moment I was thinking about all the times in our backyard when my little brother and I were playing Wiffle ball. We reenacted this scene over and over as we were growing up. Reid would hit a home run over the back fence, and as I ran to get it, I'd yell, "Hey, Bro, you just hit a home run. What are you going to do now?"

"I'm going to Disney World!" Reid would shout as he ran the bases.

You joke about that stuff as a kid, and now here I was living it. It was actually happening. It seemed completely surreal, but the whole time I tried to tell myself, *Enjoy the moment. Just take it all in.* And there are some images that are permanently freeze-framed in my memory. I can still see the expression on my teammates' faces. I can picture guys hugging their wives and kissing their children. I can imagine the confetti as thick as rain. I can see fans dancing and saying, "Who dat!" And on the JumboTron are the words *World Champions.*

They called me onstage, and the Lombardi Trophy was brought through the gauntlet of Saints players by Len Dawson, a Purdue great and a Super Bowl champion himself. All our guys were touching the trophy as it went past. As that was happening, Brittany was fighting her way through the mayhem and heading toward me with Baylen. From up onstage, I leaned down and gave her a kiss. Then she handed Baylen to me. That was when it really hit. All those rough patches on the journey—the injury, the rehab, the hurricane, the new team— and now we were really here, Super Bowl champions.

I stood there with my little boy, and I was overwhelmed. I told Baylen how much I loved him and how much he meant to me and what an inspiration he was to me. I thought of my mom, who I believed was smiling down from heaven, and all my family and friends who were there watching.

"We did it, little boy. We did it," I said.

He sure didn't mind all the commotion. He just seemed to take in all the excitement and the confetti and the lights and the cheering people. Of course, he had no idea what was going on. I can't wait to tell him what a special moment that was for his daddy—one of the greatest moments of my life.

I handed Baylen back to Brittany and gave her a kiss before stepping up for the trophy presentation. As Sean gave me the trophy, I couldn't believe this was actually happening. I kissed it and just stared at it for a while, looking at the reflections and knowing how long we'd waited to look in that mirror.

When I was told after the game that I had been named MVP, I was blown away. Up to that point I was still trying to soak in the fact that we'd won the game and the World Championship. I was humbled and grateful—I had a lot of teammates to thank for putting me in that position.

After the game Michael Irvin said to me, "You don't realize what just happened to you."

I didn't understand what he was saying. "What do you mean?"

Michael has won three Super Bowls and has been part of outstanding teams. He was referring to the MVP title specifically, saying that this was a life changer. Not that I'll look at myself differently or approach life differently, but that others perceive you in another light. Being a Super Bowl champion was my dream and my goal—it was what we'd worked so hard for. The MVP honor was just icing on the cake.

That was a great moment—for our team and for the entire

city of New Orleans. Nobody would have believed after August 29, 2005, that this was possible, but here we were. Dreams had become reality. We had won the Super Bowl, and we had done it for our city and our fans. I couldn't think of anyone who deserved it more.

The Parade

If there's any city that knows how to put on a parade, it's New Orleans. In most places, the Super Bowl parade is something the winning city starts planning after the game is over. You win on Sunday, and you have a celebration in your city on Tuesday. It's usually pretty basic: the city puts together a route, the team rides around in convertibles, and the coaches and players go up to a microphone and say a few words. The community embraces the excitement for a day and then goes on about their business. Not so in New Orleans.

It didn't matter if we won or lost—our city was determined to have a parade for us. And in a way, they'd been preparing for the parade all year, since Mardi Gras was a week after the Super Bowl. We came home to find that many of the Mardi Gras floats had been donated for us to use in our parade. This was no cobbled-together parade of cars. We had legitimate floats to ride in—some of the best floats from each parade.

Before Katrina the population of New Orleans was about 455,000. When I came to New Orleans in 2006, we were roughly half that size. But over the next few years, people started coming back and rebuilding. At one point the estimate was that three thousand to four thousand people were coming back every month. By 2009 we were back to about 80 percent of the original population. So at the time of the parade, somewhere around 355,000 people were living in the city.

The turnout for that parade was almost a million people—

about twice the population of the entire city. Who knows where they all came from—probably some from the Gulf Coast region, some from other parts of the state, and others who had been transplanted elsewhere. I heard that some fans flew to New Orleans to watch the game on TV and then stuck around for the parade. They wanted to be here to experience the homecoming, the celebration.

As exhilarating as it was to win the Super Bowl, it was just as exciting to see the sheer joy on the faces of everyone lining the streets of downtown New Orleans. This was about so much more than football. We knew it, and the fans knew it. Finally, after forty-three years, we'd accomplished something that most people thought would never happen in New Orleans. We had really pulled it off! And we'd done it together, with the help of our fans.

People screamed and cheered and sang as we passed by. But some of the most meaningful moments for me were when I made eye contact with people in the crowd and read their lips: "Thank you. We love you. Bless you, boys." I've never seen an outpouring from fans that was so genuine and straight from the heart.

Not long ago I was talking with the woman who cuts my hair, and she told me about her friend who works at the New Orleans police department. She said that on the day of the parade, people were calling 911 about me. I was throwing beads to the crowd from the top of a float, and apparently people were concerned I was going to hurt myself. They thought I was walking too close to the edge, and they were worried I was going to fall off. I'm not sure many police officers would have been available to respond because every motorcycle cop in the city was there with their blue lights flashing. They were just as excited as the people on the parade route.

The plan was for the parade to last two to three hours, but

it took twice that long. With such a huge crush of people, it was all we could do to inch our way through those historic streets. We started at the Superdome and wound through Howard to Lee Circle, down St. Charles, up and down Canal, and then ended at Mardi Gras World on Convention Center Boulevard.

In some areas the crowd was fifty people deep. Everywhere we went, they were singing "When the Saints Go Marching In" and chanting, "Who dat say dey gonna beat dem Saints?" People held up signs for us that read, *Bless you, boys* and *Greatest year of my life*. I was blown away by the masses of people—young and old, from many different backgrounds and nationalities. They all rallied together over the one thing they had in common: the Saints.

Postgame Media Blitz

I wasn't surprised by the media hype immediately following the Super Bowl, but I hadn't been expecting it to go much beyond that evening.

The first week after the game proved to be eventful from the beginning, starting with the NFL commissioner's press conference, followed by the Disney parade in Orlando and then a trip to New York for the *Late Show with David Letterman*. Letterman is from Indiana, so I knew he was rooting for the Colts. But when he saw the *Sports Illustrated* cover with Baylen and me on the front, he really seemed to identify with that picture, being a father with a young son himself. We talked about how much a child puts your life and everything that happens to you in perspective.

By the time I got home that night it was really late, but I wasn't able to sleep. My mind was whirling, trying to take in everything that had happened. Not long after nodding off,

I woke to the sound of Brittany and Baylen enjoying a loud, music-filled breakfast. They like to play the sound track from *Glee*, with Brittany singing at the top of her lungs while Baylen throws food all over the floor and claps. Life is good. I came downstairs and held Brittany in my arms for a long time.

"We did it," I said.

"I know, baby. I am so proud of you. You are so blessed— do you know that?" Then after a pause, she said, "How did you manage to win the Super Bowl and get your wife pregnant?"

I stared at her.

"That's right. I just took a pregnancy test. Baby Brees number two was there with us at that game."

I had no words. I held her as the tears gathered in my eyes. She was right—I am truly blessed.

Life didn't slow down at all that week. The next adventure was my appearance on *The Oprah Winfrey Show* with Brittany and Baylen. We weren't sure how our little man would do flying up to Chicago the night before and then going on a live show, with all the lights and people, but he was a champ. Yet another item to check off his list of accomplishments at the age of one!

And then there was *Ellen*. Prior to the Super Bowl, my wife and her mom, Kathie, had been watching Ellen DeGeneres's show, and Ellen said that when she was a kid, she lived near Tulane Stadium, where the Saints had played before the Superdome was built. The games were free after halftime, so she would go to the stadium and watch the second half. Ellen has a real attachment to the people in the New Orleans area, and she has done a lot on her program about the city's struggles post-Katrina.

The Tuesday after we won the NFC championship, Ellen said on her show, "My Saints are going to the Super Bowl!" And then she was having fun with her mother—Mama, as she calls her. She said that Mama wanted to go to the Super Bowl, but she had to find two tickets. It was just a funny little segment, not intended to be a true request to go to the game. But Brittany and her mom took it seriously and immediately jumped into action. Brittany called my marketing agent, Chris Stuart.

"Chris, stop whatever you're doing. We're getting Ellen tickets to the Super Bowl."

"Ellen who?" Chris said. "What are you talking about?"

Brittany explained the whole story, and Chris called the producer of the show. There was a gasp on the other end of the line. They never in a million years thought someone would actually give Mama tickets.

"Are you serious?" the producer asked.

"Yeah, I'm completely serious," Chris said. "Brittany and Drew want to do this for Mama."

The next day Ellen read an e-mail from Brittany on the air with Mama sitting in the audience, beaming. Brittany had written that we were both huge fans of the show and that the only prerequisite was Ellen's mother had to paint her face black and gold for the game. The audience loved it. Ellen wished us good luck and said I had to chat with her after the Super Bowl.

After we won, I made good on the promise, and she had me on her show. We talked about what New Orleans had done for my career—how I felt like the city had saved me, not the other way around. We discussed what this season meant not just to the people of New Orleans but to the whole region. Then she "retired" my jersey, hanging it from the rafters of her studio, and made a surprise presentation for Brittany and me. "Since you gave Mama seats . . . we want to give you per-manent seats, you and your wife. . . . We will name the seats after you too."

There's a connection you have with people from this area—
it doesn't matter who you are or where you've been—there's
just something at a heart level that connects. No matter where
in the world you go, New Orleans is always part of you.

When I was on the podium after the game, looking out into
the stadium with all the people on the field, I made eye contact with an older, white-haired woman. I had seen her only a
couple of times before, but I knew immediately it was Mama.
She must have wiped black and gold off her face before going
on the field. I blew her a kiss anyway.

EPILOGUE

NOW THAT THE SAINTS have scaled the ultimate football mountain and won a Super Bowl, it would be easy to sit back and enjoy our World Championship. But success presents as many challenges as setbacks do. I know every team we play is going to want to knock us off the pedestal. We'll have targets on us all year. It's up to us to find the motivation to push forward and build on the work that's been done. Will we be better in the new season? Only our commitment to growing stronger and getting better will answer that question. There aren't any shortcuts on the path to success. The way to do it is the same as it's always been: take things one game at a time, one drive at a time, one play at a time.

Winning the Super Bowl is not the end of the adventure. There's more to our journey—we have not arrived. Now it's time to prepare for the next challenge.

The story isn't over for New Orleans, either. We've made a lot of progress, but it's too soon to relax. It's not like every part of the city has suddenly been rebuilt overnight. If you drove through the Lower Ninth Ward with me, I'd show you some areas that look amazing, where people have rolled up their sleeves and banded together to rebuild. But I'd also show you houses where it looks like Katrina happened yesterday, places where there's nothing left but a slab. We've done some great work. But the story of our recovery is still being written.

The people of New Orleans are up to that task. And so are you.

I might as well tell you that whatever your struggle is, there is no final exclamation point that says, "You're done!" Yes, there was immense satisfaction for our team when we held up that trophy, especially after everything we had been through. The tougher the journey, the sweeter the celebration at the end. But that was only one major milestone on our long list of goals.

When I set out to write this book, my ultimate goal was not to get you excited about my career or the Saints, or even to make you want to move to New Orleans (although we'd love to have you at least visit us!). My desire was to have you turn the last page and become excited about waking up tomorrow. You will undoubtedly have challenges ahead that you will have to face and overcome. But don't forget that adversity is not your enemy. It can unleash a power in your life that will make you stronger and help you achieve amazing things—things you may have never thought were possible . . . until now.

Now that you've heard some of my story and the events and influences that have contributed to the person I am today, I'd like to make this personal for you. If I could sit down with you and have a face-to-face talk, these are some things I would say.

- *Find a mentor.* No matter who you are or what your profession is, we all need someone who can keep us grounded and speak truth into our lives. Find people who have built their lives on a solid foundation, and humble yourself to learn from them. I've never known a successful athlete, businessperson, or anyone else who has made an impact on the world who didn't stand on the shoulders of other great men and women.

- *Don't give up.* The worst thing that could happen in life is not getting knocked down; it's getting knocked down and then staying down. If you lose a job, if your relationships crumble, if you face a health setback—get up. You may fall again and it may hurt, but get back on the horse. And once you're up, hold your ground. Commitment is when you refuse to give yourself an excuse.

- *Turn your defeats into triumphs.* Any difficulty you face—whether it's a tear to your shoulder, a person who betrays you, a dysfunctional family, or the bad luck you have with the economy—can unleash power within you for good. Use that negative to help you not only climb out of the hole you're in, but rise to greater heights. The greatest opportunities in life are the ones that test us the most.

- *Dream.* If your mind can conceive it, you can achieve it. Not on your own, and not without struggle and hardship and effort. But when that vision mixes with hard work and commitment, you'll be amazed at what you can accomplish.

- *Hope.* In order to come back after a disappointment and accomplish something great, you have to believe in something bigger than yourself. But it's not enough to just put your hope in hope. You have to have an object of hope. For me, God is the center of that hope, and I lean on him to order my steps and show me the right path. Having hope in the Lord means I trust in his plan and believe he's never going to put anything in front of me that's too hard to handle with his help.

- *Be flexible.* My dream was to win a championship with San Diego and play my whole career with that one team. That didn't happen—it wasn't the plan. And it took a devastating injury to tear me away from that city. Be flexible enough to know when you're being led in another direction, and then follow that new vision with all your heart. You are being led there for a reason—coincidence is usually God working anonymously.

- *See adversity as an opportunity.* Remember, experience is what you get when you don't get what you want. No matter what comes your way, remember that God can use everything in your life for good, even though it may seem unfair or insurmountable at the time. Seize that adversity and let it make you stronger. Welcome it, and unleash its power.

- *Don't be afraid of taking a few steps back.* A step back is not necessarily a setback. Sometimes you have to take a few steps backward before you can get the momentum to jump over a chasm in your life. The goal may be farther than you thought, and what you see as backtracking may really just be helping you get up the speed to make the final jump.

- *Don't spectate—be ready.* Instead of standing on the sidelines watching, spend that time getting ready for the next play. Too many of us are caught sleeping at life's traffic lights. When the next opportunity comes your way, make sure you have prepared yourself well enough to seize the chance you've been given. You never know if you will get that opportunity again.

- *Remember who you are.* God created each one of us for a purpose. You will find that purpose in doing the small things well, in taking things one day at a time. That purpose will always have an element of serving others. If you're well grounded in who you really are, and if you do the right thing for long enough, eventually you will start to see the fruit of those decisions.

  When people think you're not big enough, not smart enough, not wise enough, or not experienced enough for a task, remember that faith will carry you through. The test of adversity is one that's fought with faith.

- *Finish strong.* It is not where you start in life, but rather how you finish. It's that last play that can make all the difference in the outcome. Keep it simple: in everything you do, make your last rep your best rep.

If you take away only one thing from this book, never forget that sometimes your greatest victories can come from your greatest defeats. The next time adversity knocks on your door, stand up tall and do the right thing. You can do more than just survive. You can come back—stronger.

248.86 BREES
Brees, Drew,
Coming back stronger :
R2000559118 PALMETTO

ODC

Atlanta-Fulton Public Library